DERRIDA'S
WRITING AND DIFFERENCE

Continuum Reader's Guides

Continuum's *Reader's Guides* are clear, concise and accessible introductions to classic works of philosophy. Each book explores the major themes, historical and philosophical context and key passages of a major philosophical text, guiding the reader towards a thorough understanding of often demanding material. Ideal for undergraduate students, the guides provide an essential resource for anyone who needs to get to grips with a philosophical text.

Reader's Guides Available from Continuum:

Aristotle's Nicomachean Ethics – Christopher Warne
Berkeley's Principles of Human Knowledge – Alasdair Richmond
Berkeley's Three Dialogues – Aaron Garrett
Deleuze and Guattari's Capitalism and Schizophrenia – Ian Buchanan
Deleuze's Difference and Repetition – Joe Hughes
Descartes' Meditations – Richard Francks
Hegel's Philosophy of Right – David Rose
Heidegger's Being and Time – William Blattner
Heidegger's Later Writings – Lee Braver
Hobbes's Leviathan – Laurie M. Johnson Bagby
Hume's Dialogues Concerning Natural Religion – Andrew Pyle
Hume's Enquiry Concerning Human Understanding – Alan Bailey and Dan O'Brien
Kant's Critique of Pure Reason – James Luchte
Kant's Groundwork for the Metaphysics of Morals – Paul Guyer
Kuhn's The Structure of Scientific Revolutions – John Preston
Locke's Essay Concerning Human Understanding – William Uzgalis
Locke's Second Treatise of Government – Paul Kelly
Mill's On Liberty – Geoffrey Scarre
Mill's Utilitarianism – Henry West
Nietzsche's On the Genealogy of Morals – Daniel Conway
Plato's Republic – Luke Purshouse
Rousseau's The Social Contract – Christopher Wraight
Sartre's Being and Nothingness – Sebastian Gardner
Spinoza's Ethics – Thomas J. Cook
Wittgenstein's Tractatus Logico Philosophicus – Roger M. White

DERRIDA'S
WRITING AND DIFFERENCE

A Reader's Guide

SARAH WOOD

continuum

Continuum International Publishing Group
The Tower Building   80 Maiden Lane
11 York Road   Suite 704
London SE1 7NX   New York, NY 10038

www.continuumbooks.com

© Sarah Wood 2009

All rights reserved. No part of this publication may be reproduced or transmitted in any form or by any means, electronic or mechanical, including photocopying, recording, or any information storage or retrieval system, without prior permission in writing from the publishers.

British Library Cataloguing-in-Publication Data
A catalogue record for this book is available from the British Library.

ISBN-10: HB: 0-8264-9191-X
          PB: 0-8264-9192-8
ISBN-13: HB: 978-0-8264-9191-6
          PB: 978-0-8264-9192-3

Library of Congress Cataloging-in-Publication Data
Wood, Sarah, 1963–
Derrida's Writing and difference: a reader's guide / Sarah Wood.
p. cm.
Includes bibliographical references and index.
ISBN-13: 978-0-8264-9191-6 (HB)
ISBN-13: 978-0-8264-9192-3 (pbk.)
ISBN-10: 0-8264-9191-X (HB)
ISBN-10: 0-8264-9192-8 (pbk.)
1. Derrida, Jacques. Écriture et la différence. 2. Philosophy. I. Title.

B2430.D483E27 2009
194—dc22
2008038899

Typeset by Newgen Imaging Systems Pvt Ltd, Chennai, India
Printed and bound in Great Britain by
CPI Antony Rowe, Chippenham, Wiltshire

To my Mum

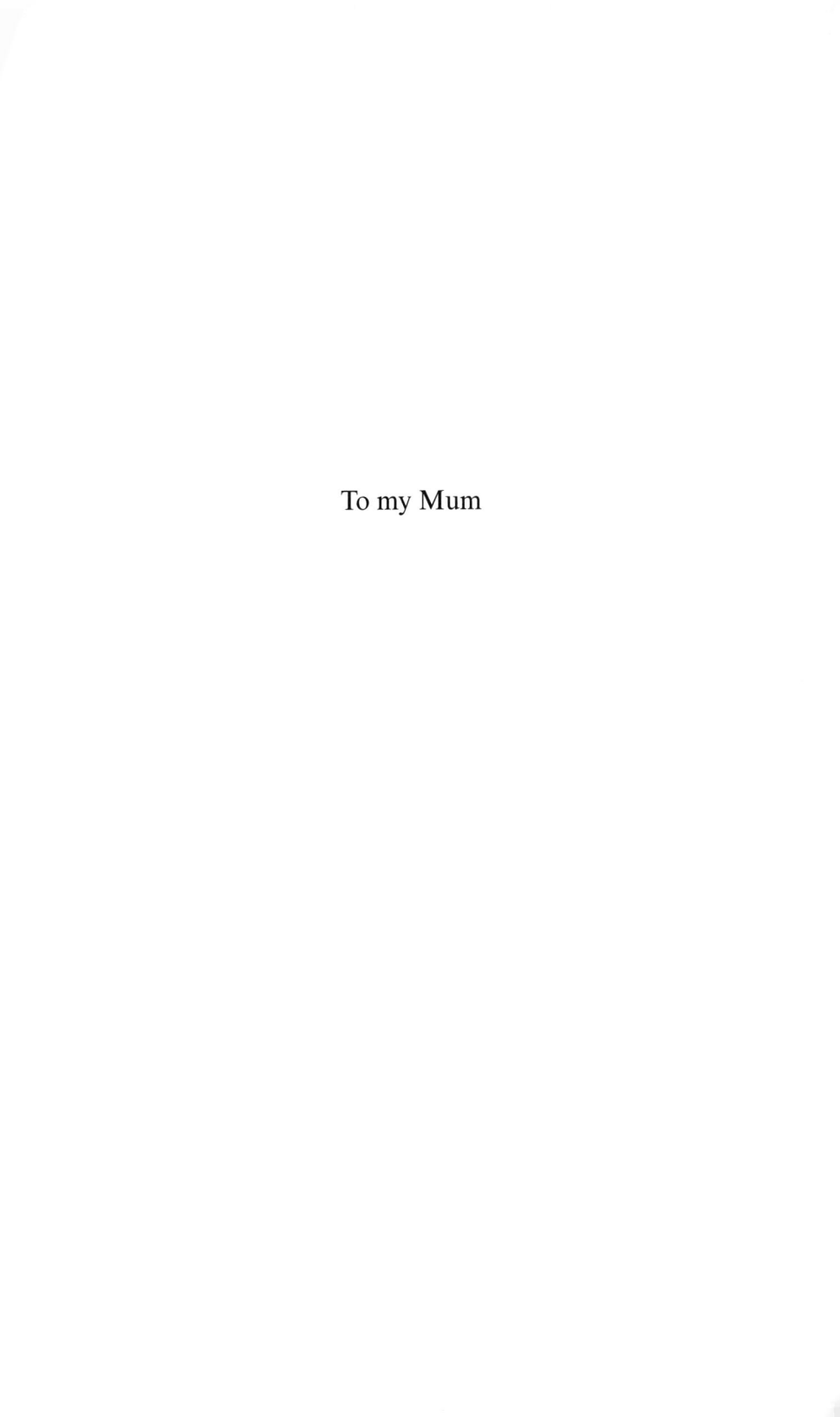

CONTENTS

Acknowledgements	viii
1. Context	1
2. Overview of Themes	16
3. Reading the Text	27
4. Reception and Influence	164
Notes	170
Further Reading	179
Index	183

ACKNOWLEDGEMENTS

Thanks to Graham Allen, David Bean, Tom Boncza-Tomaszewski, Clare Connors, Tom Dutoit, Yuli Goulimari, James Harris, John Hughes, Elissa Marder, Ariane Mildenberg, Forbes Morlock, Joke Murray, Marion O'Connor, John Phillips, Lydia Rainford, Caroline Rooney, Nicholas Royle, Roy Sellars, Linda Squire, Jonathan Tiplady, Shane Weller, Ann Wordsworth – my universities. Thanks also to Sarah Douglas and Tom Crick at Continuum, to Taylor and Francis and the University of Chicago Press for permission to cite from the Routledge Classics reprint of *Writing and Difference* translated by Alan Bass.

CHAPTER 1

CONTEXT

A text escapes: 'the text is not the book, it is not confined in a volume itself confined to a library.'[1] According to what Jacques Derrida calls 'the history of facts', *L'écriture et la différence* [*Writing and Difference*] was published in 1967.[2] It contains essays and papers written in France between 1959 and 1967 and published in a number of venues. Among these, the *Revue métaphysique et morale*, edited by Jean Wahl, was France's leading philosophical journal. *Critique* was founded by the non-academic thinker Georges Bataille and combined interests in philosophy, literature and the human sciences. It also published two excerpts from what was to be *De la grammatologie* [*Of Grammatology*] in 1965. *L'Arc* addressed similar subjects by way of special issues devoted to a single writer, philosopher, artist or topic. *Tel Quel* was set up in 1960 as an avant-garde literary and critical journal supported by Seuil, the publishing house that brought out *Writing and Difference* in its *Tel Quel* series.

A text refers 'to history, to the world, to reality, to being, and especially . . . to the other'.[3] The essays in *Writing and Difference* mostly engage with recently published French writing by men, contemporaries older than Derrida, some of whom were his teachers, some of whom were Jewish: 'Force and Signification' reviews *Forme et signification: Essais sur les structures littéraires de Corneille à Claudel*, Jean Rousset's 1962 study of literary structure. 'Cogito and the History of Madness' reads Michel Foucault's 1961 book of and about history, *Madness and Civilisation: A History of Insanity in the Age of Reason*. The two essays on Edmond Jabès respond to the 1963 and 1965 instalments in his *Livre des questions* [*Book of Questions*] series. 'Violence and Metaphysics' reads the philosophical works of Emmanuel Levinas published up to 1964 and was written on the occasion of Levinas's first book on Edmund Husserl being reissued in 1963. 'Genesis and Structure' addresses Husserl and the way phenomenology was being read in France in the 1960s. '*La parole soufflée*' and 'The Theatre of Cruelty and the Closure of Representation' return to Antonin Artaud in the light of recent attention to his work from writer and critic Maurice Blanchot, from Michel Foucault and from psychoanalytic theorist Jean Laplanche. These two essays put to the test some of the arguments put forward in *Of Grammatology* (1967). 'Freud and the Scene of Writing' is exceptional: the recent work it relates to is Derrida's own. It too elaborates some of the propositions in *Of Grammatology*. Its return to the question of writing in Freud proposes something different from the language-oriented 'return to Freud' launched by Jacques Lacan in the 1950s. Lacan's lectures at the École Normale Supérieure (ENS) in the mid-1960s were attracting the attention of philosophers and philosophy students as well as psychoanalysts. 'From a Restricted to a General Economy' takes up Bataille's reading of G. W. F. Hegel from the mid-1950s, in part to engage with the Hegel put forward by Derrida's teacher Jean Hyppolite. 'Structure, Sign and Play' continues to respond to Hyppolite and Foucault while turning to the recent ethnological writings of Claude Lévi-Strauss, which are also vital to *Of Grammatology*.

Derrida described *Writing and Difference* as part of a 'confluence of small texts, none of which on its own was sufficient to make up a book'.[4] He linked *Writing and Difference* with the two other books that he published in 1967, *Of Grammatology* and *Speech and Phenomena*, saying: 'not one of them was a book.'

EVERYTHING IN THE WORLD AND AN IMPOSSIBLE MACHINE

Writing and Difference works with what Derrida later called a 'concept of text or of context' that 'embraces and does not exclude the world, reality, history'.[5] The history of facts would be part of a larger and irredeemably diverse category that he playfully referred to as 'the entire "real-history-of-the-world"'.[6] Arguments about historicity (for now we can take this to refer to the conditions of possibility of history or the context in which history becomes thinkable as such) are crucial to many of the essays in *Writing and Difference*. Derrida believed that reality always appeared 'in an experience, hence in a movement of interpretation'. We read the appearances of the world, reality and history, which come to us thanks to what Derrida has called *différance*. For now, we can take our sense of what *différance* means from Geoffrey Bennington, who describes it as something that 'constantly folds the infinite back into the finite' and reminds us that it 'cannot fail to upset our common representations of history and time'.[7] One such representation is autobiography.

Derrida wrote explicitly about his own life and desire in a number of texts notably *Glas* (1974), *The Post Card* (1980) and 'Circumfessions' (1991). His account of his own wish to write as an adolescent helps us recognize what he means by 'text' and 'context'. He spoke of experiencing 'an obsessive desire to save in an uninterrupted inscription, in the form of a memory, what happens – or *fails to happen*'.[8] He wanted to write down everything, and felt himself to be, in André Gide's word 'proteiform'.[9] He recalled:

> I was able to take whatever form, to write in whatever tone, which I knew was never really mine; I responded to what was expected of me or recognised myself in the mirror which offered me the other. I said to myself: I can write everything and therefore I can write nothing.[10]

Elsewhere, he spoke of wanting, first of all, not to produce a philosophical work or a work of art but for there to be a machine that could 'preserve memory':

> Let's imagine a kind of machine, which by definition is an impossible one, that would be like a machine for ingrammatizing [*engrammer*] everything that happens and such that the smallest thoughts, the smallest movements of the body, the least traces of desire, the ray of sunlight, the encounter with someone, a phrase heard in passing, are inscribed somewhere; imagine that a general electroencephalocardiosomatopsychogram were possible: at that moment my desire would be absolutely fulfilled – and finitude accepted (and by the same token denied).[11]

It was impossible, but this impossibility was an inspiration. His desire to keep memory exceeded what could actually come to pass.

He wanted to be able to retain the movements of life. He wanted what, rigorously, he could not hope to possess. Edmond Jabès, subject of two essays in *Writing and Difference* recognized this when he commented: 'Rare, very rare, to live writing with such intensity.'[12] The essays in *Writing and Difference* were written by someone who was kept going by a desire to save, to remember and to read not only what is or has been said or done in texts by Foucault, Husserl or Freud but also traces of what might have been (and therefore perhaps still could be) happening in their texts. *Legein*, the Greek verb 'to read', which gives us French *lecture*, concretely means 'gathering up', as one gathers flowers. Derrida said of his writing: 'What I should be tempted to denounce as a lure – i.e. totalization or gathering up – isn't this what keeps me going?'[13] *Writing and Difference* is a book of readings and a book about reading. It opens out the reading project begun in *Of Grammatology*, where Derrida makes explicit his principles of reading, to a further multiplicity of authors, texts and disciplines.

QUESTIONS

Writing and Difference is an opportunity to recognize a repetitive insistence in Derrida's thinking as he extends his attention beyond phenomenology, philosophy of language, linguistics and ethnography to literary criticism, history, poetry, dramaturgy and psychoanalysis. Recurrent preoccupations include force and violence, madness, the book, economy, the sign and reading itself. Derrida's themes permeate his text: it is a matter of what writing can do as well as what it might say. In the process he writes into being a wide border zone where familiar critical categories come into question. For example, it is sometimes hard to tell Derrida's own thoughts apart from those of the writer he is reading or to establish a hard and fast distinction between the form of the text and its content or meaning. His work propels readers towards an unprecedented experience of writing. *Writing and Difference* is an adventure. Conventionally we might expect a book to settle differences, an expectation that treats writing as if it were a means, a tool or a route, but Derrida argues that the book has lived on an enticing illusion: 'to have given us to believe that passion, having been originally impassioned by *something*, could in the end be appeased by the return of that something.

Lure of the origin, the end, the line, the ring, the volume, the center' (372). *Writing and Difference*, on the other hand, is not appeasing: it affirms the agitation and multiplicity of writing. Thematic exposition takes place, of course, as does commentary, a philosophical and critical genre that these essays comment on frequently. He does not give up any possible writing voice but no single way of organizing writing comes to dominate the whole.

READING

Derrida pinpoints the distinguishing aspect of Rousset's *Forme et signification* as 'the quality of an attention' (25/38). The quality of Derrida's attention is the most extraordinary thing about *Writing and Difference*. Nobody writes like him, and approaching the question of how to read these essays it will be vital to think about how he *reads*. There is much to be learned from the experience of reading him, from what it feels like, what it provokes and what it does to the reader's experience of language. The book also reads you. Derrida considers beginners more open to experiencing and accurately describing the effects of texts than those, better read in philosophy, for whom 'culture, sometimes of a very refined kind, organises a prohibition of reading'.[14] '"Wild"' or '"naïve"' readers could 'have better access' to a 'trembling of the text', an effect of reading 'that in the end has to do with the body, a body, the reader's body or my body'. I begin to understand what he means by 'force' in general when his writing surprises me.

Derrida took authorial intention very seriously. He was interested in the unique and the proper, in the distinctiveness of what Rousset, Foucault, Jabès or Artaud had written. *Writing and Difference* attends to philosophical writing in a traditional sense and in a traditional manner. Heidegger, Levinas, Foucault and Bataille are approached as thinkers in their own right and also as readers (of Greek philosophy, Husserl, Descartes and Hegel, respectively). At the same time, Derrida tried 'precisely, to put myself at a point so that I do not know any longer where I am going'.[15] And he believed that it was bad for readers to be 'fearful' or to be 'in a hurry to be determined'.[16] A kind of acquiescence is needed. The text is not over and needs to be given time. Reading, we find ourselves living where we cannot take direct action. Passion and passivity are important. It's true that *Writing and Difference* has historical significance and recognizes the historical significance of the thinkers that it studies. But a text is not an object and in these essays Derrida is interested in the kind of event that does not 'display itself in its entirety as an object' for the historian' (2). Interpretations spring from language. Translation is an issue for readers of a text that works by playing and that sees the opportunities offered by the French language (and sometimes by other languages too). Sometimes it helps to look at the French word, phrase or sentence hidden by an English one. Derrida has been well served by his American and English translators and we learn something more of what they have done by occasionally returning to the French text they worked from. Attention is an extension, a stretching out towards, from Indo-European *root word meaning* 'stretch'. The word 'attention' is cognate with Greek *tonos*, 'string' hence 'sound, pitch'. Sound and tone are produced by the trembling or vibration that Derrida felt less experienced might be especially aware of. *Writing and Difference* works with various forms of writing tension that come to us as feeling, by way of what eighteenth-century philosophers called 'sensibility' or contemporary ones 'affectivity'. These tensions are also made accessible as tone and at times as the sound of Derrida's writing – what he calls the 'non-discursive sonority' of words.[17] Derrida had a special relation with English. He studied in the United States in the 1950s and from the late 1960s taught there regularly. We are reading him in translation, so it needs saying all the more that he wrote in French, he read Freud and Nietzsche in German, Plato and Aristotle in Greek and so on.

WRITING AND DIFFERENCE IN ACTION

Derrida's remark about trying to reach at a point so that he did not know any longer where he was going was a response to Jean Hyppolite. Hyppolite was a noted French translator of Hegel and author of *The Genesis and Structure of the Phenomenology of Spirit* (1947), to which the title of Derrida's essay '"Genesis and Structure" and Phenomenology' partly refers. He co-supervised Derrida's uncompleted doctoral thesis on 'The

Ideality of the Literary Object' and helped Derrida's career by appointing him as his assistant at the ENS in Paris. When Derrida first delivered 'Structure, Sign and Play in the Discourse of the Human Sciences' at Johns Hopkins, Hyppolite asked him a series of questions. He was especially interested in the idea of 'the centre' he felt Derrida was putting forward.[18] He asked familiar kinds of philosophical questions, questions we might ask, concerning location, identity and direction: 'where is the centre? . . . is this the centre? . . . Is that what you are tending toward? Is this what you wanted to say, or were you getting at something else?' Hyppolite was looking for what he calls a 'constant', a notion borrowed from the natural sciences, from Einstein. He was thinking in terms of establishing the orientation of his own thought and Derrida's. But in their exchange it became clear that a classical approach, no matter how sympathetic, was of limited use in understanding Derrida. Rather than go along with the drift of his former teacher's questioning, Derrida freed himself from it by frankly resisting the very notion of knowing where he was going. He resisted the assumption that he had absolute control over his own text and was precise enough to agree *and* disagree with Hyppolite. He did not oppose himself to his questioner. He also struck a note of feeling which was absent from Hyppolite's remarks themselves. (Although the older philosopher's wish for the reassurance of knowing, his desire to be certain of what is happening by agreeing on the dominant concept, is not without pathos.) Derrida rejected a purely nostalgic or negative re-appropriation of the centre as a lost object. He insisted: 'as to this loss of the centre, I *refuse* to approach an idea of the "non-centre" which would no longer be the tragedy of the loss of the centre.' A tragic thinker, he never flinched from thinking about the experiences accompanying the inevitable, or hastened to replace metaphysical concepts with some new, albeit negative, certainty. He also marked the importance of language: 'here the words are more than mere words, as always.' Finally, he met Hyppolite on his own ground by taking up his reference to the theory of relativity:

> the Einsteinian constant is not a constant, is not a centre. It is the very concept of variability . . . it is not the concept of some*thing* – of a centre starting from which an observer could

master the field – but the very concept of the game [or 'of play'] which, after all, I was trying to elaborate.

The speed, intensity, grace and multiplicity of this response gives some idea of the quality of thought in *Writing and Difference*.

EUROPE AND AMERICA

Derrida has said that 'there are only contexts without any centre of absolute anchoring.'[19] The exchange with Hyppolite can be referred to the context of post-war France, a country marked by the Second World War, the attempt to destroy the Jews of Europe, German occupation and movements of resistance against and collaboration with the occupying forces. Derrida was also highly aware, as a politically conscious Algerian-born French citizen, of the colonial war between France and Algeria that officially ended with Algerian independence in 1962. He was a war-thinker, a responder to inner and outer conflicts. He remembered injustice and victimization and was prepared to take sides. Furthermore, *Writing and Difference* is not simply a European and postcolonial book: 'Structure, Sign and Play' was delivered at a conference at the Humanities Centre at Johns Hopkins University in the United States. It was Derrida's response to the invitation to consider 'The Languages of Criticism and the Sciences of Man' and began a long and fruitful engagement with North American and Anglophone thinking. 'The Languages of Criticism and the Sciences of Man' was not a philosophy conference, nor was it a one-off event. It led to two years of seminars and colloquia exploring the effects of structuralist thought on the contemporary humanities and social sciences. It began Derrida's explicit engagement with 'the humanities' and his thinking about the university as an institution. It was also the beginning of his tireless travelling to speak and teach in the United States and all over the world.

☐ STRUCTURALISM

The Johns Hopkins conference in part explains why 'structuralism' has been a favourite context for many introductions to Derrida, although it isn't a strongly recurrent term in his thought. *Writing and Difference* engages with what 'Force and Signification' calls 'the *structuralist* invasion' by reading particular texts: a literary–critical book by Raymond Rousset and various works by the ethnologist Claude Levi-Strauss (1/9). The term 'structuralism' appears in two of the eleven essays. Those who want to locate the book in the history of ideas would first have to think about what Derrida says about the history of ideas at the beginning of 'Force and Signification'. The classical history of ideas 'naively belongs' to language, while structuralism is 'astonished . . . by language as the origin of history' (2).

DERRIDA'S CHILDHOOD AND YOUTH

The writer and thinker Hélène Cixous described what it was like to grow up in colonial Algeria, where Derrida was born in El Biar in 1930, she in Oran in 1937. They were surrounded by tensions between Arabs and French settlers. There was pervasive, sometimes brutal anti-semitism. It was an unreadable situation: 'no explicit discourse . . . But everything was sign and symptom'.[20] At school, Derrida recalled, there was 'not a word about Algeria, not a single one concerning its history and its geography, whereas we could draw the coast of Brittany and the Gironde estuary with our eyes closed'.[21] Derrida was top of his class but anti-semitism became traumatically connected with school, education and subsequently the various *Écoles* where he studied and worked in the university system. In wartime Algeria the French colonial government's anti-Jewish measures went beyond what the Germans occupying mainland France demanded. Aged 11, Derrida was excluded from school because he was Jewish: 'The only school official whose name I remember today: he had me come into his office: "you are going to go home, my little friend, your parents will get a note." At the moment I understood nothing, but since?'[22] Again, there is no explicit discourse. Derrida recalled insults, taunts and blows from classmates. He chose not to attend the alternative school set up by dismissed Jewish teachers and secretly truanted for eleven months. These experiences left him sensitive to anti-semitism and racism generally, with a heightened awareness of what was at stake in situations of belonging and group-identification. He was proud of having been part of an extraordinary generation of thinkers in France from the 1960s on but his sense that he was 'not one of the family' accompanied his participation in groups of all kinds and affected his thinking about institutions.[23] Later, Derrida involved himself in numerous institutional initiatives with a remit beyond his own particular work, for example in the 1970s, Groupe de recherches sur l'enseignement philosophique (GREPH), which investigated and promoted the teaching of philosophy in French schools, and the Collège Internationale de Philosophie in Paris, founded in 1982.

As a youth in Algeria he began to read some of the philosophers who appear in *Writing and Difference* and *Of Grammatology*: Nietzsche, Rousseau, Kierkegaard and Heidegger. Rousseau is the major figure in *Of Grammatology* and while *Writing and Difference* contains no essay about Nietzsche, 'the philosopher who speaks in the first person while all the time multiplying proper names, masks and signatures', it makes numerous important references to his thought. Later, Derrida connected these two favourite philosophers with the writer André Gide, as writers having what he calls a 'desire for *everything + n*'.[24] This desire and the transformations it prompts are very strong in his own writing. The books he got interested in as an adolescent 'had that in them . . . texts which were neither simply literary nor philosophical, but confessions'. *Writing and Difference* is not a confessional text but its range and depth of interests and its resistance to being dominated by a single voice, philosophical project or cultural situation shows Derrida's commitment to 'the fact of not giving anything up, not even the things one deprives oneself of'.[25] French literature influenced the accent of Derrida's writing, de-regionalizing it, and left him willing and able to 'surrender himself to language' and its secrets.[26] At the time of the Johns Hopkins conference in 1966, Derrida had been living outside Algeria for 15 years. He had gone back for two years 1957–1959 to do his military service as a school teacher, and in 1962, at the time of Algerian independence, his parents moved to France.

HIGHER EDUCATION AND EARLY ACADEMIC CAREER

Some career facts: Derrida studied at the ENS from 1952–1956, working under Foucault and Louis Althusser. He became interested in phenomenology during this period and wrote a dissertation on the problem of genesis in Husserl's philosophy. Husserl is the single most important philosopher to *Writing and Difference* and was also the main subject of *Speech and Phenomena*. In 1956 Derrida became qualified to teach in the French university system. After some work on Husserl at Harvard and his national service as a teacher in Algeria, he taught students preparing for study at one of the major *Écoles* for a year and then took up a position at the Sorbonne. Derrida's first book was published in 1962, a translation and introduction of Edmund Husserl's *Origin of Geometry* which won a prize for the year's best study in epistemology. In 1964 he began teaching at the ENS, at the invitation of Jean Hyppolite and Derrida's friend and fellow Franco-Algerian, Louis Althusser. He stayed there, in a relatively lowly position at a highly regarded institution, until he moved to the *École des hautes Études en Sciences sociales* in 1983 as elected Director. He remained there until his death, also regularly visiting the United States to teach there. After giving 'Structure, Sign and Play' at Johns Hopkins in 1966 and the publication of his three books in 1967, Derrida became more than France's most promising phenomenologist. He was recognized as a major international figure. His published work continued to address the philosophical canon: Plato and Aristotle, German philosophers Kant, Hegel, Nietzsche and Heidegger and the English philosopher of language J. L. Austin. At the same time, through the 1970s there were experiments with writing that surged beyond anything academia could imagine, without abandoning commentary and the question of tradition (e.g. *Glas*, 'Living On/Border Lines,' the 'Envois' section of *The Post Card*).

READER AND WRITER

Derrida's thinking about reading was influenced by Martial Guéroult's philosophy lectures at the Collège de France. For Guéroult, philosophy did not come to its students as ideas, concepts, thoughts or general possibilities but as *texts*. Derrida recalled Guéroult's way of reading as respectful, patient and precise: he set out to reconstruct the connections sustaining a given system of thought. He did this 'step by step . . . with the maximum care for detail' and 'respect for the way the text works'.[27] This method did not depend on an assumed coherence guaranteed by the unifying figure of an author. The text had its own coherence but writing was not taken to be simply *there*, revealed or given. From this perspective, which Derrida called 'a sort of philosophical technology', it was not a matter of agreeing or disagreeing with what the text says but of coming to terms with its logic. At the same time Guéroult paid 'attention to the letter, to literality: not to the breath that breathes through a text, to what it means, but to its literal working, its functioning'. Attention to the letter underpins a 'literariness' that is sometimes too rapidly ascribed to Derrida. The concern with literality marks a departure from the assumptions underlying the tradition of philosophical commentary which has thrived since late antiquity.

Deconstruction is deeply traditional. In general, Derrida's texts respond to what is already at work, trying to obey what he recognized as a sort of secret law written inside language. This response sometimes took him beyond the conventions of writing, although he prided himself on very accurate French. He sometimes neglected the relatively superficial constraints of 'style' in order to 'bow to a more hidden rule . . . a law of the language that would entrust itself only to me'.[28] He devoted attention to something in language that was unknown but powerful and necessary, and bade readers: 'invent in *your* language if you can or want to hear mine.'[29] There is of course no excuse for assuming that politics, culture and philosophical tradition are therefore irrelevant to Derrida or to us when we read him, but no history can provide the key to this secret theme that is everywhere in *Writing and Difference*.

PHILOSOPHICAL CONTEXT

Writing and Difference shakes philosophical assumptions about the proper place, function and nature of traditional disciplines. In the course of his readings Derrida explores several kinds of vocabulary. The following philosophical terms are important: 'metaphysics' from Leibniz and others; the '*Cogito*' of Descartes; from Hegel, 'dialectics' and 'sovereignty'; 'structure' and 'genesis' in Husserl's phenomenology and the 'other' in the work of Emmanuel Levinas. This collection takes on philosophical themes of force, necessity, repetition, decision and memory, among others. Philosophy would routinely refer to these as 'concepts' but we should hesitate to read this book in those terms. Derrida found effects of detour, delay, delegation, division, inequality and spacing at work in the effects he analysed, so that they no longer have the simplicity and predictability that make concepts

CONTEXT

indispensable to the consistency of philosophical systems. His work sets out to change the 'accredited, authorized relation between a word and a concept', an effect that can only emerge in the course of some kind of reading.[30] Derrida redefined or added fresh emphasis to certain words and occasionally coined new ones but always with a sense that to do so is to repeat, as well as to break new ground. Sometimes these effects of repetition and fragmentation emerge as reiterated syllables that play across his French text as if it were a poem. Not only the category of the concept but also that of the word is being rigorously worked over.

OVERVIEW OF DERRIDA'S WORK

The two other great texts published in 1967, *Of Grammatology* and *Speech and Phenomena* look like books, single volumes. But Derrida has emphasized that they are not unified projects. They are apparent unities, phenomenally speaking, but their true wholeness consists of multiple voices, additions, gaps, temporal shifts and crossings. Derrida is not advancing a theory or setting out a programme. His piercing awareness of system, of the connections and articulations and interrelations in the texts he reads, does not point in a single direction. Later works take this issue up in a reading of the two great modern philosophers of system, and therefore also of politics: Kant and Hegel.[31]

Derrida wrote more than forty books and dozens of essays. His later work ceases to emphasize themes such as the centre, or metaphysics, that are crucial to *Writing and Difference*. Nonetheless certain movements of thought characterizing this collection return throughout his oeuvre: opening and closure, the monstrosity of what is to come, spacing and impossibility as a precondition of experience. Derrida continued to respond to what was happening and not happening, politically, historically, academically and artistically in the world around him – a world never simply taken to be present. We see in *Writing and Difference* the distinctive notions of *supplement* and *différance* also developed in *Of Grammatology* and *Dissemination* (1972). 'Freud and the Scene of Writing' opens up questions explored further in *The Post Card* (1980) and *Archive Fever* (1995). Derrida's engagement with psychoanalysis continued throughout his life, addressing institutional and political aspects of that movement, as well as the activity of psychoanalytic interpretation itself.

13

The essays on Jabès and the book were followed by work on many French literary writers, including Mallarmé, his *Tel Quel* comrade Philippe Sollers, Genet, Flaubert, Blanchot, Valéry and Francis Ponge. He also wrote on Kafka and Celan, Shakespeare, Poe, Melville and Joyce and gave an important interview on the 'strange institution called literature' in 1989. The questions of the book and the material support of writing were taken up again in the collection *Paper Machine* (2001). The interest in law that emerges particularly in the essays on Jabès continues in 'Force of Law: the Mystical Foundation of Authority' (1990). The 1990s also saw an explicit focus on religion, extending the thinking around Levinas and Jabès in *Writing and Difference* to a consideration of Kierkegaard in *The Gift of Death* (1990). *Adieu to Emmanuel Levinas* came out in 1997. There were two essays on Artaud after *Writing and Difference*: 'To Unsense the Subjectile' (1986) and *Artaud le Moma* (2002). There are also two interviews: 'Artaud et ses doubles' (1987) and 'Les voix d'Artaud' (2004).

The logic of reading and writing that informs not only this guide but also Derrida's continual return as a teacher and writer to the texts of the Western canon, especially in philosophy but also in literature and the humanities, cannot be periodized. The specific temporal movements of writing and difference require precise attention to texts: generalizations about 'late' and 'early' work are of very limited relevance to the process of actually reading sentences, paragraphs and pages of Derrida's work. He writes in a way that refuses to be limited by themes or by the authors of the texts he reads, so that what follows is a compromise, designed to facilitate reading rather than to outline an area of research. Still, Derrida's responsiveness led to essays, books, colloquium proceedings, open letters and interviews on a wide variety of topics, increasingly quickly translated into English and other languages. The range of topics he addressed included sexual difference, literature and the nuclear threat, relations between signature and proper name in literary writing, architecture, the university, drawing, photography, apartheid, friendship and occasionally deconstruction itself. In the last two decades 'Readers' on Derrida and deconstruction began to appear. The beautiful autobiographical text 'Circumfessions' came out to accompany and disconcert Geoffrey Bennington's introduction to his work. A constant and pervasive concern with politics became more recognizable in conventional terms, for example in *Specters of Marx* (1994), where Derrida directly addresses the notion of a 'new world order' in the wake of the collapse of communist regimes in Russia and Eastern Europe. *The Politics of Friendship* (1994) explored allegiance, love, enmity and partisanship. There was a book on Blanchot, a collection of writings on religion and *Voiles*, a collaboration with Cixous (1998).

From 2000 to the present, books, essays and interviews appeared on the university, animality, mourning, cosmopolitanism and forgiveness, on Jean-Luc Nancy and Cixous, on so-called rogue states and much besides. The publication and translation of Derrida's remaining unpublished seminars is under way, including work on the death penalty and 'The Beast and the Sovereign'. The last interview Derrida gave before his death from pancreatic cancer in 2004 was published in 2007 as *Learning to Live Finally*. Without compromising the richness and precision of his thought it is as direct and broad as life.

CHAPTER 2

OVERVIEW OF THEMES

The way Derrida reads and writes makes it possible, and advisable, to find new themes as you read and reread him. His great themes of life, experience and the secret open on to all the others. They are what open his writing to you and they are the least obedient to the logic of a guide. (Imagine a book: *Jacques Derrida's Guide to Your Life*...) The themes listed below focus on words, ideas and systems of thought that *Writing and Difference* refers to, by highlighting them in its title, or repeatedly invoking them, or inviting us to rediscover their meaning.

WRITING

For Derrida *writing*, in a sense that *Of Grammatology* and *Writing and Difference* do much to explain, 'is the stage of history and the play of the world' (287). The 'fundamental property of writing' is '*spacing*' (272). *Writing and Difference* draws our attention to spacing in its epigraph, a fragment from Stéphane Mallarmé's preface to the experimental poem *Un coup de dés jamais n'abolira le hasard* (1897). It can be translated as: 'the whole [is] without any novelty except in the spacing of the act of reading.'[1] The novelty of these essays may not be in their propositions, ideas, interpretations, *content* – but perhaps consists in reorganization or displacement of something that philosophy has neglected: reading. The effects of this displacement are nothing less than revolutionary.

DIFFERENCE

Derrida's writing encompasses the unnameable in sentences that are daring and complex, moving between a familiar way of thinking and thoughts that are both necessary and unprecedented. For example, the possibility of the trace is 'a common and radical possibility that no determined science, no abstract discipline, can think as such'.² 'Trace' is therefore not put forward as the new name for 'writing' – the fruit of Derrida's researches. Rigorously, the provocative thought of the trace can only be broached within existing modes of knowledge and scientific discovery. The trace is a 'common root' that gives rise to the law but has no law and is 'not a root but the concealment of the origin'. Furthermore, it is

> not common because it does not amount to the same thing except with the unmonotonous insistence of difference, this unnameable movement of *difference-itself*, that I have strategically nicknamed *trace*, *reserve*, or *difference*, could be called writing only within the *historical* closure, that is to say within the limits of science and philosophy.

Thus the noun 'writing', *écriture*, is not itself, and is opened and dispersed as an 'unnameable movement'.

FORCE AND VIOLENCE

'Force is the other of language without which language would not be what it is' (32). *Of Grammatology* delineates a notion of 'originary violence' that has to do with 'writing in general' and with names.³ There is a violence of language which consists 'in inscribing within a difference, in classifying'.⁴ When we use names to 'think the unique within the system' and 'inscribe it there' we lose 'the proper' along with 'absolute proximity' and 'self-presence'. The latter was, anyway, 'only dreamed of and always already split, repeated, incapable of appearing to itself except in its own disappearance'. Violence has to do with difference and writing as the phenomena that trouble the illusions of presence and self-sameness. Doubling divides and opening breaks. For example, what 'Freud and the Scene of Writing' calls 'breaching' (Freud's *Bahnung*, pathbreaking) puts violence at the heart of memory and the psyche (252). Freud's notion of psychical writing opens the way to an exploration of repetition, which makes language possible: 'Force produces meaning (and space) through the power of "repetition" alone, which inhabits it originarily as its death' (268). Repetition is indispensable for the action of force but it also dissipates force into form, which can be translated and therefore understood. And concepts themselves, which function by always amounting to the same thing, are violent in their abstraction and their denial of the movements of *différance*. Derrida opens up the question of how this kind of structural violence relates to the more familiar concept of violence as it is understood in terms of moral law and transgression.

HISTORICITY

Geoffrey Bennington's work on Derrida refers to history as a 'necessary complicity' and reminds us that questions of historical responsibility are grounded in the non-coincidence of the present with itself.[5] In general, we can't help but accept what we would like to resist, even if only in order to resist it more effectively. To resist what should be resisted we must remain in the closest possible touch with its logic, without simply adopting it. Rather than think about time in terms of duration or the instant, Derrida's texts draw on a powerful logic of division and repetition that we can never simply catch up with or otherwise surpass. His work brings us in touch with history, makes us aware of being held, caught, surprised by it.

Derrida described his work as 'just doing history, in my own way'.[6] The current practice of putting texts or ideas in 'historical context' does justice neither to the text nor to history, which is supposed to be outside the text and to determine it. Derrida's generalization of writing and text discredits this opposition and challenges a historicism that remains barely able to recognize his work:

> History does not cease to be an empirical science of 'facts' because it has reformed its methods and techniques, or because it has substituted a comprehensive structuralism for causalism, atomism and naturalism, or because it has become more attentive to cultural totalities. Its pretension to founding normativity or a better understood factuality does not become more legitimate but only increases its powers of philosophical seduction. A confusion of value and existence, and more generally, of all types of realities and all types of idealities is sheltered beneath the equivocal category of the historical. (201–2)

METAPHYSICS

Derrida's reading of Husserl sought to acknowledge phenomenology as an ultimate, necessary but still questionable development of metaphysical thinking. Metaphysics remains a delicate, difficult and urgent issue for *Writing and Difference*. The word comes up hundreds of times in the text, signalling the impossibility of any simple movement 'beyond' metaphysics. Metaphysics, after all, refers to the fundamental questions addressed and formulated by Western philosophy: the investigation of the first principles of nature and thought, ontology or the science of being. Originally, in the writings of Aristotle, the Metaphysics came after (*meta*) the Physics, which studied natural science. Our discourse belongs to metaphysics. 'Force and Signification' associates metaphysics with the classical oppositions of duration and space, quality and quantity, depth of meaning and surface value, and analyses a metaphysics implicit in all structuralism. 'Cogito and the History of Madness' detects a metaphysics at work in Foucault's notion of the archaeology of silence. 'Violence and Metaphysics' questions Levinas's redefinition of metaphysics; '*La parole soufflée*' investigates Artaud, who was bent on destroying a dualism proper to metaphysics that separated body and soul, speech and existence. 'Freud and the Scene of Writing' identifies Freudian concepts as belonging to the history of metaphysics and yet their elaboration includes the notions of trace and supplement that trouble metaphysical thinking. 'Structure, Sign and Play' says that if you want to shake metaphysics then there's no sense in doing without metaphysical concepts.

THE BOOK

The derivation of the term 'metaphysics' points to the significance of the arrangement of writings into the variety of material forms we would call the book. We can point to 'Edmond Jabès and the Question of the Book' as a crystallization of matters raised by Maurice Blanchot.[7] He is in turn responding to the poet Mallarmé's notion of an absolute Book, combining aspects of the Bible and the earth, a single true and established text. Derrida responds directly to Mallarmé when he insists that to write is 'the absence of divine writing, that is to say, first of all, the absence of the Jewish God' (10). Writing is not analogous to divine creation.

Writing and Difference suggests we should think of a book as being bound together, not by its actual cover, nor by its contents (themes, ideas, belonging to a particular academic discipline), nor even by the framework of a particular social, historical and cultural context but by the unity of a strange movement of writing that we have no specialist vocabulary to describe. *Writing and Difference* has no author's explanatory preface but in a bibliographical note Derrida gives the original provenance of each of the essays (except 'Ellipsis', written especially to end the volume) and emphasizes the flexibility of the ties between these essays gathered between a single pair of covers. The note says of the texts now drawn together into the book: 'in order to bind them together [*pour les relier*], in order to reread them [*pour les relire*] we cannot hold ourselves at an equal distance from each of them' (xiv/437). In the absence of a single author's overview, Derrida's sense of writing as both systematic and impossible to systematize leaves room for the different essays (and for the letters of words such as *relier* and *relire*) to turn round, talk to each other, dance, connect and separate. The form is such that the relation of the contents remains somewhat mobile. Derrida's note doesn't deny that the book forms a system but it emphasizes that these essays will remain in a somewhat deranged relation to spatial organization, as they constitute 'the *displacement of a question*'. Decentring is a key movement in 'Structure, Sign and Play' and 'Ellipsis', which are the last two essays in the book. Never vague or imprecise, Derrida deliberately keeps the stitching loose, does not join the dots created by his incisive readings and leaves blanks blank.

CLOSURE

Closure is hugely important in *Writing and Difference*. In 'Cogito and the History of Madness', Foucault's notion of an archaeology of silence is described as a form of 'metaphysical closure', complicit with the classical values of origin, reason and history that Derrida argues are exceeded by writing (43). In 'Violence and Metaphysics' the term helps explain the limits of philosophical discourse and the problems inherent in Levinas's attempt to use philosophy as a way of opening thinking towards the beyond of philosophy. This opening would be impossible, according to

Derrida, without either (1) moving outside language and therefore outside thought or (2) without 'a kind of unheard of graphics' that would inscribe '*formally* and *thematically*' the question of '*the relations between belonging and the opening, the question of closure*' (138). In 'Genesis and Structure', Husserl's conception of transcendental consciousness is analysed in terms of the 'principled, essential and structural impossibility of closing a structural phenomenology', on account of the 'infinite opening of what is experienced' (204). Furthermore, beyond the relationship between perceiver and perceived that constitutes intentionality, lies *hylē*, matter, which is 'the possibility of genesis itself' and is the 'essential opening' without which 'consciousness could not receive anything *other* than itself' (205). The relation to the other, must, in language, always be related to the question of opening and closure, to borders, doors, passages. The first essay on Artaud, '*La parole soufflée*', is concerned with Artaud's awareness of the metaphysics of presence as what he calls 'cruel' or in other words, necessary. What is so extraordinary about Artaud for Derrida is his capacity to be critically aware and affirmative of the '*cruel* . . . law of difference' (244). Artaud uses metaphysical notions such as 'self-presence, unity, self-identity, the proper, etc' to reveal the limits of the metaphysical. Unlike his fellow 'destructive' thinkers, Nietzsche, Heidegger and Freud, who like him attack metaphysical assumptions in a manner that makes him dependent on them, Artaud seems to have inscribed and experienced the limit of metaphysics with a fatal vividness that makes Derrida wonder about the relation between the concept of madness and the concept of metaphysics in general. 'Freud and the Scene of Writing' understands psychoanalysis as having elements that do not readily fit within the 'logocentric closure' associated with linguistics (an implicit querying of Lacan's combination of Freud and Saussure) (249). In 'The Theatre of Cruelty and the Closure of Representation', Derrida explores the space created by Artaud's dependence on the concept of theatrical representation as a form of closure. Artaud loved theatre as overflowing; he hated theatre as repetition. Derrida sees that this conflict is not only Artaud's tragedy but also the tragic condition of all representation: 'Closure is the circular limit within which the repetition of difference infinitely repeats itself' (316). There's no chance for us to learn of the originating power of difference without doing so within the very limits that are produced by difference and eluded by it. The essay on Bataille and Hegel deals with the notion of economy as a form of closure and with Bataille as a writer with philosophical concerns who does not write from within philosophy. Bataille undertakes a 'calculated sliding' in writing that relates classical concepts to 'expenditure without reserve' and a 'nonmeaning which is . . . beyond the horizon or closure of absolute knowledge' (339). Absolute knowledge is Hegel's attempt to establish an impassable limit for deciding the relation between the known and the unknown, the knowable and the unknowable, within metaphysics. Bataille takes seriously Hegel's thinking of 'the completion of history and the closure of absolute knowledge' and then betrays them 'by exceeding them or by simulating them in play' (341). And 'Structure, Sign and Play' refers to closure in the context of language as play, as a field of 'infinite substitutions only because it is finite ['*substitutions infinies dans la clôture d'un ensemble fini*' – literally 'a field of infinite substitutions within the closure of a finite whole'] (365/423). Wherever Derrida wants to think either the movement beyond metaphysics, or play, he must appeal to the fact and concept of closure.

ECONOMY

This is an explicit preoccupation in the essay on Bataille, whose strange notion of 'general economy' opens up a reading of Hegel. But it is also crucial elsewhere, especially in Derrida's readings of Levinas and Freud. Derrida is interested in economies, plural. This account from *Dissemination* helps us to see how the relative domestication of an economy (from Greek, *oikos*, household) relates to the movements of difference, deferral and detour known as *différance*. *Différance* is the name of a 'kind of economy' (Derrida stresses its violent constitution by calling it a 'war economy') which brings 'the radical otherness or the absolute exteriority of the outside into relation with the closed, agonistic, hierarchical field of philosophical oppositions, of . . . "difference."'[8] An economy implies unreconciled tensions that cannot be mastered. In Levinas this concerns the relation to the other, in Freud, the relation between life and death. In Derrida there is an economic movement of the trace that implies both its mark and its erasure – the margin of its impossibility – according to a relation that no speculative dialectic of the same and the other can master, for the simple reason that such a dialectic always remains an operation of mastery.

The alternative to mastery is irreconcilable conflict. 'Violence and Metaphysics' insists, contra Levinas, 'One never escapes the *economy of war*' (185).

SIGNS

Derrida is not, despite a keen interest in these matters, a philosopher of language or a scientist of signs. *Speech and Phenomena* reads Husserl's theory of signs, as does 'Différance'. A large part of *Of Grammatology* consists of an exploration of philosophical thinking about language from the eighteenth century to the present in the form of a reading of Rousseau's 'Essay on the Origin of Languages'. The book also engages with the notion of the sign in Levi-Strauss's anthropology and in the linguistics of Ferdinand de Saussure. Derrida says in *Of Grammatology*: 'If it seems to us in principle impossible to separate, through interpretation and commentary, the signified from the signifier, and thus to destroy writing by the writing that is yet reading, we nevertheless believe that this impossibility is historically articulated.'[9] It is in *Of Grammatology* that Derrida writes most about linguistics, but the notion of signification is indispensable for a reading of *Writing and Difference*, where he approaches 'the question of the sign' as 'more, or less, or in any event something other, than a sign of the times' (2).

Structural linguistics described language as a system of signs and defined the sign as the combination of a signifier, the part of the sign we can hear and see, an 'acoustic image' and a signified, a concept. The relation between a signifier and its signified is understood to be arbitrary. Structural linguistics thereby makes a powerful attempt to contain and conceptualize the look and sound of words in relation to their meaning. But the aspect of Saussurean linguistics that interests Derrida most is its insistence on difference. According to Saussure, *difference* is what allows particular signifiers and signifieds to emerge from the indistinct mass of acoustic material or of thought. As Samuel Weber glosses it:

> Instead of language being considered from the vantage point of a hierarchically and temporally prior presence as its point of departure, it is construed as an articulation, determined and defined by a difference that produces identities only belatedly and retroactively: as concrete and individual signifiers and signifieds.[10]

Derrida eases writing and signification apart in 'Force and Signification', and 'Cogito and the History of Madness' insists that reading is not a simple passage from sign to signified. 'Edmond Jabès and the Question of the Book' offers us signs interrupted by silence, and commentary that is, according to Jabès's ear for writing, a lesson in being quiet (*comment taire*).[11] Derrida argues against the Saussurean notion of a 'transcendental signified', exempt from the system of signifiers, which would 'refer to no signifier, would exceed the chain of signs, and would no longer itself function as a signifier'.[12]

LIGHT

Reading makes us blind. Signification does not depend on vision. But thought has for a very long time arranged itself around the hierarchical opposition of light and dark. *Writing and Difference* insists that illumination can hide as well as reveal. 'Force and Signification' explores this through Nietzsche's Greek Gods Apollo (light, form, structure) and Dionysus (blindness, formlessness, frenzy). One does not read by natural light: 'Cogito and the History of Madness' works by the strange 'light of . . . rereading' and takes us beyond the totality of what is, to plant us in the 'light of a hidden sun' that is not the 'natural light' by which Descartes proves the existence of God (38, 69, 72). Jabès finds illumination in what Derrida calls 'the generous distance between signs': The *Book of Questions* finds a 'light' in the 'absence [of signs] which you read' (87). Phenomenology (etymologically from Greek *phainomenon*, 'that which appears or is seen') develops from a Greek notion of philosophical illumination. 'It is difficult', Derrida remarks, 'to maintain a philosophical discourse against light' (105). He traces the complexity of Levinas's attempt to philosophize without violence in terms of this problem and cites the philosophical and poetic commonplace that the 'heart of light is black' (106). 'Freud and the Scene of Writing' notes Freud's frequent use of photographic metaphors to elaborate the notion of psychic writing and 'From a Restricted to a General Economy' closes with a strange evocation of text and reading in terms of the impossibility of seeing (428n.18, 350).

NOTHING

Structuralism may be an efficient reading method, but it may not be fully alert to the possibilities of its own movement, and history rightly concerns itself with 'the immense region of somnambulism, the *almost-everything* that is not the pure waking state, the sterile and silent acidity of the question itself, the *almost-nothing*' (3). Derrida felt as a young man that he had nothing to say, but he also recognized that it is 'the consciousness of nothing, upon which all consciousness of something enriches itself, takes on meaning and shape' (8). An arresting and enigmatic interest in what is scarcely there, that which traditional philosophy would tend to exclude, is taken up in 'Violence and Metaphysics', where Derrida writes about 'certain problems put to philosophy as problems philosophy can't resolve' (98). These are for him the only questions capable of founding a community of philosophers in the wake of or beyond philosophy. This would be a community

> of decision, of initiative, of absolute initiality, but also a threatened community, in which the question has not yet found the language it has decided to seek, is not yet sure of its own possibility within the community ... This is very little – almost nothing – but within it, today, is sheltered and encapsulated an unbreachable dignity and duty of decision.

We will return to this passage. *Of Grammatology* also concerns itself with a thought without weight: 'a *thought* of the trace, of differance or of reserve' that has arrived at the limits of the knowable and that points beyond it.[13] This *thought* at this point is for Derrida 'a perfectly neutral name, the blank part of the text, the necessarily indeterminate index of a future epoch of difference. *In a certain sense, "thought" means nothing.*' And thinking is 'what we already know we have not yet begun'. So irony, negativity, doubt are not the rallying points. Perhaps what constitutes this community of thinkers is the secret.

CHAPTER 3

READING THE TEXT

'FORCE AND SIGNIFICATION'

'Force and Signification' is a call to work, to read and write, made *through reading and writing* and marks the possibility of a turning point in the history of literary criticism. Derrida reconsiders the notion of the work of art (*oeuvre*) and in the process gives us a text that understands itself, and asks to be understood, not as an object but as an incarnate movement of writing. The laborious connotations of 'work', of the writer applying himself to a task and creating some kind of object, engage with a wilder notion of writing as Dionysian excess – a dance that arises from passion. It is part of the universality of Derrida's work that he pays attention to states of body and soul. Hélène Cixous called him a 'surreptitious mathematician of moods [*états de l'âme*]'.[1] One could associate this kind of interest with literature, psychology or the investigations of consciousness undertaken by the branch of philosophy called phenomenology. Derrida's readings of Jabès and Artaud, of Freud, the founder of psychoanalysis, and of Husserl, the founder of phenomenology, affirm the direct interest these writers share in thinking about lived experience. Derrida, however, consciously begins with writing, using the term with a poet's sense that is not simply opposed to lived experience. One can *live writing*. 'Force and Signification' is packed with references to sleep, waking, somnambulism, dreaming, anxiety, desire and mental reflection as well as bodily movements such as sliding, dancing, sitting and bending over to read or write. However these states and acts are not Derrida's themes. They don't become the basis of a Derridean explanation of consciousness or bodily life in general. Themes take us in the direction of the signified 'content' of a text and for Derrida there is no 'general psychological structure that could rightly be separated from the signifier' and therefore, we might add, from the movement of reading.[2]

The essay opens our eyes and ears to the restlessness of writing and to writing's progression by way of difference. It favours the fluidity of reading over the fixity desired by interpretation. 'Force and Signification' suggests that signification, the work of language understood as a sign system, is not an adequate framework to understand force, which is neutralized by attempts to present it in a discourse. Ruin and fragmentation become means to break away from the melancholy passion for literary form articulated in the essay's epigraph from Flaubert. The desire for pure structure is a desire to deny the other, time and history. The essay closes with two different approaches to writing: Flaubert's formalist conviction that the man is nothing, the work is everything and Nietzsche's wish for a bodily writing, a dance of the pen. If Derrida agrees that writing 'cannot be thoroughly Dionysiac' and that one must sit down to write, he still manages to dance and to call others to take to the floor (34). The essay ends with Nietzsche's Zarathustra asking who will help him to take writing down from the mountaintop and engrave it in 'hearts of flesh' (35). It is a moment of the kind evoked in Derrida's *Monolingualism of the Other*:

> Each time I write a word, a word that I love and love to write; in the time of this word, at the instant of a single syllable, the song of this New International awakens in me. I never resist it, I am in the street at its call, even if, apparently, I have been working silently since dawn at my table.[3]

Structures

'Force and Signification' considers the limits and openings instituted by Jean Rousset's 1962 study of the form and genesis of literary texts by Corneille, Marivaux and others. This reading immediately engages the larger question of relations between on the one hand, the methods and assumptions of structural analysis and, on the other, literature. Rousset and structuralism are not just examples of a way of thinking prevalent in France in the 1960s: for reasons Derrida will explain, 'literary criticism is structuralist in every age' (3). Rousset wants, ultimately, to unify and make simultaneous two ways of reading that initially appear to be distinct from each other. His book treats as 'a homogenous reality' the authors' developing imaginative projects *and* formal patterns of language that cannot be reduced to authorial intention (16). According to Derrida, Rousset aims directly at the 'totality of thing and act, form and intention, entelechy [realized end] and becoming, the totality that is the literary fact as concrete form'. If writing is as Derrida argues, then Rousset's attempt to reconcile the history of a writer's work as a creative process and the analysis of the complete works as a formal structure cannot succeed. There is a resonance here with phenomenology and Husserl's vexed attempt to account for the constitution of a transcendental ego as an adventure that happens in time *and* to make the transcendental ego the foundation of the structure of experience. For according to Derrida, one can only oppose force to force and writing to writing: the unity of force is never going to be present as itself. There are forms without one single form. Derrida identifies as metaphysical the 'aesthetic that neutralises duration and force' and the conviction that 'truth is absolute simultaneity' (27, 28).

Moving Off

The first sentence of 'Force and Signification' evokes structuralism as an act of war, part of history but not yet past: 'If it recedes one day, leaving behind its works and signs on the shores of our civilisation, the *structuralist* invasion might become a question for the historian of ideas, or perhaps even an object' (1/9). We should note the 'if': the structuralist invasion has the temporality of a text and consists of multiple works and signs that we do not yet know how to interpret. An invasion is a presence, like the current Allied 'presence' in Iraq. It is also something that happens to presence and it is not simply *there* to be examined. (A war journalist's job is complex and dangerous: even turning up where the fighting is can be difficult.) Presence is neither neutral nor simple. Signification, the process of language as understood by structural linguistics, takes time. And writing, Derrida will emphasize, endures. Reading will take time. Our civilization is made of archives and remains. The first sentence sets up a hypothesis. Structuralism is not, or not yet, a question, an object or a theme for our civilization to reflect upon at leisure. It remains ready to be, not yet formed or formalized, while already generating effects.

Derrida finds various words for structuralism's action, an important one being the verbs *s'ébranler* (meaning 'to move off, start off or activate') and *ébranler* ('shake'). They are translated as 'activation' (2) and 'shaking' (5) in 'Force and Signification'.[4] These words also describe the effect of Derrida's text. If a motivating force can affect history and language, while resisting being placed by history, linguistics, philosophy or literary criticism, it becomes necessary to open up a new reading awareness in order to engage with the effects of the said force. That would be the way to see for oneself in 'Force and Signification', but not only there, what Derrida is talking about when he says: 'Force is the other of language without which language would not be what it is' (31). That sentence may be elliptical (how could a remark about something other than language be anything else?) but awareness of the play of forces in writing is the route to understanding Derrida. While Derrida patiently observes the strategies Rousset uses, what he likes best about Rousset is not to be formalized: it is the quality of Rousset's attention to texts. Cixous recalls that Derrida himself gave and deserved special attention: '"A bloke who pays attention to what he says," he said to me one day about Heidegger, as about himself. . . . Pay attention to what he says, he who pays attention to what he says.'[5]

'Force and Signification' suggests that no image or concept of force can avoid separating force from itself. Force is neither an entity nor a movement; it may get something moving, but it never appears itself. When history, philosophy, psychology or literary criticism take force as a theme, it undergoes a formalization that makes force appear but in the same gesture freezes and thereby de-natures the very thing that is being brought to our attention. We get an image or a memorial of force and not the thing itself. History, philosophy and the rest reduce the quality of what they are pursuing to something quantifiable. Something similar happens when language is conceptualized as system of signs, as it is in the various kinds of work (literary–critical, linguistic, anthropological and so on) that are covered by the umbrella term 'structuralism'.

Letters, Literature and Literality

For Derrida the visible and audible aspects of language bring our attention to difference and to words' ability to escape their fixed, proper or natural form. Especially when we come across reiterated fragments of words, pairs or groups of letters that are less than complete signifiers and which cannot therefore be understood as the acoustic image of a concept. His writing often becomes loud with these reiterations of sounds. He is a poet. In some later works word fragments are recognized as key players: *Glas* gives us *gl-* and the section of *The Truth in Painting* (called '+R (Into the Bargain)' is laced with *tr-*. The gathering (we could just as well name it a scattering) of syllables shows language being marked by something that cannot appear in the words themselves, if a word is understood to be the bearer of meaning. Only in the original French can we experience this aspect of Derrida's attitude to force. A reading that paid attention to force as that-which-escapes-articulation-while-making-it-possible, would note the insistence of certain syllables in the French version of 'Force and Signification': beginning with '*Si*', the 'If' that itself begins the essay. The phoneme [*si*] occurs twice in the French pronunciation of 'signification' and its letters, side by side, scattered or inverted, recur densely across Derrida's text. That this may still seem an eccentric thing to mention, a riskily slight phenomenon to make much of, is a measure of where we are in the reception of Derrida's work.

Derrida does not philosophize by making propositions. 'Force and Signification' would be of little interest if it either agreed or disagreed with Raymond Rousset's readings of French literary texts, or noted that structuralism, while having certain limits, has something to contribute to the progress of thought that phenomenology lacks. Noticing the syllables allows us to experience, at a level deeper than the explicit, how writing is inhabited and worked over by force. To pick out some important words in the opening of the essay: *signification* itself is inhabited, *civilization* is being entered, the *historian* of ideas (in French, *des idées*) is delayed in his desire to take structuralism as an object, dead and done with, by this trifling hiss on the line, this sibilant 'if,' this sly or shy glimpsed *si* or *is* or *xi* or *s'y* or *ici* (or *ti*, thanks to the 't' in some French words that is phonetically [*s*]). *Si* transmits its force, like the insistent argumentative affirmative '*mais si*', right across the essay, and in a way that won't go away, that *insists* (an important word for the remains and ruins that interest Derrida), as much as it resists being fixed as a structure, an underpinning, the foundation of a system. As Derrida says: 'What is at stake, first of all, is an adventure of vision, a conversion of the way of putting questions . . .' (1). 'Force and Signification' does not formalize or aestheticize the effects of its own writing by laying down in advance the philosophical framework that would dominate its reading. The unheard of music of writing is the displacing force that Derrida puts before signification in his title because in his thinking, the force of writing comes first.

Derrida's concern is 'the literary object' or, less scientifically, the literary *thing, la chose littéraire* (1/9). 'Force and Signification' accentuates the verbal and etymological connection between literature and the letters that make up writing; Derrida reads *to the letter* and, ideally, should be read in the same way. This way of reading transforms critical writing: letters keep working in an active and unruly fashion, even while we try to get a handle on what they are doing. Their movement destabilizes what literary criticism, not just Rousset's criticism, and not to mention history and philosophy, usually takes to be the stability of textual structures. Force escapes description from the point of view of philosophical writing with its implicit claim to exemption from the contingencies of language, which are hypostasized as literary form. Force escapes form. It also drives and troubles signification. This is explicitly argued by Derrida but it also rigorously affects the composition of the text.

The ideal of objectivity in history and, by implication, in philosophy and the study of language and literature is at stake. The opening of 'Force and Signification' suggests that structuralism would have to be done with in order to become an object for the attention of historians. The history of ideas neutralizes tensions and conflicts by containing them within an apparently impartial discourse and describing ideas as if from an impartial point of view. Structuralism is progressive because it challenges the assumption that objectivity of this kind can itself go unquestioned. Structuralism 'first of all, is an adventure of vision [*regard*], a conversion of the way of putting questions to any object posed before us'. Derrida's text does not show us that adventure of vision but invites us to undergo it, to be invaded and inhabited by it. At the end of the essay Derrida reminds us that the notion of literary form adopted by structuralism was already contested in the nineteenth century in Nietzsche's responses to Flaubert's remarks on writing. There is a risk to literary aesthetics in the notion of writing as letter. It endangers our current sense of what literature is by 'dissolving the notion of art and the value of "beauty" by which literature is currently distinguished from the letter in general' (14). However, 'removing the specificity of beauty from aesthetic values' would *liberate* beauty from the visual register. Derrida uses the word 'literature' quite rarely in this chapter. 'Letter', 'literal' and 'literality' occur more often. On the basis of these terms we are invited to understand anew what Derrida will later call 'this strange institution called literature'. For now we should mark his preference for liberated beauty, beauty that does not wait for the conceptual framework of aesthetics and entails movement and breakthrough. At the beginning of the chapter he dreamed of a literary criticism that would not wait for philosophy and towards its end cites Nietzsche saying that music should not be confused with acoustics. The letter for Derrida seems to be a way to a sort of raw, indescribable energy.

Anxiety

The structuralist invasion is something that is happening to universal thought. Derrida calls it *réflexion universelle*, keeping up the notion of an adventure of *looking*, of something happening to *vision*. It is receiving something from language itself. This is not an isolable episode, but takes the form of a shudder passing through language itself. This 'formidable' movement is happening all over, by all routes and despite all differences. The movement *is* the mode of reception, and the anxiety *is* the movement. The notion of force that Derrida entertains here affects the familiar opposition between thought and language. Throughout his work we learn of the strange continuities between the two; here at the beginning of *Writing and Difference*, an agitation of and in language itself comes to our attention. Language is *unquiet* – it is anxious but also more literally not at peace. In the next few pages a lexical–graphical–universal disquiet will emerge under the names 'shaking', '*solicitation*', which can be glossed as 'making everything move', and '*angustia*', the Latin root of 'anxiety' (5, 8). Like the recurrence of a reiterated syllable playing across the processes of signification that interest structuralist thought about language, this widespread anxiety resists formalization. It is 'not . . . able to display itself in its entirety as a spectacle for the historian' (1–2/9). The adventure of vision entails disconcerting blind spots. Rhythmic intervals of light and dark, clarity and obscurity, waking and sleep pulse across the essay. The Nietzschean gods Dionysus and Apollo, respectively identified with ardour and structure, necessarily variable in their behaviour and not simply opposed, emerge as avatars of force and form. Rather than domesticate difference into a fixed structure of oppositions, the text attends to them and articulates them in a discourse for which they are not objects on display, but conditions of possibility for our reading.

Derrida is interested in what historians do to thought: they care more for the signified than the movements of the signifier. The historian sees signs and symptoms but does not necessarily hear syllables. However, our pet sound, the sample *si* or *ci* or *is* becomes very insistent when Derrida writes about the historian's attempts to recognize the disturbance of language as a locatable moment within the unquestioned continuity of historical time: 'if (*si*) by chance he (*celui-ci*) were to attempt to recognise in [language] the sign (*signe*) of an epoch, the fashion of a season (*saison*), or the symptom (*symptôme*) of a crisis (*crise*)' (2/9). These *si*'s only insist; they do not discuss or discover. They neither hamper nor clinch the argument. But they do point to something other than signification. He will say later that 'access to free speech' consists in the release of language from its 'signalizing function' (13). Poetry gives access to free speech in this way, but so does writing:

> By enregistering speech, inscription has as its essential objective, and indeed takes this fatal risk, the emancipation of meaning – as concerns any actual field of perception – from the natural disposition in which everything refers to the disposition of a contingent situation.

The contingent becomes thoroughly contingent for the first time when it passes beyond the boundaries guaranteed by a particular situation where speech takes place. The risk is 'fatal' for reasons that are articulated elsewhere.

All writing ... in order to be what it is, must be able to function in the radical absence of every empirically determined addressee [and sender, and producer], in general. And this absence is not a continuous modification of presence; it is a break in presence, 'death', or the possibility of the 'death' of the addressee [or sender, or producer], inscribed in the structure of the mark.⁶

Fascination

The question of the sign is historical, Derrida agrees, but in an unaccustomed sense. Meaning is undergoing a shake-up, 'an operation called, from the Latin, *soliciting*' (5). We speak of something or someone 'soliciting our attention' and the writing here does that by its way of addressing itself to signification and by a certain kind of attention to force. It works in the reading and therefore in the reader. Derrida describes how structuralism has brought thought about signs to a point where the 'simply signicative' nature of language appears to be much less than the whole story. (The undisciplined whispering of inscription in these sentences is strong even in English on this page.) Somewhere in the becoming 'uncertain, partial and inessential' of signification we are invited by the consonance of letters and sounds to reconsider beauty as force, an irreducible power to fascinate that inhabits, but is not reducible to, the notion of structure. This fascination fuels 'the structuralist obsession' and the anxiety of language. Derrida suggests that we reconsider 'the meanings of imagination, affectivity [*sensibilité*] and fashion' in the light of structure's power to fascinate. A footnote cites the American anthropologist Alfred Kroeber, who says:

> 'Structure' appears to be just a yielding to a word that has a perfectly good meaning [*signification*] but suddenly becomes fashionably attractive for a decade or so ... and during its vogue tends to be applied indiscriminately because of the pleasurable connotations of its sound [*l'agrément de ... consonance*]. (379n.2/10n.2)

Derrida points to the value of differentiating the meaning of the words one uses, giving a long list of terms roughly synonymous with 'structure', implying that the word 'structure' can be more precisely differentiated from, and is more inhabited by other words, than we might guess from Kroeber's airy remark that it has a 'perfectly good meaning'.

Still, one can have a weakness, a soft spot, for favourite words. Derrida's notion of force works with, and on, susceptibility, imagination and sensibility. He will write in 'Circumfessions' of 'seeing a word' as if for the first time, 'as happens to me so often, and each time it's the birth of a love affair, the origin of the earth'.[7] Imagination, fashion and sensibility are open to charm, which suspends our powers of discrimination between objects on the basis of their meaning and draws our attention to the qualities of the thing itself. When the thing is 'the literary thing', a text, that means a fascination with letters: consonance, chiming, the play of the letter and vocalic repetition. Fascination does not want to arrive at a just valuation of what fascinates it. That would mean having done with being invaded by it and being ready to write its history. Derrida acknowledges that '*Form* fascinates when one no longer has the force to understand force from within itself. That is, to create' (3). For this reason literary criticism has always been essentially structuralist and at the time Derrida is writing, criticism has begun to recognize its own melancholy relation to force as that of which it is itself bereft. Perhaps it is time for a new understanding of the opposition between 'critical' and 'creative' writing?

Historicity

So 'the structuralist stance, as well as our attitudes assumed before or within language, are not only moments of history. They are an astonishment, rather, by language as the origin of history. By historicity itself' (2). We are, Derrida insists, surprised by writing, held in it, already in a text. An indirect approach to force, an avowed lack of philosophical originality and muscle makes structuralism, preoccupied with (and astonished by) language and form, the most able to articulate the relation between repetition and surprise that is, for Derrida, the possibility of history.

Structuralist analyses, Derrida says, 'are possible only after a certain defeat of force and within the movement of a diminished ardour' (3). This defeat comes just when Derrida seems to be going large, extending his account of the structuralist invasion to a discussion of world culture and speaking of nothing less than the 'activation [*ébranler*]' of Western thought. The destiny of Western thought is to extend its reign while, correspondingly, the West draws back its boundaries. That sounds like a big historical generalization. But Derrida's concern with historicity insists on 'language as the origin of history'. Being 'before [in front of] or within language', and 'before the possibility of speech' is like being in front of a door that we are already through, because we are 'always already within' the possibility of speech. This doesn't mean we are in the presence of something. In this state or possible state how could one indicate the possibilities? Structuralism's astonishment at language escapes the classical history of ideas. However Derrida stresses that because structuralism is surprisable, and to that extent unreflective and spontaneous, it deserves the attention of historians.

Haunting

Structuralism may celebrate its interpretive triumphs but knows itself to be bereft of force. This weakness has a clarifying effect because 'the relief and design of structures appears more clearly when content, which is the living energy of meaning, is neutralised' (4). But to neutralize a structure is inevitably destructive. (Derrida insisted that deconstruction was not neutral.[8] It is, on the contrary, affirmative.) Derrida thinks of structure as an emptied city 'reduced to its skeleton by some catastrophe of nature or art' and 'now only haunted by meaning and culture'. The 'state of being haunted which keeps the city from returning to nature, is perhaps the general mode of presence or absence of the thing itself in pure language'. This haunting is disturbing but inner disquiet is the very movement of language as consciousness rather than a psychic state that could exist outside language. It is an *ébranlement*: a jolt of force, a vibration or trembling, the jolt at the setting off of a vehicle or by analogy the threat of ruin or the nervous shock produced by a vivid emotion. Everything shakes: consciousness begins as an earthquake.

The care and conscientiousness of structuralist literary criticism such as Rousset's are, Derrida shows, powered by a force that that consciousness separates itself from in order to come into existence as such. Structuralism's awareness of language is nothing other than its succumbing to a movement or violence. It can take this movement as its object in a critical act that thereby transforms itself into an act of purifying destruction, which empties out force as living presence. 'Structuralist solicitude and solicitation . . . reproduce, in the register of method, a solicitude and solicitation of being' (5). (The English text capitalizes 'Being' here but Derrida just has *l'être*, not a philosophical term so much as an ordinary French word and a homonym for *lettre*, letter.) Structuralism has transformed the shaking of the letter into a method. Deconstruction does not do that: Rousset's book is not an empty town for Derrida. He values *Forme et signification* not for methodological reasons but because its readings relieve an anxiety of language that seems to conform, 'beneath the language, operations, and greatest achievements of this book' to the anxiety of the author himself. Rousset is able to feel the impurity and haunted quality of language.

Freedom

Rousset reflects on the literary–critical idea that 'language is one with meaning, that form belongs to the content of the work' (6). This would depend on a neutralized or transparent text that formal analysis could in principle fully understand. The play and letters and sounds by which we have been reading the opening of 'Force and Signification' already shake the supposed unity of language and meaning, form and content. The letter does not simply belong within language; neither does it direct our attention towards a unity of meaning, a matrix or a set of key terms for the interpretation of the text. Literary criticism doesn't quite know what to do with letters. Wayward and indispensable, literality has a rapport with the imagination as Derrida recognizes it in Rousset and, beyond Rousset, in Kant. Literary criticism seeks to conceptualize imagination as the 'mediation or synthesis between meaning (*sens*) and literality (*lettre*).' But Kant insists that imagination is a hidden art that cannot be expounded or conceptualized. Derrida agrees that to understand creative imagination one must 'turn oneself toward the invisible interior of poetic freedom' and admires Rousset's attention to 'the enigmatic origin of the work' (7). Reading must engage with the unknowable if it is to engage force.

Imagination 'is a freedom that reveals itself only in its works' (6). The notion of poetic freedom will recur in the essays on Jabès, and Derrida discusses freedom more generally in his readings of

Levinas, Artaud and Hegel. Imaginative freedom manifests itself in works that do not exist within nature, 'but neither do they inhabit a world *other* than ours.' This gives us a new insight into the book's epigraph, Mallarmé's remark that 'the whole [is] without any novelty except in the spacing of the act of reading.' Derrida has been working with notions of space and location in writing and now we find that writing and reading both concern a 'departure from the world towards a place which is neither a *non-place* nor an *other* world, neither a utopia nor an alibi' (7). To read or write a literary work, a work of imagination, is to be divided: 'separated from oneself in order to be reunited with the blind origin of the work in its darkness'. Familiar notions of the work of art (*oeuvre*) and of the book will be touched by this sense that reading and writing are not responsible to the phenomenal world. Derrida refers to a number of literary writers at this point including Blanchot, Artaud and Flaubert, and by implication Mallarmé and others. It is hard not to be conscious of the resemblance and etymological relation between the French words for book and freedom, *livre* and *liberté*. ('Edmond Jabès and the Question of the Book' does so too, extending the chain through *lieu*, place, and a number of other signifiers in *li-*.) Latin *liber* happens to have meant both 'book, paper, parchment' from Indo-European *leub-h* 'to strip or peel' and 'free' from *leudho*, 'people', also a root of Greek *eleutheria*. But writing is not what we tend to think of as freedom. It is not freedom of choice. There is a politics in Derrida's discussion of poetic freedom and force, but it is a politics that gives space to nothing and to what may appear to be a woeful lack of force, for example to the 'consciousness of having something to say as the consciousness of nothing' which is, he adds, 'not the poorest but the most oppressed of consciousnesses' (8). Artaud had this difficult gift.

Writing between Heaven and Earth

The oppressed consciousness of nothing inherits an untold wealth because it is that 'upon which all consciousness of something enriches itself, takes on meaning and shape. And on whose basis speech can be brought forth'. Freedom is not the prize of a struggle nor the acceptance of some external reality or other. It doesn't seem to be a state one can enter. It is not won by the writer's personal suffering ('not an empirical modification or state of the writer') but does involve a return to anxiety – this time not the *inquietude* of language but an *angoisse* of writing. *Angustia*, the Latin root of *angoisse* and *anxiety* means 'constriction, distress' or more concretely, 'choking'. This is how Derrida defines it:

> the necessarily restricted passageway of speech against which all possible meanings push each other, preventing each other's emergence. Preventing, but calling upon each other, provoking each other too, unforeseeably and as if despite oneself, in a kind of autonomous overassemblage of meanings, a power of pure equivocality that makes the creativity of the classical God appear all too poor. (8)

What's more, 'if the necessity of becoming breath or speech restricts meaning – and our responsibility for it – writing restricts and constrains speech further still' (9). The content or message of writing has been neutralized – made nothing – to allow a new account of writing to emerge as the experience of being between the air and the earth. For Derrida that is between permanently jostling possibilities of meaning, universal but unstructured, vaporous and ethereal and the 'no less universal element in which meaning is engraved', Derrida tells us in a note, 'so that it will last' (383n.23). The link between heaven and earth is as if in the writer's body, which is the site of both passage and blockage. The writer takes responsibility for the experience of not being able to take responsibility for writing. You can't take responsibility for writing, Derrida suggests, any more than you could take responsibility for the air by breathing. Writing 'is the moment at which we must *decide* whether we will engrave what we hear' (9). That decision cannot be made on the basis of meaning because it is the decision that decides meaning.

Poetry is 'access to free speech'; it frees language from signification, which is a kind of sleep. Poetry awakens speech and frees it from being '*utilised*' as information or as the communicating passage from one being to another or from the signifier to the signified (13). Poetry creates meaning by 'enregistering (*consignant*) it, entrusting it to an engraving, a groove (*sillon*), a relief, to a surface' that wants meaning to be 'transmissible' to infinity.

The groove is a *sillon*, literally a furrow that keeps faith with the earth Derrida identifies with the endurance of writing. The notion of a writing that *wants* something (not rendered in the translation) opens a discussion of *vouloir-écrire*, literally of *to want-to write*. The earth of writing wants the mark endlessly there, endlessly moving off.

Vouloir-écrire, which the English translation gives as 'the attempt-to-write' or as 'the will to write', is defined in a series of negations of all the things you might think it is: not free will, not primal will, not desire. It's not a philosophical concept either. Derrida even defines it against something familiar to all of us. Writing is the only possibility of an escape from personal feeling and emotional susceptibility: 'It is a question here not of affectivity but of freedom and duty . . . To be affected is still to be finite: to write still could be to deceive finitude, and to reach being.' Derrida's notion of 'being' here is more Beckettian than Heideggerian. His 'finitude' corresponds to the notion of 'habit' in Samuel Beckett's study of Proust. For Beckett the times between the continuity of periods of habit 'represent the perilous zones in the life of the individual, dangerous, precarious, mysterious and fertile, when for the moment the boredom of living is replaced by the suffering of being'.[9]

The Work of Art

Derrida is interested in the attempt to account for the act of writing by a particular writer, in a particular work, without 'historicism, biographism or psychologism', all of which are forms of storytelling ready to distract reading from 'the internal historicity of the work itself, in its relation to a subjective origin that is not simply psychological or mental' (15). This 'historicity of the work is not only its past, the eve or the sleep in which it precedes itself in an author's intentions, but it is also the impossibility of its ever being present, of its ever being summarized by some absolute simultaneity or instantaneousness' (15/25). The stories literary criticism tells about the historical, biographical or psychic origin of a work are, Rousset and Derrida believe, fictions. These critical fictions have been written; they therefore have historicity, but they are not true accounts. The structure of the work is not its history but nor is it objective or formal.

Derrida emphasizes historicity because by defining 'the *internal* truth and meaning of the work' Rousset risks losing a sense of that historicity, which has to do with what Derrida said earlier makes the work work – 'pure absence – not the absence of this or that' (7). Only that can *'inspire'*. This helps us to understand how it is that there is 'no *space* of the work, if by space we mean *presence* and *synopsis*' (15). The history of the work is another story, the story of the 'operation' of the work. 'Operation' comes from Latin *opus*, origin of *oeuvre*, the word for both 'work' and 'work of art' in French. The 'proper history and temporality' of the work of art can't be taken as objects. Structuralism is a 'restraint' (*garde-fou*, an important word in *Of Grammatology* where it refers to a safety-barrier or guard-rail rather than an actual restraint) in relation to an 'internal geneticism' that reconstitutes and reawakens value and meaning. This history doesn't come to light and can't be made present but shakes, startles or haunts presence, making it what it so strangely is.

Structure for Rousset is no longer a matter of space but of words and letters. It is 'the literary thing itself' but the literary thing this time taken, or at least practised, *literally* (*à la lettre*). Rousset is interested almost exclusively in 'relational configuration' and takes the correlation of linguistic forms to be the essence of the work. He 'grants an absolute privilege to spatial models, mathematical functions, lines and forms' (18). But not in the accepted metaphorical sense of these structures as entities in space, and of literary structure therefore as a spatial form in which the writer places or arranges his material. This section is worth slowing over because Derrida's work is itself often read in terms of topics or 'the theory of commonplaces in language and the manipulation of motifs or arguments' (17). Is this, as he asks, because of 'the fact that language can determine things only by spatialising them'? That seems to provoke a 'sliding as unnoticed as it is efficacious' that confuses meaning with its 'geometric, morphological, or in the best of cases, cinematic model' (18). 'Metaphor is never innocent' (19). Our attention is being directed towards something in writing that has no place. There is something other than metaphor, even if historicism would be mistaken in believing itself exempt from metaphoricity or in believing that it can simply take metaphor as its object without asking how a history of metaphor might be possible.

Surprise

Structures imply simultaneity: a theory of space must also imply a theory of time, however limited. In literature and literary criticism in particular, 'duration and force' are neutralized as 'the difference between the acorn and the oak' (27). This aesthetic of encasement can be traced in Proust and Claudel as well as Rousset but it 'translates' the more general thought-pattern of a metaphysics. This metaphysics also implies a particular way of thinking about the book: 'a structuralist reading, by its own activity, always presupposes and appeals to the theological simultaneity of the book' (28). All fragments contribute towards a work that is, in Rousset's words, 'simultaneously present in all its parts'. Rousset acknowledges an irregular counter-tendency to fragmentariness in the book but sets up the 'task of the demanding reader' as to overturn this tendency and render the work present, all at once. The book becomes a way of totalizing writing and the kind of reading Rousset practises is a confirmation of fundamental relationships that persist despite the fact that reading takes place in time. By contrast Derrida gives us a very powerful experience of rereading as surprise. Difference is neutralized by comparison and can only be experienced as some sort of surprise, which is itself the experience of being sur-*prised*, taken, beyond any possible intention, by writing as power. When Rousset speaks, perhaps rather complacently, of the surprises revealed by transforming the book into a 'simultaneous network of reciprocal relationships,' Derrida expostulates: 'What surprises? How can simultaneity hold surprises in store? Rather, it neutralises the surprises of non-simultaneity. Surprises emerge from the dialogue between the simultaneous and the nonsimultaneous. Which suffices to say that structural simultaneity *itself* serves to reassure' (28).

All this means a return to the notion of the spacing of reading set forth in the epigraph to *Writing and Difference*. Space differs from simultaneity: 'by saying "simultaneity" instead of space, one attempts to concentrate time instead of *forgetting* it' (29). Forgetting would be an experience of the same order as surprise: an experience that cannot be mastered. Later, Cixous comes up with the word *oublire* (*oublier*, to forget, condensed with *lire*, to read) to describe how, each time one reads the text, it is the same and different.[10] Force can't be ironed out. It nests in *volumes*.

A note points out that structuralist critics hold to 'the letter of the flattened, established Law; the commandment on the Tables' (388n.53).

Broken Tables

In the extraordinary closing pages of the essay Derrida finds in this very Law what the note calls 'the letter of books – movement, infinity, lability and instability of meaning rolled up in itself in the wrapping, the volume'. The letter is on the side of spacing and meaning that is not restricted to the operations of signification. There are elements of signification that cannot, Derrida insists, 'be spread out into the simultaneity of a form'. Writing is not identical to itself and is not at peace. The disquiet, the suspicion of all reassurances, the anxiety and trembling of language that inhabit the essay must also be explicitly stated, formulated, for example when Derrida asks 'is it by chance' that the force of meaning in the broad sense is 'a certain pure and infinite equivocality which gives signified meaning no respite, no rest, but engages it in its own economy so that it always signifies again and differs?' (29). Real books are unrealized and unrealizable because of this restless differencing; they make the categories in which they are supposed to be securely conceptualized 'tremble'.

So what has happened to philosophy? Structuralism has a 'dependence on phenomenology' and its 'conceptualization not only of direction but of power' which Derrida addresses throughout *Writing and Difference* (32). 'Force and Signification' has been concerned with giving a non-conceptual account of force that does not leave philosophy intact. The language of sleep, waking, forgetting and dream that Derrida has been using throughout, apparently metaphorically, engages with Husserl's phenomenological thought about consciousness and beyond that with a language of form and images of dark and light. At the end of the essay it is clear that Western philosophy is not competent to understand force because images of dark and light, and the oppositions form/substance, form/matter or form/crypt cannot conceive force. The dream of emancipation from this language is preferable to the attempt, which would involve a denial of the history that makes this language inevitable (33). A dream implies a wish that is fulfilled in and by the dream and not a utopian project that denies necessity. A dream is unrealized, like the book as Derrida understands it. Freedom and the experience of force in deconstruction always entail a sense of what is impossible, what one cannot do. It has to do with acceptance but also with resistance and it does not wait for philosophical formulations that would guide and protect its resistance – because that resistance would precisely counter a philosophical language inadequate to force. Criticism will have to renounce the 'privilege given to vision' and 'Apollonian ecstasy'.

Apollo and Dionysus are characters from Nietzsche's *Birth of Tragedy* and Nietzsche, a philosopher who is also a writer of troubling books, also comes on stage at the end of the essay in a double-act with Flaubert. But Derrida's anticipation of a literary criticism capable of loving force exceeds identification with any one writing-master. Instead he advocates a new kind of exchange between literature and criticism in which criticism renounces the kind of pleasure Rousset takes in form and goes on to

> exceed itself to the point of embracing (*aimer*, to love) both force and the movement that displaces lines, . . . to the point of embracing (*aimer*) force as movement, as desire, for itself, and not as the accident or epiphany of lines. To the point of embracing it as writing. (33/47)

Writing is an extension of the love of force as movement and desire. Criticism must learn to be writing and not the contemplation of writing as form.

'Historicity itself' now returns as 'the difference between Dionysus and Apollo, between ardour and structure'. This difference 'cannot be erased in history, for it is not in history. It too, in an unexpected sense, is an original structure: the opening of history, historicity itself. *Difference* does not simply belong either to history or to structure' (34). A purely Dionysian writing, the mobile, energetic conception of writing resisted by Flaubert and recommended by Nietzsche, may be desirable but not possible. Language is not capable of formlessness: 'Dionysus is worked by difference. He sees and lets himself be seen.' He has form too. And the exaltation of writing as a new kind of master concept would not be true to its affinity with roots, earth and the lowly.

Writing is down among the letters. It is 'better still when letters are no longer figures of fire in the heavens' (35). In accordance with the earlier account of writing as written in the earth, to write one must 'descend, work, bend down in order to engrave and carry the new Tables down to the valleys, to read them and have them read'. We must begin where we are, as he says elsewhere. The last page or so of the essay must be read in terms of the letter but also to the letter. The 'v' of engraving, and the '*si*' of, for example, 'incidence and insistence of inscription' take us right into writing, into an unpacified energy of writing that is not reducible to meaning, form or concept. It can never, therefore, win an argument, make a point or manifest a position. How can we think about it? By writing. What will you write? That would be the question.

Study Question
What kind of writing would be most forceful? Would it be a private letter, a speech by Shakespeare, a philosophical argument, a newspaper editorial, a set of instructions? How do you measure writing-force or writing as the difference between forces?

'COGITO AND THE HISTORY OF MADNESS'
The essay's epigraphs from Kierkegaard and Joyce suggest that the maddest thing about madness may be how close it is to reason. Madness haunts reasonable enterprises like making a decision or writing a book. According to Kierkegaard: 'The Instant of Decision is Madness.'[11] Kierkegaard's *Philosophical Fragments* (1844) asks the following questions: 'Can a historical point of departure be given for an eternal consciousness; how can such a point of departure be of more than historical interest; can an eternal happiness be built on historical knowledge?'[12] The remark about madness is part of Kierkegaard's interrogation of historicity: what are we to make of experience in, of and as time, given that consciousness may be an illusory representation that bears an unknown relation to the eternal and the true? How are the vagaries of what happens to and in my consciousness be gathered up into a totality? The indispensable thinker of such questions is Hegel, whose *Phenomenology of Spirit* (1807) describes the relation of consciousness to the truth of reason. For Derrida, Joyce was akin to Hegel. When he read *Ulysses* at Harvard in

1956–1957, he recognized the resemblance. Joyce attempted to gather together a number of languages, cultures and religions in a single work. For Derrida that 'impossible task of precisely gathering in a totality, in a potential totality, the potentially infinite memory of humanity' was new and modern but also 'very classical in its philosophical form. That's why I have often compared Joyce's Ulysses to Hegel's, for instance, the *Encyclopaedia* or the *Logic*. It is an attempt to reach absolute knowledge through a single act of memory'.[13] So when Derrida cites Joyce saying that only a transparent sheet separated his 'terribly risky' book *Ulysses* (1922) from madness, he is alluding to the intimacy between madness and a crowning work of reason (36). Joyce's sheet (*feuille*) seems alarmingly permeable, given that it already shares so many letters with madness (*folie*).

Derrida is about to take a decisive step and a risk. 'Cogito and the History of Madness' was initially a paper delivered at the Collège Philosophique in 1963. It addresses Foucault's *Madness and Civilisation: A History of Insanity in the Age of Reason* (1961). Derrida speaks of his gratitude to Foucault as a teacher. He had begun to read Husserl in his first year at the École Normale Supérieure (ENS) while attending Foucault's lectures on Husserl's *Ideas II* and on Merleau-Ponty. He states, somewhat formally: 'I retain the consciousness of an admiring and grateful disciple.' In a phrase of Hegel's, Derrida calls this an 'unhappy consciousness'. Derrida describes how, when he starts to respond to the master in public, the disciple feels 'challenged by the master who speaks within him and before him' (37). The mental torment of inner division silences him. He is both master and disciple and neither; he has no choice but to speak.

Hegel's *Phenomenology of Spirit* says that the '*unhappy, inwardly disrupted* consciousness' is a divided unity.[14] The division of self-contradiction is essential for the progressive movement of reason but the Unhappy Consciousness is 'not as yet explicitly aware' that it *is* a unity. Instead it is, like Kierkegaard's instant or moment of decision, preoccupied with the immediate contradiction. Derrida is about to challenge Foucault, who occupies the position of a master. He does not know what will happen. He is unhappy: this is a moment of folly, the kind of moment that Foucault's book insists cannot and should not be reduced to the language of reason. We have here a foretaste of 'the war and the ruses' between writer and reader that, 'Freud and the Scene of Writing' will insist, cannot be read on the basis of classical subjectivity. The war is inside Derrida, he admits. When he speaks, when he begins to read Foucault publicly, who will he be? Will there be a new experience of contradiction? If so, it will involve knowledge *and* feeling: a difficult, exciting, dangerous sense of writing as difference.

'You're crazy to write this'

The out-takes on the US DVD of *Derrida: The Movie* (2002) include a confession that although nothing intimidated Derrida when he was writing, at other times he felt afraid of what he had done:

> there is a very strange moment when I go to sleep . . . At that moment, in a sort of half sleep all of a sudden I'm terrified by what I'm doing. And I tell myself: 'You're crazy to write this' 'You're crazy to attack such a thing!' 'You're crazy to criticize such and such a person!' 'You're crazy to contest such an authority, be it textual, institutional or personal.' . . . In this half sleep I have the impression I have done something criminal, disgraceful, unavowable, that I shouldn't have done. And somebody is telling me: 'But you're mad to have done that.'[15]

The account of Derrida's unhappy consciousness at the beginning of 'Cogito and the History of Madness' dramatizes the essay's argument that madness cannot be described or contained in the apparent neutrality of a discourse, for discourse must always be on the side of reason that radically excludes madness. Such safeguards as are possible come from the practice of reading that Derrida adopts, in an inventive movement that takes the risk of being 'neither direct nor unilinear' in order to come as close to madness as possible (37). For Derrida, madness was inevitable and necessary to thought. According to his ethic of reading, the absence of a neutral or common measure between his language and the language of the other meant that such a common measure 'has to be invented at every moment, with every sentence, without assurance, without absolute guardrails [*garde-fou*]'.[16] Which is to say that 'a certain "madness" must watch over thinking, as reason does also.'

The Absent Addressee

Derrida's text retains traces of spoken delivery. He writes in the first person that characterizes the 'Cogito' and some of his own most provocative statements. And he addresses someone who, it turns out, 'may always be absent' (37). Who is being addressed? In one sense this is easy: it's Foucault, in reality or perhaps as Derrida imagines him. But writing, for Derrida, always haunts speech and the structure of the written mark implies the death or radical absence of any addressee. He is starting to speak in a scene of teaching and writing still in progress long after the master delivered his lectures and wrote his book. Derrida's relation to Foucault's teaching has to be, but can't be, assimilated. It would be wrong to totally absorb the other's text, wrong also to be inhospitable to it. The student feels 'challenged by the master who speaks within him and before him' (37). (Foucault did indeed respond angrily to Derrida's reading of his work.)[17] Learning, as Kierkegaard knew, is the untimely experience of a paradox. What we read teaches us: at the same time as we sift the text for what we might accept or reject in it, the text already gives us that which we sift and the experience of sifting that begins before one can know what one is receiving, or even whether it is in fact or in principle acceptable. The difficult feelings that go with being a disciple who wants to respond to the master arise because of a necessary forgetting of reading. The endless argument between oneself and a master's voice within that precedes one's own stems from not having yet realised that the master 'like real life, may always be absent'. That absence is the possibility of speech. Derrida is taking risks by means of writing in a way that does not flatten out Foucault's book into a structure.

A Summary of the Argument

To summarize too briefly and not madly enough: in this essay Derrida insists that the division of reason from madness was not, as *Madness and Civilisation* had argued, a historically determined and determinable event but is, as Geoffrey Bennington puts it, 'a problematic of "Reason in general"'.[18] Derrida connects recent developments in the human sciences with the history of metaphysics by taking up Foucault's reading of René Descartes' *Meditations* (1641). Foucault, Derrida makes it clear, missed a 'project of a singular and unprecedented excess' in the

Cogito (69). 'Cogito', meaning 'I think', is a crucial philosophical statement and gesture. The hugely influential Cartesian aphorism, '*Cogito ergo sum*' ('I think, therefore I am') does not actually occur in the *Meditations* but it encapsulates three important things: Descartes' interest in the first principles of philosophy; the importance of first person, present tense propositions to metaphysics and the attempt to use presence, as mind or consciousness stating its own current activity, to guarantee philosophical certainty. 'Cogito and the History of Madness' reads Descartes' daring, rigorous and complex text very closely. Derrida demonstrates that if its obvious meaning is followed, the passage resists Foucault's attempt to interpret it. That is, it resists attempts to enclose it within 'the totality of that which can be thought, the totality of beings and determined meanings, the totality of factual history'. Further, any discourse would, as discourse and meaning, risk missing the point of what Descartes has written by bringing its 'excess in the direction of the nondetermined' into relation with a determined and communicable meaning. Foucault's historicism therefore runs a risk of being totalitarian, despite his book's generous and admirable philosophical interest in the nature and possibility of history: 'the question of the origin of historicity *in general*' (69–70). Foucault has read Descartes too fast and with too little sense of the pathos of philosophical writing as it duels with madness.

Derrida takes his straightforward reading of the Cartesian text to the point of what 'cannot be recounted, cannot be objectified as an event in a determined history' (70). He is at once meticulous and empathic. We have presented the essay in terms of a dialogue or a dispute. We have glimpsed Derrida's avowal of anxiety about speaking out against certain aspects of Foucault's book. One of the implications of Descartes' philosophy is that thought should not bow to tradition or authority but proceed independently by a process of analysis and discovery. Husserl paid tribute to this desire for independence at the beginning of his own *Cartesian Meditations*:

> anyone who seriously intends to become a philosopher must 'once in his life' withdraw into himself and attempt, within himself, to overthrow and build anew all the sciences that, up

to then, he has been accepting. Philosophy . . . is the philosophizer's quite personal affair. It must arise as his wisdom, as his self-acquired knowledge tending towards universality, a knowledge for which he can answer from the beginning, and at each step, by virtue of his own absolute insights.[19]

In contrast with the drive to self-communion in the *Meditations* of Descartes and Husserl, Derrida describes himself as a disciple and pays close attention to the relation between Foucault's arguments and his teacher's way of reading. How would we come to think and reason if we took reading seriously? What would history be, if it did not take the form of a narrative that rendered a continuous course of events from the point of view of a transcendent subject?

Madness Itself

Derrida uses the Kierkegaardian phrase 'point of departure' [*point de depart*] twice in the early pages of the essay: to refer to Foucault's book, and to a specific passage where Foucault writes about Descartes and finds in the *Meditations* an alibi for the exclusion of madness from philosophical reason (36/51, 37/52). *Point de depart* also means 'no departure': at the moment when a writer distinguishes his text from another's, nothing separates them. The clear differentiation of subject from object depends on a departure that the French language won't allow. Derrida observes:

> Foucault wanted to write a history of madness *itself*, that is madness speaking on the basis of its own experience and under its own authority, and not a history of madness described from within the language of reason, the language of psychiatry *on* madness . . . (39)

For Derrida this wish not to be in a state of contradiction is the best and the impossible thing about Foucault's book. The expression 'on the basis of its own experience and on the basis of its own authority [*à partir de son propre instant, de sa propre instance*]' refers to the 'instant of departure' and the 'instance' of madness itself. Pure madness, madness proper would be associated with a single, undivided, unmediated moment. Foucault's notion of *decision* as a historical moment when madness and reason parted ways implies a reduction of the instant or the point to something simply identical with itself. Derrida sticks by difference much more tenaciously, notably in his replacement of Foucault's notion of *Decision* with that of *dissension*, which Derrida prefers because it is generally madder, being able 'to underline that in question is a self-dividing action, a cleavage and torment interior to meaning [*sens*] *in general*, interior to *logos* in general, a division within the very act of *sentire*' (46). The emphasis on sense corresponds to Derrida's emphasis on reading and writing as experiences.

Decision in Foucault's sense implies 'a discourse arrested by *command*', that powerfully secured the border between reason and madness. For Foucault, Derrida argues, madness once had the power to speak with reason and 'the issue is . . . to reach the point at which the dialogue was broken off' (45). The word 'decision' comes from the Latin *caedere*, to cut, as if a cut had been made at a particular moment in the wholeness of a unified and non-self-contradictory *logos*. This Greek word *logos* combines a large number of meanings. To list some of them will show how much is at stake in the notion of *logos* being at one with itself. *Logos* means 'speech, discourse' but also 'principle, promise, order, command, condition and decision.' It means 'legend, book' and also 'incident'. It means 'thought' and 'reasoning' but also 'cause, end, argument and meaning'. Philosophy wants to find a way to gather each and all of these meanings together.

We might contrast Foucault's emphasis on the historical instant or point with Derrida's remark that his own lecture will be 'neither direct nor unilinear'. The root of the French word *sens*, Latin *sentire, means to* 'perceive, feel, know', and further back its roots lie in a figurative use of the literal expression 'to find one's way' from the Indo-European base *sent* 'to go'. In French a path is a '*sentier*'. '*Sens*' occurs frequently in *Writing and Difference*. Derrida's sensitivity and sensibility move and find their way without making appeal to a former state of 'free circulation and exchange' supposed to precede writing's difference from itself.

Commentary

How does this movement of sense relate to reading? This is where Derrida's traditional practice of *commentary* comes in.

READING THE TEXT

This practice would not be possible or necessary were a text identical with itself. Derrida undertakes his commentary in order to reopen Foucault's '*interpretation* of Descartes's intention' (37). A commentary and an interpretation of authorial intention are not the same. Derrida glosses '*interpretation*' as follows:

> a certain passage, a certain semantic relationship proposed by Foucault between, *on the one hand*, what Descartes said – or what he is believed to have said and meant – and *on the other hand*, let us say, with intentional vagueness for the moment, a certain 'historical structure', as it is called, a certain meaningful historical totality, a total historical project through which we think what Descartes said, or what he is believed to have meant – can *particularly* be demonstrated.

Derrida insists in *Of Grammatology* that commentary, the production of a signifying structure by a critical reading, 'has always only *protected*, it has never *opened*, a reading'.[20] It is a more limited but perhaps less limiting operation than interpretation. Derrida calls his reading of Descartes 'most classical, banal' and blandly insists that 'when one attempts . . . to pass from an obvious to a latent language, one must first be rigorously sure of the obvious meaning' (38). Derrida respects the unity of Descartes' language at the level of what the text says. He has found something in the *Meditations* that he wants to protect by re-marking it: hyperbole: 'the project of exceeding every finite and determined totality' an 'absolute opening' which is nonetheless fated to be 'reembraced' and 'overcome [*surprise*] by economy' (73, 75/95). Foucault claimed that 'protective barriers [*garde-fous*]' were set up by reason to put an end to its formerly unrestricted dealings with madness (45/62). But as far as Derrida is concerned, there is no escape from being held within a language and a logic, and historical narrative cannot describe this general predicament that even the boldest thinking suffers.

Meaning as Signification and as Sense

Derrida asks repeatedly and with didactic emphasis whether Descartes' intention has '*the historical meaning* [*signification historique*] *assigned to it*' by Foucault (38/53). The reference to signification foregrounds semantics: what does the text mean?

Derrida's commentary stops to ask questions. It does not leap from the 'immediate materiality' of Descartes' text to what it signifies (38). It is indispensable to understand what the writer wants to say. Respect for the original language in which the text was written (Latin, here) and the principle of reading to the letter are tremendously important to Derrida's readings. The stakes are these: Derrida takes the passage in Descartes to be the 'index of a more general problematic' that intersects with, and challenges, the presuppositions of Foucault's history of madness.

According to the seventeenth-century aphorist Blaise Pascal: 'Men are so necessarily mad that not to be mad would be another form of madness.'[21] Pascal's *other* form of madness' is reason (39). And Descartes' reasoning is an experience of the division (*partage*, 'sharing') between reason and madness. The philosopher is exploring rather than policing the border between the two. Derrida comments that this experience, at its furthest reaches, 'is perhaps no less adventurous, perilous, nocturnal and pathetic than the experience of madness, and is . . . much less *adverse* to and accusatory of madness, that is, accusative and objectifying of it, than Foucault seems to think' (39/55). The 'meaning [*sens*] of the Cogito' is not, it would seem, exhausted by its *signification*, which would be reducible to what the text says. Derrida uses '*sens*' to describe Descartes' experience of the dangerous adventure of writing.

Derrida wanted to protect experience from further rationalist aggression by the inventive reasoning of reading that neither assimilates nor loses what it reads. He insisted that when he wrote there must always be 'more than one language, mine and the other'.[22] 'Cogito and the History of Madness' asks 'Is there a history [*histoire*, 'story'] of silence?' (41/57). Does silence have a story? Who could tell it? Derrida cautions against ignoring what the psychiatrist, delegate of a certain 'rational or political order' might have to say about madness: 'perhaps it does not suffice to imprison or to exile the delegate, or to stifle him: and perhaps it does not suffice to deny oneself the conceptual material of psychiatry in order to exculpate one's own language.' Derrida's readings try to avoid repeating what has been done to madness. He doesn't set out to maintain a good conscience at the expense of the other.

Logos and pathos

Foucault's book makes the silence of madness metaphorically present by means of *pathos*, feeling, rather than *logos*, discourse or reason. Philosophy has tended to set reason above passion. Derrida calls *Madness and Civilisation*: 'a new and radical praise of folly whose intentions cannot be admitted because the *praise* [*éloge*] of silence always takes place *within logos*, the language of objectification' (44/60). He pays tribute to Foucault's sensitivity to the less obvious forms of mastering madness. A number of things interest him: why Foucault's book is like it is; the thinking behind its silences; its projects of an archaeology of silence and of locating the origin of the command that Foucault believed had put an end to the supposed dialogue between reason and madness. Derrida doubts that this dialogue existed or ever could. In order to clarify the point, he follows Foucault back to the Greeks. A long parenthetical discussion analyses a short passage in which Foucault refers to the Greek notion of *hybris*. *Hybris* refers to a kind of folly: insolence, over-confidence or arrogance, such as invites disaster or ruin. But it was not incompatible with *logos*, Foucault suggests. If, later in history, madness was intolerable to reason, Greek *logos* had no contrary. He cites Socratic dialectic as 'reassuring' because it envelops the contested notion of *hybris* and brings it within *logos*. Derrida contests this claim.

In order to reassure, Socratic dialectic must have already implicitly recognized *hybris* as a threat. It must have 'expulsed, excluded, objectified, or (curiously amounting to the same thing) assimilated and mastered as one of its moments . . . the contrary of reason' (47). If there was reassurance there must have already been contradiction. And if Socrates remained within a discourse that knew no contrary, then his dialectic could not have been reassuring. The whole history of philosophy is a smoothing over of a difference within *logos* from the start. This difference cannot be reduced to a contradiction and furthermore, Foucault's attempt to historicize *différance* is problematic. 'The attempt to write the history of the decision, division, difference, runs the risk of construing the division as an event or a structure subsequent to the unity of an original presence, thereby confirming metaphysics in its fundamental operation' (48).

We note that Derrida identifies the 'heart of the matter' as the assumption that reason can have a contrary, that there can be an other of reason known to reason and that the opposition of reason to its other is symmetrical – and then defers the question in order to examine Foucault's assumptions about madness. 'Everything transpires as if, in a continuous and underlying way, an assured and rigorous precomprehension of the concept of madness, or at least of its nominal definition, were possible and acquired' (49). There is perhaps an implicit reprimand here: it won't do to write a history of madness and reason without reading philosophy first.

Reading *before* historical context

Derrida wants history to be open to the philosophical tradition. He also wants it to be as accurate as possible. Foucault's history raises 'banal but inevitable problems of periodization and of geographical, political and ethnological limitation' (50). Most important, perhaps, Derrida is suspicious of something that *Of Grammatology* calls 'the tranquil assurance that leaps over the text towards its presumed content, in the direction of the pure signified'.[23]

'Cogito and the History of Madness' pursues the notion of 'a historicity proper to reason in general' and argues that if there is such a thing, 'the history of reason cannot be the history of its origin' (50). Historicity would be something more dynamic than the condition of the possibility of history or the circumstances under which the concepts 'history' and 'tradition' are possible and take on their particular value. It would give rise to meaning and nonmeaning and could not be comprehended as part of the history of meaning. In spite of his claim that in the middle of the seventeenth century an original event or decision separated reason from madness Foucault's book can still be shown to refer to something more like the general dissension within meaning that Derrida proposes. Derrida cites Foucault's wish to uncover a 'perpetual exchange, the obscure common root, the original confrontation that gives meaning to the unity, as well as to the opposition, of sense and non-sense' (51). This historical question leads not to this or that moment in the history of facts, nor to an ahistorical structure, but to the question of historicity itself.

The Reading of Descartes

Derrida insists that the prerequisite for a response to it must be:

> the internal and autonomous analysis of the philosophical content of philosophical discourse. Only when the totality of this content will have become manifest in its meaning for me (but this is impossible) will I rigorously be able to situate it in its total historical form. (53)

There will be time enough for historicism and other forms of totalization when we have finished reading. He cites the passage from Descartes' *Meditations* cited by Foucault. He looks at how Foucault reads the passage, moving very slowly. He rereads Descartes, still with an eye to Foucault's reading-moves. Derrida's way of proceeding is classical but at the same time dramatic. He applies the logic of Foucault's book to the passage: Descartes appears to Foucault to be boxing madness in as an example of sensory error. Derrida's text works patiently but also moves incredibly fast between the landscape and rhythms of the *Meditations* and Foucault's history of madness. What comes over is the force of Descartes' thought, somehow amplified by Foucault's unsuccessful attempt to recruit it in support of his theorizing. References to Foucault's project, to his silences (some attributed to discretion dictated by the logic of his aims, others revealed as troubling shortfalls in reading) aim precisely at the terrain identified by *Of Grammatology*: 'a certain relationship, unperceived by the writer, between what he commands and what he does not command of the patterns that he uses. This relationship is . . . a signifying structure that a critical reading should *produce*.'[24] Command, mastery or power, Foucault's great theme, emerges as a limited stratagem within what 'Cogito and the History of Madness' calls 'the possibility of meaning in general' (66).

In the *Meditations* a 'natural comfort' and 'apparently prephilosophical confidence' allow Descartes to risk extreme hypotheses such as that of an evil genius that meddles his mind (64–5). This hypothesis welcomes 'everything that was previously set aside as insanity . . . into the most essential interiority of thought' (64). But at the same time it is not a mad hypothesis. The *Meditations* are part of language, and language – not the mathematical and geometrical truths that underpin the possibility of even deluded perception and dreaming – *language* both welcomes and escapes madness. Descartes' extreme hypothesis carries a recognition that Descartes never articulates because it is part of his articulation:

> if discourse and philosophical communication (that is, language itself) are to have an intelligible meaning, that is to say, if they are to conform to their essence and vocation as discourse, they must simultaneously in fact and in principle escape madness. They must carry normality within themselves. (65)

Normality would not mean being responsible to a given set of norms. It would remain to be invented in the adventure of writing.

Reassurance

'It is through the relationship to the other as another self that meaning reassures itself against madness and nonmeaning [*nonsens*] . . .' (72/92). This relationship is an economy that allows the writer poetic freedom. Cixous puts it like this, in a passage '*About the person whose name is You*':

> . . . it is not *for* you that I write: it is *by* you, passing through you, because of you – And thanks to you each book takes every liberty. Crazy liberty, as you say. The liberty not to resemble, not to obey. But the book itself is not crazy. It has its deep logic. But without you I would be afraid of never being able to return from Mount Crazy.[25]

There are moments in writing that orient themselves in relation to a reader, who is present to the writer as anonymous, absent, a passage rather than a destination. Then writing is not a discourse but a movement of invention capable of, in Derrida's words 'what the world calls crises of madness' (76). These episodes of writing are not incompatible with reason, even if their inventions take the risk of going beyond reason in order to extend it. The reader Cixous imagines would be capable of sensing the *feeling* of this hidden duel in the text of philosophy. Pathos – feeling – is a necessary part of philosophy. Derrida asks whether philosophy 'is perhaps the reassurance given against the anguish of being mad at the point of greatest proximity to madness. This silent and specific moment could be called *pathetic*' (72). The movement traced in Descartes, whose crisis is the 'fugitive' and 'ungraspable' moment when the Cogito escapes reason, could also open a reading of Husserl, questioning 'the profound *reassurance* of the certainty of *meaning*' offered by Husserl's notion of the living present (73).

Derrida sees Foucault as an ally and is grateful to his book for helping him imagine a future philosophizing that would 'no longer be in memory of Cartesianism' (75). Philosophy, in the closing pages of 'Cogito and the History of Madness' emerges as an economy of writing thanks to which reason is madder than madness: 'I philosophize only in *terror*, but in the *confessed* terror of going mad. The confession is simultaneously, as its *present* moment, oblivion [*oubli*, forgetting] and unveiling, protection and exposure: economy' (76/96). Its history is a series of crises. Derrida takes Foucault's empathy with madness to a further extreme. He envelops the abstract philosophical 'I' with a confessional impulse that, as Hegel predicts, exposes him to reason and to the judgement: 'You're crazy to write this.'

Study question

What differences would it make to you and your work if you were a psychiatrist and read what Foucault and Derrida have to say about madness? Or if you were a person diagnosed as suffering from a mental illness?

'EDMOND JABÈS AND THE QUESTION OF THE BOOK'

What is a book? And how would we phrase the question of the book? In the course of some remarks on the books he published in 1967 Derrida described what he wrote as 'articles, not books'.[26] There was 'a sort of confluence of small texts, none of which on its own was sufficient to make up a book'. The word 'confluence' in 'Edmond Jabès and the Question of the Book' describes Jabès's attempt to regain possession of his language, 'by any means, through all routes' (90). And Derrida's more general thoughts on his own three publications emphasize chance, variety and fluidity:

> not one of them is a book, not one of them was planned as a book... *Writing and Difference* is a collection of texts, dating from 1962–3 to 1967; *Of Grammatology* is made up of two heterogeneous passages put together somewhat artificially (the first part and the part on Rousseau), and this logic of supplementarity is a logic of incompleteness; as for *Speech and Phenomena*, that was a conference presentation, I wrote it in a few weeks in the summer for a conference in the United States, and then I showed it to Jean Hyppolite who said to me 'it could be made into a book'... it was anything but a project for a book.[27]

Derrida identified a book with the appearance of 'blossoming or a completeness' and his 1967 books with something 'rather like impromptus, fits and starts'. This very 'incompleteness and... non-coincidence' made him want to continue writing. Discontinuity nourished continuity, he explained, 'because I wanted to prevent misunderstandings, to be more specific, but also in order to prolong the non-coincidence'.

For him, completeness would be the enemy of our understanding and of the life of writing which is difference. *Of Grammatology* speaks of a 'good' writing, which was not in fact what Derrida understood writing to be:

> The good writing [*la bonne écriture*] has therefore always been *comprehended*. Comprehended as that which had to be comprehended within a nature or a natural law, created or not, but first thought within an eternal presence. Comprehended, therefore, within a totality, and enveloped in a volume or a book.[28]

What would a book be – could it even strictly be said to 'be'? – if it were not thought of as already understood, natural like a blossoming, legitimate, good, a totality existing within the greater totality of eternal presence? Perhaps books cannot know that writing is endless. However, readers know that books are not totalities. They move from book to book and between books.

They can reread and can affirm as Derrida did that they have not done with reading and perhaps that they have not even begun to read the books they return to most often.[29] Books written by readers or lovers of writing are not closed forms but passages.

Derrida greets *Le livre des questions* [*The Book of Questions*] (1963) as an uncovering of powerful and ancient roots that would change how Jabès's collected poems, *Je bâtis ma demeure* [*I Build My Dwelling*] (1957), are read. In spite of the remarkable work of the American poet Rosmarie Waldrop and others, Jabès is still little known in the English-speaking world, especially compared with the writers that preoccupy other essays in *Writing and Difference*. But as a poet, a Jew and a powerful thinker about writing and the relation of writing to Judaism and Jewish experience, Jabès is very important to Derrida. So much so that when Derrida writes a last short piece with which to finish the book it is to Jabès that he returns.

The Radical Origin of Meaning as Letter

Derrida begins 'Edmond Jabès and the Question of the Book' by thinking about rereading and how a later work can transform an earlier one by changing how it is read. He also draws attention to what he calls the 'radical origin of meaning as literality [*comme lettre*]', where 'literal' doesn't mean the opposite of 'figurative' but refers directly to the letters that are the atoms of language (78/99). He explains that by the radical origin of meaning as letter, he means 'historicity itself.' He quotes Jabès's phrase 'people born of the book': the notion of the Jews as a race issuing from the book offers a way of connecting the letter, meaning and the possibility of history in a way that is more ancient, vivid, serious and powerful than structuralist analysis or Cartesian metaphysics. Derrida describes the poetry Jabès wrote between the early 1940s and the late 1950s and published in *Je bâtis ma demeure* in a metaphor that owes its force to the letter's power to generate unexpected truths. Jabès's earlier poetry was for Derrida a kind of pliant tree that risked being weakened by the ivy [*lierre*] of its distracting levity. This ivy twines through the whole essay with tendrils of words and letters. Later in the text, Derrida speaks of 'the adventure of the text as weed' (81). In French, *lierre* suggests, as well as *livre*, 'book', and '*leurre*', 'illusion', the verbs *lire*, 'to read' and *errer*, 'to wander', as the Jew wanders and as genuine reading and writing always depart from known paths. That departure does not mean entering into mere confusion but it accepts the risk of not making sense that is essential to poetry. *Relier* is the verb used to describe the binding of a book: we recall Derrida's bibliographical note to *L'écriture et la différence*, which points up this kind of anagrammatical liaison when it explains that 'in order to bind [*relier*]' together these essays, 'in rereading [*relire*] them, we cannot maintain an equal distance from each of them' (xiv/437). Binding apparently fixes the book, stitches it together – at least as far as the order of the pages; reading opens up the text, for example by means of the flicking to and fro that allows us to see connections between one part of the book and another or the smaller movements back and forth that are prompted by the play of letters marking the closeness and difference of *relier* and *relire*. This transformation of space and time by the reader's recombination of the fragments that make up the text is widely recognized as a poetic strategy but it also has deep, politically and humanly significant roots in Jewish Kabbalistic traditions of reading. And in roots and in the earth, Derrida insists, lies the possibility of freedom.

A Certain Judaism

Rosmarie Waldrop's invaluable study of Jabès explains the importance to the poet of the notion that each word is a detached shard of the name of God. This means

> that breaking open words and recombining their letters is neither just fun nor impious. It is not even just the Kabbalistic tradition of 'travelling inside the word'. For Edmond Jabès, this method 'permits a rediscovery, a rereading of the word. One opens a word as one opens a book: it is the same gesture'.[30]

In a world that the poet finds unreadable, still to be read, God is the promise of meaning that comes close to us as the fragmentation and rereading of texts. In the explicit engagement with the notion of the book and with Judeity offered by *The Book of Questions*, Derrida finds an opportunity to once more explore a kind of poetry fundamental to thinking and irreducible to the formal playfulness of a literary genre. One might think that the so-called word play would hide, absorb or introvert meaning but the opening of 'Edmond Jabès and the Question of the Book' suggests that attention to the word liaisons around *lierre*, 'ivy' and *relire*, 'reread' will take readers away from the immediately visible foliage of writing, down to roots that are not merely verbal. The first paragraphs insist on these roots, 'true', 'powerful and ancient', able to talk and shared by a people and a writing. Many poems in *Je bâtis ma demeure* are not obviously concerned with Judaism; they advertise a relation to French lyric and are full of girls, flowers and graceful romanticism. *The Book of Questions* is a love story of a different kind. Jabès calls it 'the story of a love destroyed by men and by words' (79). More than once Derrida's opening paragraphs on Jabès mention love. Discourse can love; letters can love and be loved. Writing is not a formal game. There is a 'passion *of* writing', something distinct from a passion *for* writing or a passion that writing articulates (77). 'Passion' signifies 'love' but also a passive endurance that Derrida and Jabès associate with the enigmatic insistence of the letter. And the root here is 'a certain Judaism'. At times we will wonder – is it the Jew that loves and survives and perpetuates Judaism or the letter?

The epigraph to Jabès's complete poems *Le seuil et le sable* (1990) invokes a staying power that owes its existence to a faculty of memory [*mémoire*] 'more ancient than personal recollections [*souvenirs*]' and which is 'bound [*liée*] to language, to music, to sound, to noise, to silence'.[31] However, Derrida does not invoke Jabès's developed sense of the letter, to override the particular historical experience of Jews. (Steven Jaron points out that *The Book of Questions* was received in France as a work of universal import, even while it inscribed specifically Jewish suffering and drew on the interpretative practices of rabbinic scriptural commentary.)[32] And yet his claim is unequivocal: 'there could be no history without the gravity and the labour of literality. The painful folding [*pli*] of itself by which history reflects on itself as it ciphers itself' (78/99–100). Folding, like binding, reminds us of the formation of actual books but it's also a kind of doubling that makes historical consciousness possible, for history 'begins by reflecting itself'. Those who associate the play of the letter with frivolity or a formalist lack of historical awareness should think again in the light of Derrida's concern with roots, radical origins and suffering: Jabès and Derrida take very seriously the play between levity and gravity in writing. The folding of words and letters that we see in Derrida's language here relates to a theory of history. The Jew, in Jabès's thinking, is the fold [*pli*] necessary for history to begin. The Jew who chooses to write is already chosen by writing because of being a Jew, who accepts the divine origin of the Torah (the first five books of the Bible). These sacred texts, along with certain traditions and the learned rabbis who interpret both texts and traditions, are the source of authority in Judaism. The need for interpretation arises because the Tablets on which God's law was written were broken by Moses, enraged that the people of Israel had turned to idolatry. Yet another word in *li-* resounds in the sentence describing the 'Jew who elects [*élit*] writing which elects [*élit*] the Jew'. The Jew has both a passive and an active relation to writing. Judaism is a religion of the book, founded on silence and interruption, on an original breaking of the Tables upon which God wrote the law (Exod. 32:15–16; 32:19).

Poetic Freedom

According to Jabès the poem writes the poet. There is a primal folding of subjectivity: so that the book 'becomes a subject in itself and for itself' (79). This is not the self-consciousness of 'critical or speculative reflection' but is, 'first of all, poetry and history'. Freedom (in French that's another word in *li-*, *liberté*) must be a thing of the earth and the root 'or it is merely wind' (80/101). For Jabès, freedom is awakened by a sense of our 'ties [*liens*]'. We return here, in a subtle way, to the opening of the essay and the arboreal poetic discourse of *Je bâtis ma demeure* that 'bent a bit in the wind' and was yet to love its roots. Ties suggest being held in one place, with the restraint of roots – here called 'buried origin' and 'the gravity that situates [freedom's] centre and its site (*lieu*)'. Jabès mentions in an interview that his books are

> both a place of passage and the only place where I might live. Isn't it surprising that the word of God should come from the desert, that one of the names of God in Hebrew should be PLACE, and that the book should have been lived as the place of the word by the Jews for millennia?[33]

At this point Derrida starts to capitalize Site (*Lieu*). This is partly for political reasons, to indicate that neither he nor Jabès is talking about a place in the world: Zion or the State of Israel.[34] The capital 'S' suggests a proper name, a place without concept and a referent that is unknown to history: 'When it lets itself be articulated by poetic discourse, the Land (*Terre*) always keeps itself beyond any proximity, *illic*.' The Latin word *illic* means 'there, at that place, therein, in that matter.' The word indicates a specificity as yet without content, a space, a poetic opening to the unknown other that resonates with and through all the other words we have been collecting: *livre, relire, lierre, relier, pli, élit, liberté, lien, lieu* . . . possibilities of meaning, the alluring promised lands of writing.

At this point, partly again for political reasons but also for others that have to do with negotiating the question of law and of God, Derrida distinguishes what Jabès's poetry is doing from prophecy, and the Site referred to by Jabès from any terrestrial location. The Bible is in the background here. The notion of a promised land comes up in Genesis, where God first tells Abraham to go to a new land. The formation of the people of Israel occurs through a series of movements, wars and migrations, heading towards a settled homeland that never materializes. These movements are prompted by God speaking to prophets and interwoven with the establishing of divinely dictated laws and traditions. In the Book of Exodus, the prophet is Moses and the Law takes the form of the Ten Commandments. The Law comes to the people of Israel as writing, entrusted to Tables which can be broken, which Moses breaks and which God writes or dictates a second time. A trace would not be a trace if it could not be erased: the condition of the Law reaching the Israelites is the condition of the possibility of the destruction of the Law, which opens Jewish history by separating the people from the commandments and making commentary, interpretation and exile essential Jewish traditions. If the Promised Land as Jabès writes it cannot be confused with Canaan or Palestine, remaining definitively 'elsewhere', then the Jew has been given 'tradition as adventure.' ('Tradition as adventure' would be a possible definition of deconstruction.) For Jabès this also defines poetic discourse.

The book, for Jabès and for Derrida, is not a programme and is not accompanied by authoritative reading instructions. The ancient deserts wandered by the exiled Israelites are empty of theory. This is their paradoxical fertility, which perhaps only poetry can articulate. Jabès, responding directly to 'Edmond Jabès and the Question of the Book' spoke out against pre-decided reading in which the

> code is known, transmitted, and our reading is based on it, on this knowledge, this confidence in the written. A reading called open at the level of the text. But of which text? since, once drafted – of this reading I shall make my writing, – the text is nothing but an application of a theory accepted in advance...[35]

Jabès resisted the modern habit of approaching important texts 'in terms of what we have gotten out of them and remembered, of what we can cheerfully refer to'. On the contrary, '[e]verything is again set in motion – called into question – by writing'. And what made Jabès love Derrida's writing was its 'total acceptance of risk'.

Exile and Brokenness

Exile, 'separation from their true birth', is the condition of both Poet and Jew (80). But Derrida is careful to distinguish one from the other in order to understand their relation in a more precise way. *The Book of Questions* is, Derrida points out, a 'self-justification' addressed to the Jewish community. That community 'lives under heteronomy', subject to the law given by God, while the poet 'does not simply receive his speech and his law from God'. Poetry 'presupposes broken Tables' and makes its own law (81). The law given by God can neither liberate nor control the poet. Both poet and rabbi must interpret but each interprets interpretation differently. Reading, here in the form of 'hermeneutics' and 'exegesis', is where everything starts. In a phrase that returns in 'Structure, Sign and Play', there are 'two interpretations of interpretation'. And this is not incidental. God himself is divided, spaced out, interrupted. This is what makes questioning possible.

READING THE TEXT

Although he is not mentioned by name, Nietzsche is here, along with a sense of the originary force of broken signs. 'Force and Signification' ends with broken tables and the new half-tables surrounding Nietzsche's prophet Zarathustra. And in 'Structure, Sign and Play' one of the 'two interpretations of interpretation' is described as 'Nietzschean *affirmation*': 'the joyous affirmation of the play of the world and of the innocence of becoming, the affirmation of a world of signs without fault, without truth, and without origin which is offered to an active interpretation' (369). This is contrasted with what is perhaps the more conventionally rabbinical way of reading that 'seeks to decipher, dreams of deciphering a truth or an origin which escapes play and the order of the sign, and which lives the necessity of interpretation as exile'. This latter set of aims would perhaps correspond to what 'Edmond Jabès and the Question of the Book' calls 'the unhappy consciousness' of the Jew. Two stances, but Derrida emphasises that these are lived simultaneously. No division in deconstruction can be reduced to an opposition through which experience is to be read *either* forwards *or* backwards. Jabès has written a book of questions that incorporates the commentary of imaginary rabbis into a poetic fiction. The breaking of the Tables of the Law is not an event in a narrative that begins in unity and ends in division. It is not a Fall or 'some accident *within* history'. The rupture is in God. For Jabès and Derrida, God has 'separated himself from himself', and by writing the Law and allowing the Tables to be broken and writing the Law again, he has made questioning possible. In the previous essay, 'Cogito and the History of Madness', we saw a God who guaranteed meaning for Descartes. Jabès's God (who is not an invention because He accords with the account of God in Exodus) is questionable, 'does not act in the simplest of ways . . . is not truthful . . . is not sincere' (82).

All Writing Is Aphoristic

If sincerity is false, then the way through the Desert should be duplicitous and indirect. It proceeds by way of lie and ruse: the 'infinite detour' (83). At the opening of the essay, Derrida referred to the 'rigour and rigidity of poetic obligation' that was lacking in Jabès's poetry to 1958. Now, still reading Jabès, he recommends 'the virtue of the lie' and a path that lacks the 'prescription of truth's rigour' (82, 83). In a theme that he develops everywhere, separation – here from a God already separated from himself – gives birth to writing which cannot reduce separation but thrives on it. The theme of separation returns later in a discussion of the letter's effect on meaning, where Derrida makes claims that are crucial for our understanding of his writing:

> If absence does not allow itself to be reduced by the letter, this is so because it is the letter's ether and respiration. The letter is the separation and limit in which meaning is liberated from its emprisonment in aphoristic solitude. For all writing is aphoristic.[36] No 'logic', no proliferation of conjunctive undergrowth [*lianes*] can reach the end of its essential discontinuity and non-contemporaneousness, the ingenuity of its *under-stood* [*sous-entendu*] silences. (86/107)

The letter liberates meaning. It is the ultimate fragment of language, and language is in essence fragmentary, interrupted, spaced out. Unlike the word, the letter or word fragment has no meaning alone and yet appears (think of the *li-* we have been noticing) at a distance from itself. The letter has an especial connection with spacing. An aphorism (the word is derived from Greek *aphorizein*, to mark off, divide) derives its force from its limits. It stimulates commentary and interpretation precisely by not continuing, not elaborating or explaining itself. An aphorism allows itself to be interrupted. Meaning is not the product of a logic or of discursive connections: rather, the letter and spacing give rise to these things: 'without interruption – between letters, words, sentences, books – no signification could be awakened' (87). Derrida talks about 'leaps' and about writing as the risk of death: 'Death strolls between letters. To write, what is called writing, assumes an access to the mind through having the courage to lose one's life, to die away from nature.' The letter and its spacing also make possible a relation to the other built on solitude and difference. The letter would be a dead letter 'if it left its solitude [*solitude*, another *li-* word, much repeated here], or put an end to interruption, to distance, to respect, and to its relation to the other, that is, a certain nonrelation'. Certain phenomenological themes concerning otherness and a relationality founded on the monadic solitude of each of us, which will be explored more explicitly in the next essay, 'Violence and Metaphysics', can be glimpsed here.

The Animality of the Letter

The letter lives: its life is not human life, nor can it simply be opposed to human life: for Jabès and Derrida there is 'an animality [*animalité*] of the letter'. Letters have soul (Latin *anima*, Greek *psyche*) and life, they are not the servants of proper meaning, as philosophy and the common sense derived from it, would tend to assume they are. And letters are the life of metaphor, lived as exile from proper meaning and beyond the possession and control of man, in 'a wandering of language always richer than knowledge' (89). Our words in *li-* give 'Edmond Jabès and the Question of the Book' something of what Derrida calls, referring to Jabès's writing, 'the organised power of the song'. This power is not redeemable by commentary because it is not conceptual or thematic and cannot be captured by the opposition between literal and metaphorical language. Derrida insists that the animality of the letter *is* metaphor itself, metaphor understood in a non-classical way as a movement of meaning that will not return to itself, that cannot be grasped or worked out as a stable rhetorical architecture of thoughts. Derrida is also implicitly touching on notions he will discuss in 'White Mythology: Metaphor in the Text of Philosophy' (1972), such as Aristotle's claim that the power to form letters distinguishes man from the animals, and the philosophical notion of metaphor as a 'provisional loss of meaning . . . within the horizon of, the circular reappropriation of literal, proper meaning'.[37] Jabès describes the vital strangeness of writing's energy in terms of animals: squirrels and fish. Derrida had a constant and profound interest in animals, always particular kinds of creature rather than the abusively generic philosophical category, and Cixous has written a remarkable account of Derrida as Proteus, the Greek divinity who assumed the form of various animals in order to avoid foretelling the future.[38] The animality of the letter means that the letter does not speak to explain itself or its frame of reference; it is metaphor without end, equivocal and uncertain and, Derrida insists, *alive*. His reading of Jabès challenges Western notions of the dead letter, of metaphor as death, or of a literality that finally closes meaning, even the assumption that there is an inevitable opposition between (organic) life and writing. The poem, like the animal, 'does not articulate its own justification' (90). It is without alibi. Risk, which was there at the essay's opening, as the ivy that 'could have [*risquait*] hidden or absorbed' the meaning of *Je bâtis ma demeure*, is absolutely crucial to poetry and to Derrida's thought, which is faithful to necessity of thoughts generated by the primal power of song. Song here is not a separate genre but a mode of writing related to the cry rather than the discursive intelligibility of speech. We understand it in a different way. Derrida strongly resists the idea that the elements combined in Jabès's writing are united by 'confluence', a meeting of already established and understood strands of meaning (Judaism, literature, tradition, etc.). *The Book of Questions* is a song and as such it comes out of a wound in a miraculous way: 'This cry sings because in its enigma, it brings forth water from a cleft rock, the unique source, the unity of a spurting rupture . . . A poem always runs the risk of being meaningless and would be nothing without this risk.'[39] Poetry has for too long been regarded as singular in a secondary way, a sort of individual response to a historical or philosophical context that claims absolute primacy. From the point of view of conceptual thought, difference has been regarded as that which comes along and happens to being. On the contrary, the poem for Derrida is ahead of all concepts, and difference, which interrupts presence, gives presence to us in the very same gesture. This is an event that defies narrative. The passage quietly flows with the language of moving water that springs from a broken rock and the source that Derrida writes about is not a simple beginning. We have to presume: 'that the unity of the source is not due to a chance encounter, but that beneath this encounter another encounter takes place today'. The encounter is always with what is other, with a difference that is not assimilated, even now. The verb to be becomes fragile under these conditions. Thus: 'Encounter *is* separation', for 'Being never *is*, never shows *itself*, is never *present*. Is never *now*, outside difference.' One can only encounter it in the mode of non-encounter, missing, distance and detour.

The book is where this can happen – not as a metaphor or a literary representation but as an experience of difference as the origin of meaning. Derrida takes Jabès as an accomplice who allows him to articulate extremely strange and powerful aspects of writing. For Jabès the book is terrifically capacious: everything will come to inhabit it. It is not a finite container but a passage where everything comes to pass. The book defies commentary because it is never finished. It is not an artistic creation, for writing must be 'a tearing of the self toward the other within a confession of infinite separation' or it will destroy itself. 'The other and the threshold can only be written, can only affirm themselves in writing [*en lui*, referring to the book]' (93/113).

Still, at the end of the essay, Derrida questions the book and asks things of it that Jabès does not, at least not in *The Book of Questions*. There are questions that don't fit into the book but make it possible. What if 'the form of the book was no longer to be the model of meaning'? Or what if 'Being . . . revealed itself only in . . . a radical illegibility' (94)? This illegibility is not to be thought within reason or *logos*. Literature is to be read within life:

> The written questions addressed to literature, all the tortures inflicted on it, are always transfigured, drained, forgotten by literature, within literature; having become modifications of itself, by itself, in itself, they are mortifications, that is to say, as always, ruses of life. Life negates itself in literature only so that it may survive better. So that it may *be* better. It does not negate itself any more than it affirms itself: it differs from itself, defers itself, and writes itself as *différance*. Books are always books of *life* . . . or of *afterlife* . . . (95).

Study Question

James Joyce wanted to write books that gathered together 'the potentially infinite memory of humanity'. Derrida imagined a writing machine capable of registering everything that happens 'such that the smallest thoughts, the smallest movements of the body, the least traces of desire, the ray of sunlight, the encounter with someone, a phrase heard in passing, are inscribed somewhere; imagine that a general electroencephalocardiosomatopsychogram were possible . . .'. What form do you think would be the most longlasting and the most sensitive for receiving impressions? Books? Film? E-mail? Things made into symbols?

'VIOLENCE AND METAPHYSICS'

The unthinkable truth of living experience, to which Levinas returns ceaselessly, cannot possibly be encompassed by philosophical speech without immediately revealing, by philosophy's own light, that philosophy's surface is severely cracked, and that what was taken for its solidity is its rigidity. (112)

Questions

This essay continues to think about questioning, as did the response to Edmond Jabès and his *Book of Questions*. Cixous comments on Derrida's capacity to startle and provoke:

> I translate the flea you put into my ear into *question*. Barely have I put an ear to your text before I feel myself summoned, given notice to wonder, questioned, dislodged from any response that I might think I was able to lodge, pushed further, further and further.[40]

The curious relational powers of the question will be an important theme in the essay: there are 'problems put to philosophy as problems philosophy cannot resolve' and these questions without answers are of decisive importance in the history of philosophy because they bring philosophers together in a particular way (98). Derrida claims that 'Violence and Metaphysics' is written in 'disenchanted prose', but it is no less intense to read than any of the essays in *Writing and Difference*, and contains the most patient and prolonged reading in the book (398n). It has a relentless quality: 'Yes', it seems to say to yet another aspect of the thought of Emmanuel Levinas, 'yes, and yet . . .' 'Violence and Metaphysics' announces itself as working 'in the style of commentary', so that any objections that emerge in the course of the essay will not, Derrida insists, be Derrida's own but 'questions put to *us*' by Emmanuel Levinas himself (103).

Otherness and Violence

The whole essay will be preoccupied with the impossibility of non-violence in human relations, thought and language. It reflects on separation, solitude and the radical absence of objective common ground between individuals, but Derrida also stresses, early on, the effect, in the world, of the openness and uncertainty of questions without answers. He holds fast to Husserl's desire to think 'a *transcendental theory of experiencing someone else*, a transcendental theory of so-called "empathy"'.[41] He also accepts Husserl's recognition that there is no direct experience of the other and that if there were, 'if what belongs to the other's own essence were directly accessible, it would be merely a moment of my own essence, and ultimately he himself and I myself would be the same.'[42] By this logic, what would seem to be immediate confirmation that I am not alone, turns out, on reflection, to leave me more alone than ever.

Derrida affirms the possibility of love, friendship and community in the absence of empirical or theoretical proof that there is anyone beyond 'me'. As a thinker and philosopher, he knew that for example, there is no simple presence and that being together with someone else could not be a matter of co-existing in the shared space of 'here' and 'now'. And yet he knew he lived and wanted to live as if there were. He wanted to see his friends, or to speak to them on the telephone and so on. 'Violence and Metaphysics' affirms early on that 'the impossible has already occurred' (98). For the paradoxes and severe laws that are the daily bread of Derrida's thinking, and that make up our lives whether we recognize them or not, do not take place in some abstract world of principle but in what Derrida calls *history*. When he refers to 'history' he does not mean that the experiences that interest him are necessarily to be found in the written record of the past, but that for all their elusiveness, they do happen. For Derrida history is *what happens*, not excluding the impossible. All this 'Violence and Metaphysics' affirms. Or rather, Derrida *wants* to affirm the experience of the impossible. Can an affirmation worth making ever be more or less than a *desire* to affirm, an affirmation stubbornly looking for the possibility of its taking place? Why affirm the undisputed and indisputable truth? I cannot affirm except on my own behalf; it is something I do *through* but never *for* you.)

Derrida observes that it is in the strange space opened by a radical uncertainty about the future of philosophy that a community may be formed, not thanks to the positive effects of empirical or institutional relations, but first of all in relation to the difference of questioning:

> within that fragile moment when the question is not determined enough for the hypocrisy of an answer to have already initiated itself beneath the mask of the question, and not yet determined enough for its voice to have been already and fraudulently articulated within the very syntax of the question. (98)

Philosophy itself may turn out to have been a moment within the more enduring adventure of the question.

Why Levinas?

In an interview shortly before his own death, Derrida named Levinas, among others, and explained what it would mean to be faithful to the values of their generation. It would mean

> to adhere, sometimes in opposition to everyone and everything, to certain shared exigencies . . . to an *ethos* of writing and thinking, an intransigent or indeed incorruptible *ethos* . . . that does not let itself be scared off by what public opinion, the media, or the phantasm of an intimidating readership might presume to simplify or to repress.[43]

And yet Derrida did not forget the *differences* that 'ran rampant in that milieu, which was anything but a homogenous whole,' so that fidelity sometimes took the form of 'infidelity and a parting of the ways'.[44]

Levinas had written the 'first major work devoted to the entirety of Husserl's thought' in French, a critique influenced by Heidegger (104). *Théorie d'intuition dans la phénoménologie de Husserl* (1930) was reissued in 1963. Husserl is perhaps the true hero of the virtual community of living and dead philosophers that Derrida's essay convenes. 'Violence and Metaphysics', which appeared as a very long essay, spread between two issues of the philosophy journal *Revue de métaphysique et morale* in 1964. Derrida's second book on Husserl, *Speech and Phenomena*, came out at the same time as *Writing and Difference* and his introduction to Husserl's *Origin of Geometry* had been published, with Derrida's translation of that text, in 1962. Derrida found in Husserl's transcendental phenomenology 'the most modern, critical and vigilant' form of metaphysics.[45] Husserl's phenomenology is devoted to the pursuit of the secret of living experience, for what he calls 'my pure living' and 'all the pure subjective processes making this up', so that for Husserl the universe of phenomena is understood not as the context for, but as being 'meant' by those subjective processes.[46] Derrida's thought is itself a differentiating passion for the 'unthinkable truth of lived experience' and the question of how such an unthinkable truth might possibly relate to language (especially the language of philosophy) seethes in his work. In 'Violence and Metaphysics' he refers to a 'wounding' of language in Levinas's writing: Levinas's insistence that the truth he seeks is neither this, nor that, opens language by negation and thus 'silently' reveals 'experience itself' (112).

If 'Violence and Metaphysics' especially highlights Levinas's contestation of Husserlian phenomenology, the essay also incorporates a long discussion of the Heideggerian concept of Being (*Dasein*). Martin Heidegger's ontology, his distinctive thinking of being, has perhaps been overemphasized as the dominant philosophical context for deconstruction. The frequent recurrence of Being with a capital 'B' in *Writing and Difference* marks Heidegger's influence on the reception of Derrida. The English translation sometimes uses 'Being' where Derrida wrote the common noun '*être*.' 'Being' with a small 'b' translates terms used by philosophers since Parmenides and is, of course, an ordinary non-philosophical word.

No Departure from Metaphysics

Derrida was never simply interested in what goes on inside philosophy. He shared with the great philosophers a concern with what is most fundamental to philosophy – those things which, by definition, don't simply belong to it. Husserl and Heidegger both display a drive towards the radical, the basic aspects of thought. Metaphysics has traditionally been the field of philosophy which asks the most fundamental questions about what things are.[47] If metaphysics articulates philosophy's desire for the earth from which it springs, then deconstruction is the shaking of that earth, and gives us the experience of something unearthly at work in it.

The historical origins of philosophy are Greek, and Derrida never stopped acknowledging this. Heidegger also recognized and thought about the roots of philosophy in the Greek language and saw the profound implications of the issue of translation in the formation of modern philosophy. 'Violence and Metaphysics' finds no end to the violence of metaphysics and will show us no final philosophical 'departure from Greece' (104).

We might ask what is still to be gained today from this essay preoccupied with 'the outer or inner reaches of philosophy', where no end emerges to the philosophy wars – wars apparently attached to a past moment, forty years ago – a moment that turns out to mark the endurance of metaphysics rather than any decisive separation from it (103). What is the lasting interest of this violence that the title mentions? We might begin with the extraordinary opening sentence:

> That philosophy died yesterday, since Hegel or Marx, Nietzsche or Heidegger – and philosophy should still wander toward the meaning of its death – or that it has always lived knowing itself to be dying (as is silently confessed in the shadow of the very discourse which declared *philosophia perennis*); that philosophy died *one day, within* history, or that it has always fed on its own agony, on the violent way it opens history by opposing itself to nonphilosophy, which is its opposite and core [*fond advers*], its past or its concern, its death and wellspring: that beyond the death, or dying nature of philosophy, perhaps even because of it, thought still has a future [*avenir*], or even, as is said today, is still entirely to come because of what philosophy has held in store; or more strangely still, that the future itself has a future – all these are unanswerable questions. (97/117)

Whether we like it or not, when we begin 'Violence and Metaphysics' we are apparently caught up in philosophical discourse. But we aren't being invited to share a certain point of view on philosophy. It's not clear who is asking these unanswerable questions or what the context of those questions should be. They relate to the future and to what philosophy may be, seen from the perspective, not of its beginnings in Greece, but of its end. Philosophy has at least since Plato formed itself around the question of how to die.[48] The preoccupation with the end is an eschatological and to an extent Judaic perspective. If philosophy seems to perhaps end in German thought (all four of the thinkers Derrida mentions are German) it returns here in French. But this isn't a re-run of the Second World War: the essay greets us with a violence that has no obvious protagonists, no positive basis, lacking the initially refreshing anthropological simplicity of polemic. This ghostly quality has to do with what the essay is about.

Phenomenology and ontology are, according to Levinas, who insists on the complicity between knowledge and power, 'philosophies of violence' (113). Light, which since Plato has been thought to give us phenomena to be known and to reveal being, has an 'ancient clandestine friendship' with power. 'Everything given to me within light appears as given to myself by myself' (114). This appropriation of the visible, in the apparent neutrality of a light that falls impartially on everything, would, according to Levinas, be violent. It could be ethically important not to see, to experience a dark aspect of being and not to seek certainty within the apparently shared space of the visible. In this context it becomes clearer why Derrida's very long opening sentence, full of 'unanswerable questions' is in the subjunctive mood, taking the form of the verb that expresses condition, hypothesis or contingency. Under certain conditions, these *might* be the questions to be asking.

Derrida never attacks, contradicts or simply refutes those he reads. 'Violence and Metaphysics' repeatedly points out the limits of a classical logic which strictly polices contradictions. The 'experience of the other' has a different type of rigour (113). This would be a very open kind of experience where we could not know what to expect. Whatever the content of the experience may be, it would have the quality of surprise. Levinas's notion of the other gives rise to an experience that contests formal logic 'in its root'. The root is where things connect down in the dark. Derrida goes underground to explore these connections, for this root 'would be not only the root of our language but the root of all Western philosophy, particularly phenomenology and ontology'. *Logos*, the Greek word that gives us English 'logic' and these 'ology' endings, also means speech, discourse, principle, promise, order, command, condition, decision, legend, book, incident, thought, reasoning, cause, end, argument and meaning. All those who live in, with, by means of language have a stake in philosophy and Derrida returns to philosophy partly for economic reasons, because reading philosophical texts is the most economical means of investigating metaphysical limits which impose themselves on all regions of thought and activity in history. He will say of Levinas that it is the mark of 'strong and faithful thought' to respect the 'zone or layer of traditional truth' (109). Any violence here is not the violence of a simple break that marks the transition from one way of thinking to another. Such breaks are, for Derrida, always in a tension with 'memory, fidelity, the preservation of something that has been given to us'.[49]

How Derrida Reads Levinas

Derrida distinguishes the themes Levinas takes up from the history of his thought. He refuses to 'sacrifice the history of Levinas's thought and works to the order and the aggregate of themes . . . assembled in the great *Totality and Infinity*' (104). He says: 'the result is nothing without its becoming. But neither will we sacrifice the self-coherent unity of an intention to the becoming, which then would be no more than pure disorder. We will not choose between the opening and the totality.' Derrida wants to be faithful to the complex detours and differences in the history of Levinas's thought *and* to its intentions assembled into a 'great book'. His reading is animated by a tension between its interest in genesis and becoming, and organized completeness.

While Derrida relates earlier and later aspects of Levinas's thought, or provides synopses of his ideas in a quite classical way, he also traces what he calls a 'displacement of concepts' (108). For Derrida no philosophy can be at one with its own fundamental notions: there will always be slippage, detour, difference and deferral at work. He does not want to reduce these inevitable movements and the tensions accompanying them to the status of mere logical contradictions. They are what make philosophy historical – they make philosophical systems happen, in time, for real, outside the necessary abstraction. So he is interested in *how* Levinas proceeds: what he does as a philosopher and also the continuities in his thinking as well as what he doesn't reject, deny or abandon (109). He also sees what is 'new, quite new' in Levinas: a 'metaphysics of radical separation and exteriority' (110). There is recognition and respect for what Levinas intends to do but there is also a sense that displacement, a disturbance of what appears to be the *space* of a discourse, will affect these notions, *separation* and *exteriority*, which are themselves apparently spatial. There will be particular difficulty for Levinas: in what kind of language must this new metaphysics be articulated, given that 'traditional' *logos* is 'entirely governed by the structure "inside–outside," "interior–exterior"' (110)? How to mark the new language off from the old? And how to restore the dimension of time, in which things happen, to a discourse dominated by spatial models of reality and experience? Derrida insists that 'there is no element of Levinas's thought that is not engaged' by the 'questions of language and the question of language' (136). Metaphor – in Greek thought, the reference to something unknown by means of what is known – sides with the violence of light.

Parmenides

To continue thinking about historicity – the conditions of the possibility of history: philosophy is both continuous and discontinuous with itself. Levinas goes back to Parmenides, the pre-Socratic philosopher who, according to Hegel 'began philosophy proper'.[50] Parmenides' Poem speaks of the opposition what is and is not, and of being as whole, homogenous, unshaken and complete. Plato, who stages his relation with Parmenides in a dialogue between Socrates and a Stranger from Elea who is a disciple of Parmenides, still failed to break with a Parmenidean notion of being. This notion of being as a unity became part of metaphysics. Levinas wants to dare to break with Parmenides, and to have a plural idea of being that 'does not fuse into any unity' (110). As a writer and a thinker he is interested in negation, he practises a 'wounding of language' that defines its concepts in terms of their being neither this nor that. He engages with Greek philosophy in order to distinguish his own thought from its violently unifying procedures. That would seem to be a kind of break in history, a historical event. But Derrida, for whom continuity and discontinuity are not simply opposed, wonders whether something important is not inscribed in the Greek language itself, that will make it impossible for us to extricate ourselves from metaphysics that is, at root, Greek? If Plato failed to break with Parmenides, will a non-Greek such as Levinas fare any better? Can philosophical dialogue be reduced to the difference between individual points of view (Plato against Parmenides, Levinas against Husserl or Heidegger, Derrida against Levinas)? Here Derrida asks what turn out to be unanswerable questions and draws attention to the importance of language in the determination of concepts. To establish the plurality and otherness of being, to intervene in and redirect the path of a philosophy that is Greek, even to bring that philosophy to an end, it is necessary for Levinas to enter into the same philosophical language and risk the same inability to break with the limitations of the Greek conception of being that affected Plato:

> ... will a non-Greek ever succeed in doing what a Greek in this case could not do, except by disguising himself as a Greek by *speaking* Greek, by feigning to speak Greek in order to get near the king? And since it is a question of killing a speech, will we ever know who is the last victim of this stratagem? Can one feign speaking a language?

These questions must necessarily affect Levinas in relation to Heidegger and his translation of Heidegger's German concepts. Derrida returns to this issue at the end of the essay. For now he marks the emergence of a 'primordial secret' – secret because it cannot be shared – the fact that the relationship to the other arises from the solitude of my existence (111). And for Levinas the mode of that relation is not as described by Heidegger, nor as described by Husserl. It consists of a 'face-to-face, the encounter with the face' (112). By thinking the relation to the other as being without the intermediary or medium of language, Levinas seeks to avoid dependence on a philosophical language that is not adequate to its proper purpose, that of fidelity to 'the unthinkable truth of lived experience'.

Jewgreeks

The epigraph to 'Violence and Metaphysics', a line from the nineteenth-century English poet and cultural critic Matthew Arnold, flags up an opposition between Greek and Jewish thought. The previous essay on Edmond Jabès is explicitly concerned with Judaism, history and God and these themes are prolonged in 'Violence and Metaphysics' which ends with a quotation from

James Joyce's mighty philosophical novel *Ulysses*, which tells in numerous different Englishes the experiences of the Jew Leopold Bloom by means of episodes modelled on those of Greek epic: 'Jewgreek is greekjew. Extremes meet.' Derrida is at this point still asking questions prompted by Levinas. If Levinas and Derrida cannot help but be Hellenic in their engagement with philosophy, the Hebraic aspect of thought does not emerge in the same way as the Greek. Derrida and Levinas were both Jewish (as was Husserl) and therefore, by the logic of oppositions, they were non-Greek, but there is no symmetry or opposition between Greek and Jew in this essay. The figure of Levinas, whose thought can make us tremble in the desert, suggests the possibility of a philosopher–prophet and eschatologist (student of last or ultimate things): a philosopher who is a stranger in his own time, a voice crying in the wilderness. As far as Derrida is concerned, there is no neutral space within which dialogue and the trajectory towards the other could be made comprehensible. No neutral totality can '*comprehend* dialogue' (121). This is 'not the beginning of irrationalism but the wound or inspiration which opens speech and then makes possible every logos or every rationalism' (121–2).

Hear, and tremble

The essay introduces the eschatological thought of Emmanuel Levinas as something that 'can make us tremble' (101). Shaking and trembling are characteristic movements of being in deconstruction. An important form of trembling is sound vibration: its differences of rhythm produce tone, which is a kind of variant tension. 'Violence and Metaphysics' points out the relation between trembling and sound with reference to *trembling* in Hegel's *Aesthetics* (124). Hearing is, according to Hegel, closer to the ideal (and to soul, thought and language), than sight. The trembling that vibrates as sound is not the opposite of light but is perhaps the profound movement of those apparently stable organizations of continuous space that light seems to give us. A slightly frightening thought. Hear, and tremble, as the Bible says (see Isa. 66.5). As movement, trembling is related to the possibility of history. Derrida quotes the storywriter Jorge-Luis Borges saying: 'Perhaps universal history is but the history of the diverse *intonations* of several metaphors' (114). In his valorization of the ear, Levinas is 'very close' to Hegel – 'much closer than he admits' (123).

Levinas and Husserl on the Experience of the Other

Derrida locates a fundamental disagreement between Levinas and Husserl in their notion of the other. Levinas mistakenly claims that the other in Husserl is assimilated to the ego; it is 'the ego's phenomenon' and therefore Husserl has reduced the other to the same, to part of oneself (153). Directing attention to Husserl's fifth Cartesian Meditation, Derrida insists that for Husserl the other is 'presented to me . . . as originary nonpresence. It is the other as other which is the ego's phenomenon: the phenomenon of a certain non-phenomenality which is irreducible for the ego . . .'. He goes on to clarify: 'One could neither speak, nor have any sense of the totally other, if there was not a phenomenon of the totally other, or evidence of the totally other as such' (154). He goes on to say that:

> Husserl's most central affirmation concerns the *irreducibly mediate* nature of the intentionality aiming at the other as other. It is evident, by an essential, absolute and definitive self-evidence that the other as transcendental other (other absolute origin and other zero point of the origin of the world), can never be given to me in an original way and in person but only through analogical appresentation.

To gloss this we need to go back to Husserl, who argues that:

> properly speaking, neither the other Ego himself, nor his subjective processes and appearances themselves, nor anything else belonging to his own essence, becomes given in our experience originally. If it were, if what belongs to the other's own essence were directly accessible, it would merely be a moment of my own essence, and ultimately he himself and I myself would be the same.[51]

Appresentation is a 'making co-present' that brings the other to me, but indirectly and by way of a divided present, one that comes to me as a result of mediation. In the absence of any possibility of verification, Husserl explains, an appresentation motivates a recognition of someone else, rather as, when I experience a physical thing it 'perceptually motivates "belief in" something else being there too'. I constitute my relation to the other analogically, on the basis of a similarity that connects, within me, 'that body over there' with my body.

Levinas appears to think that this understanding of the other on the basis of myself is an assimilation and a betrayal of otherness. Derrida insists that appresentation 'confirms and respects separation' and is a kind of 'nonviolent respect for the secret' (154–5). Bodies are other for Husserl but not for Levinas. Derrida is interested in noticing that Husserl recognizes, in the reality of the external world, that something of every perception 'is always hidden' and we can know that outer world only in mediated ways, by 'anticipation, analogy and appresentation'. Husserl's emphasis on bodies is important as a 'first alterity' without which my sense of others as other could not emerge: 'the Other is also a body, from the beginning'. Bodies cannot be known completely as totalities – they have more than two dimensions; they are opaque. To this another otherness is added – *history*: 'The stranger is infinitely other because by his essence no enrichment of his profile can give me the subjective face of his experience *from his perspective*, such as he has lived it.' What distinguishes Husserl from Levinas here is Husserl's emphasis on *the ego* as that which allows the infinitely other to appear. The other is, as such, still a modification of my ego. This means that we can speak about it because it is a phenomenon experienced by my ego and also that the other is, as an alter ego, still an ego and therefore not just a thing *in* the world but 'the origin of the world' (156). There is another origin of the world and I cannot own it. Derrida explores the ethical force of bringing together as closely as possible the same and the other, the ego and the other, and insists on the experience of the other as an *economy*. The other must be able to happen to me, 'speak to me, understand me, and eventually command me' (157). If he or she were absolutely other and beyond relation, as Levinas would have it, then this would not be possible: 'the other is absolutely other only if he is an ego, that is, in a certain way, if he is the same as I' (159). This economy can never be absolutely peaceful. There is a transcendental violence in every 'reduction of the other to a *real* moment of *my* life', but this reduction, thought initially by Husserl, is necessary for there to be any ethical stance, such as Levinas takes up, in relation to the other. This inevitable and 'irreducible' violence is at the same time non-violence, since it 'opens the relation to the other. It is an *economy*' (160).

Hegel becomes important in 'Violence and Metaphysics' as the philosopher who, like Husserl, is interested in philosophy as a way of understanding the relation between the immediacy of experience and the mediated activity of thought, which gives us an understanding – and arguably a more genuine experience – of the immediate phenomena of living, only after our leaving that experience in order to question it. Immediacy turns out to be an effect of certain detours and delays, rather than the hallmark, given directly to me by my living, of what is truly causal and original. One discovers – and precisely in the living experience of thinking as detour and delay – that difference is at the origin. There is a kind of tragicomedy at work in experience and Husserl and Hegel recognize this in a philosophical way. War, Derrida reminds us with reference to Hegel's *Phenomenology of Spirit*, is not only an event for mankind, with battles, generals and casualties, but is a constitutive part of experience and consciousness. Derrida manages to take this tragicomic state of affairs – that war is the 'very emergence of speech and of appearing' – and make it something more than an economy that might implicitly justify violence (162). The books remain unbalanced, still to be balanced. There must be an economy of violence but Derrida never uses this thought (as both Hegel and Heidegger on occasion do) to silently or explicitly justify the wrongs and brutalities of history on the grounds that they are expressions of the authentic movement of Spirit (Hegel) or Being (Heidegger). Derrida returns to a discussion of the living present 'at once the most simple and difficult of notions' and the Husserlian ego – me – as that which can only experience anything in the present and at the same time this present of the ego's living experience is where all other times come into existence and appear. Time appears in and for the ego and this necessary narrowing of temporal differences into the realm of the same, the ego, is violent.

Letting Be

Whereas for Heidegger the term 'metaphysics' suggested an inheritance which urgently needs further thought, for Levinas metaphysics was a resource, freeing the other from the neutralization imposed by ontology and phenomenology (119–20). The last third of 'Violence and Metaphysics' focuses on the violence of being and returns to Heidegger's notion of 'letting be'. We are still, in a way, thinking the interplay of sameness and difference as the living present, as the present participle of the verb 'to be', Being. Thinking it, rather than thinking about it, which would imply that Being was a category, with contents, that I could recognize. Between activity and passivity, letting be is not the same as ignoring or letting alone. It means an opening of thinking towards what is nameless, towards Being before social organization and therefore before ethics. So letting be is what would make ethics possible. Letting be may allow comprehension but it also acknowledges the forms of an existing thing or person that cannot be transformed into an object of understanding. Letting be would encounter beings where they are not yet entirely nameable, where they are not even recognizable as animate rather than inanimate, or human rather than animal, or abstract rather than concrete, or you rather than me. The obvious differences and samenesses of people in their relation to each other are traced to a foreignness of Being. This ontology, or philosophy of Being, persists in Levinas's thought, even where he wants to poise his arguments against Heidegger and ontology. One could see these pages of Derrida, with their multiple sources and addressees – Derrida himself, Levinas, Heidegger but also Husserl (still), Descartes, Hegel and Nietzsche, not to mention you – as the summoning of a community by means of questioning. It perhaps helps us to understand better the experience of reading 'Violence and Metaphysics' if we bear this call in mind, along with the thought that the 'best liberation from violence is a certain putting into question, which makes the search for an *archia* [Greek: commander and origin] tremble. Only the thought of Being can do so, and not traditional "philosophy" or "metaphysics"' (176). Look for the leader, like a dissatisfied customer who demands to see the person in charge of this essay, and the writing will be less able to loosen the grip of violence on thought. But of course, cease to respect the distinctions between the thinking of the cast members of Derrida's essay, and it would lose its means of articulation and say nothing to us.

Empiricism and the Inevitability of Philosophy

We have talked a lot about experience in this chapter. Doesn't everything start there? Even before philosophy calls on or seeks out the truth of experience? The philosophical name for a thinking grounded in experience rather than philosophy is *empiricism*, but as we have seen, if experience includes the experience of thinking (Heidegger), and if a phenomenology of living experience begins with the ego and not with the world (Husserl), then a radical empiricism such as the one that Levinas wants, must have its more mediated philosophical moments. Derrida asks explicit questions which also silently animate the rest of the essay:

> But can one speak of an experience of the other or of difference? Has not the concept of experience always been determined by the metaphysics of presence? Is not experience always an encountering of an irreducible presence, the perception of a phenomenality? (190)

These questions are necessary: Derrida is not contradicting Levinas's thought or even neutrally pointing out contradictions within it (the latter is a favourite thing to detect Derrida doing), but he is perhaps slowing it down just by reading it, by reading what Levinas does not say alongside what he says, by reading those whom Levinas has read and by refusing to reduce those others to moments within Levinas's argument. At the same time, the slowing provokes a tremendous sense of speed and the numerousness of the things that can happen in an instant.

Empiricism in the Greek philosophical tradition has always been determined as '*nonphilosophy*' (190). But Derrida insists that what philosophy recognizes as empiricism's inability to philosophize, can, when adopted with resolution, make the unity of thought and meaning (Greek *logos*) tremble. Derrida uses again a term he introduced in 'Force and Signification,' *soliciter*, from the Latin *sollicitare*, to shake or make tremble. Soliciting also suggests that this trembling asks us for a response. The trembling reminds us of the promise that 'the thought of Emmanuel Levinas can make us tremble'. Derrida continues 'At the heart of the desert, in the growing wasteland, this thought, which fundamentally no longer seeks to be the thought of Being and phenomenality, makes us dream of an inconceivable process of dismantling and dispossession' (101). In the Old Testament, trembling is the classic response to the presence of God. If Levinas's thought can stir a dying Greek philosophy it may be through something incommensurate with that philosophy. We could call this awakening of philosophy, this experience of the infinitely other, *Judaism*. If so, Derrida is interested in thinking about how, in history, it has been possible for Judaism to become the other of Greek thought, given that it may be Judaism that accomplishes something that Greek thought does not know how to experience, the experience of the infinitely other. Derrida is intrigued by the way that Judaism happens to philosophy, 'is ordered to occur as logos, and to reawaken the Greek in the autistic syntax of his own dream' (190–1).

Dreaming stands for the invention of a new syntax, particular to the dreamer and therefore autistic, a language conceived on the basis of the *autos*, the same, the self-same. Dream would be the condition of philosophy. For Derrida, Levinas is making philosophy aware of itself in a new way, allowing it to dream of its own dispossession and dismantling and at the same time rendering it hospitable to Judaism. There is no escape into Judaism, which does not exist in itself for Greek thought and therefore cannot ever surprise philosophy. We cannot choose between alternatives to determine our identity as either Greek or Jew: 'We live in and of difference, that is, in *hypocrisy*, about which Levinas so profoundly says that it is "not only a base contingent defect of man, but the underlying rending of a world attached to both the philosophers and the prophets"' (192).

Study Question
Must the otherness of other lives, of our own unconscious life, always escape us? If so, what would be good and what bad about that?

'"GENESIS AND STRUCTURE" AND PHENOMENOLOGY'
This essay returns to Husserl. It is laid out in terms of two concepts and reads Husserl's project and oeuvre in terms of them. Derrida is clearly interested in what becomes of phenomenology and in that which, within phenomenology, makes new acts of philosophising necessary. Derrida's *historical* interest in how and

why things are understood to happen in a particular form will demand that a kind of violence be done to the integrity of Husserl's philosophy. It means a 'putting into question, that is, an abusive investigation which introduces beforehand what it seeks to find, and does violence to the physiology proper to a body of thought' (193). The readymade couple 'genesis and structure' implies a whole tradition and a long-debated opposition. The essay's title silently refers to Jean Hyppolite's landmark study of Hegel, *The Genesis and Structure of the Phenomenology of Spirit* (1947), and implicitly engages with a certain way of reading philosophy. 'Debate' is foreign to proper philosophical thinking and especially foreign to the way Husserl thinks and yet, after honouring this fact with some care, Derrida reveals his own conviction that a debate between 'genesis' and 'structure' in fact 'animates' phenomenology and makes it 'unbalanced' at 'every major stage' (196). The 'new reductions and explications' that are the future of phenomenology are necessary because of this imbalance.

Phenomenology is concerned with the origin of the world in the act of a concrete consciousness. A genetic description attempts to describe how something comes about, its becoming and its historicity. A structural description is concerned with essences and the arrangement of closed systems. However, as Derrida explains further in 'Structure, Sign and Play' something always remains *open* in a structure and this means that a descriptive and radical thinker such as Husserl, concerned with openings, works precisely in the space where a structure is open to becoming something else. There, genesis and structure cannot be simply opposed to each other. This essay has a bearing on structuralism, therefore, and suggests that phenomenology remains important in the development of thinking about structure, historicity and the relationship between psychology and philosophy.

At the time 'Genesis and Structure' was written, Derrida had already completed a dissertation on 'The Problem of Genesis in Husserl's Philosophy' (1953–1954). There he works with Husserl's movement towards locating all genesis in a transcendental consciousness. This would enable phenomenology, which locates genesis in a concrete individual consciousness, to meet the '"worldly" sciences' that currently differ from phenomenology because they seek to know the world in itself, rather than seeing consciousness as the origin of the world.[52] To understand what is at stake in this ambition of Husserl's was, according to Derrida, more than an endeavour in the 'pure history of philosophy': it would also entail a precise sense of 'the meaning of every genesis'.[53] Husserl assumed that this notion of transcendental genesis, which phenomenology points to, is achievable by phenomenology: Derrida is not so sure that it is achievable at all.

Reason and Writing

Our discussion of this already remarkably concise and elegant essay will arrange itself around a passage from near the end where *writing* and *difference* suddenly appear by name. This happens in the course of an account of genetic phenomenology as it relates to logic, the ego and history. As we read we will come up against *logos*, glossed by Derrida as 'the idea of an infinite task of reason', and the question of its relation to consciousness (207). How is *logos*, which presents itself as an essence, and which can be glossed in so many ways (we recall that it can be translated as: speech, discourse, principle, promise, order, command, decision, book, incident, thought, world, order) possible in history? The questions underlying this might be, why is life like this? Why is history like this? What is happening? Why does consciousness occur under conditions which it is so difficult – but still possible – for consciousness to understand? Why is deconstruction necessary now?

> Reason . . . unveils itself. Reason, Husserl says, is the *logos* which is produced in history. It traverses being [*être*] with itself in sight, in sight of appearing to itself, that is, to state itself and hear itself as *logos*. It is speech as auto-affection: hearing oneself speak. It emerges from itself in order to take hold of itself within itself, in the 'living present' of its self-presence. In emerging from itself, hearing oneself speak constitutes itself as the history of reason through the detour of *writing. Thus it differs from itself in order to reappropriate itself. The Origin of Geometry* describes the necessity of this exposition of reason in a worldly inscription. An exposition indispensable to the constitution of truth and of the ideality of objects, but which is also the danger to meaning from what is outside the sign. In the moment of writing, the sign can

always 'empty' itself, take flight from awakening, from 'reactivation', and may remain for ever closed and mute. . . . [W]riting here is the 'critical epoch'. (208/248)

To read this passage, we will have to backtrack through the essay with the necessarily limited aim of seeing why it is necessary for a discussion of genesis and structure and phenomenology to turn to a notion of writing in general.

The Ego as the Origin of the World

Genetic phenomenology entails three interlinked approaches, via logic, via the ego and via historicity. To describe unique events according to the radical logic of the constitution of objects by the ego, phenomenology must free itself from historicism, which would be the search for a factual, psychological account of how reason appears for consciousness. Phenomenology suspends scientific notions of logic and objectivity, and the commonsensical understanding of logic derived from the sciences, in order to be able to get past settled assumptions which operate at the level of culture but which lack philosophical value. Husserl wants to philosophize radically – to give access to living experience 'on the basis of the most untamed precultural life' (207). He locates this wild heart of life in the constitution and the modifications of concrete consciousness. The search for *eidos*, essence, begins there. One must return to the 'genesis of the ego itself', for the ego is the scene of this original and world-beginning life. Because the ego is understood to be the origin of the world, 'the genetic description of the ego at every instant prescribes the formidable task of a *universal* genetic phenomenology.' Historicity in general will have to be understood phenomenologically on the basis of an understanding of what Husserl calls 'the unity of the history of the ego'. What Derrida calls elsewhere the history of the world as the history of *différance* cannot be understood on the basis of the history of the objective world.

According to Husserl a 'teleological reason' runs throughout historicity (207). This emergence of reason in history takes the form of a play of veils. It comes each time seeming to 'tear open' a previous finitude of consciousness and seeming to 'give voice' to the energy of a silence (208). (It looks therefore like the discovery of *logos*, the coincidence of reason and speech.) But the unveilings are also 'coverings up' because the tearing open is an origin that 'dissimulates itself immediately' beneath the continuity of a new objective world where consciousness is once more caught up in the finite domain of objects newly revealed to it. Blindness to 'the power of a hidden infinity' prolongs itself by means of a seeing necessarily restricted to a limited domain. But Husserl recognizes in this movement that the events that bring to human consciousness 'the idea of an infinite task of reason' is '*always already indicated*' in the confusion and darkness of history (207, 208). Here we approach a sense of an inextricable complicity in writing, between genesis (which is an event and unrepeatable) and structure (which is a repeatable pattern). The reference to indication is a reference to *writing*, which is for Husserl the trace of 'lost intentions' that need to be reanimated by those who encounter them.[54] Derrida finds already in his *Introduction to the Origin of Geometry* that Husserl's emphasis on intention, on writing's 'pure relation to a consciousness which grounds it as such' ignores the 'factuality' of writing, which 'left to itself, is totally without signification'. The silence or illegibility of 'prehistoric arcana and buried civilisations' point to writing's ability to 'dispense with every present reading in general'. These remains are not meaningless but they do not signify. Thanks to writing, reason necessarily runs through what look like its opposites: silence, unreadability and death.

Hearing Oneself Speak

Reason amounts to a tear, a wound in consciousness. How then can we capture its essence, the value affirmed by its movement? And this event, which 'embraces the totality of beings', happens at the level of concrete individual consciousness (207). Understanding what happens in history, must, for phenomenology, begin there. This brings us to our paragraph's movement between 'the *logos* . . . produced in history' and 'hearing oneself speak'. As so often in Derrida, close reading moves us away from where we are. Something is announced in this lecture from 1959, published in 1964, that takes us to other dates and texts. Hearing oneself speak is discussed at length in Chapter 6 of *Speech and Phenomena* titled 'The Voice that Keeps Silence'. There Derrida comes up with the term '*différance*.' He traces a movement of *différance*, which, he says, 'is not something that happens to a transcendental subject: it produces a subject'.[55] *Différance* is found to be at work 'at the origin of sense and presence'. There is an affirmation of a movement here for which, Derrida says in the essay '*Différance*' (1968) 'there has never been, never will be, a unique word, a master-name'.[56] It is the destiny of *différance* to continually break up 'in a chain of different substitutions'. Our paragraph also cites Husserl's *Origin of Geometry*, the subject of Derrida's first major publication in 1962. The *Origin of Geometry* explores how mathematical truths can be discovered and become self-evident. Such truths cannot be reduced to the psychology of the geometrician, they have an 'ideal objectivity' that is the same for everyone. What makes this ideal objectivity possible is 'written, documenting linguistic expression', a 'virtual' form of communication.[57]

This paragraph is about how reason happens, about the living experience of reason. Not only does this living reasoning necessarily entail a wealth of references to vital but distracting objective content that the passage does not, cannot fully reveal, but the event of hearing oneself speak has historicity only through *writing*. Only through writing does hearing oneself speak become possible as an event in the history of reason and as an idea that has objectivity and the chance of universality. There is a writing at work already within speech and in my living presence to myself. Writing is 'indispensable for the constitution of truth and for ideal objects', but it entails a risk. It may not be awakened by my concrete consciousness. Thanks to the detour through the sign, it may 'remain forever closed and mute'. I may not be able to read it so as to return it to life. Hearing oneself speak is an experience of writing and difference but it also brings me close to death.

Reading as Opening

This paragraph is also about reading. If reading can reactivate and awaken signs, it also engages with the sign as that which takes me away from myself. Reading takes me away from my own curiosity. It may be an encounter with my own consciousness as consciousness of another consciousness but it is also the encounter with signs which may remain forever silent. In reading, the *logos* produced in history happens in and for my concrete consciousness. It unveils itself to me and at once hides itself as the objective content of what I am reading. There is an opening in reading, a movement that cannot be reduced to understanding. Opening is 'the most powerful structural a priori of historicity' and 'the concrete possibility, the very birth of history' (210). It is 'genesis itself', but as opening, it has no content. Content, is however indispensable, and Derrida makes it clear that Husserl's phenomenology can never be considered as mere food for deconstruction. This is marked in the slow pace of Derrida's reading of Husserl, in its concern with the precise detail of the connections made by phenomenology and with the 'initial distinction between different irreducible types of genesis and structure'. Derrida is concerned to read, to go back, not to know where he is going, to open his questioning to the necessary transformations dictated by his concrete unique reading. Husserl's transcendental reduction is 'but the free act of the question, which frees itself from the totality of what precedes it in order to be able to gain access to this totality, particularly to its historicity and its past'. This freedom of the question entails a 'gap', an opening in which the unity of structure and genesis and general cannot be established. One of the most powerful sentences in 'Genesis and Structure' concerns the opening or spacing that will frustrate structuralism: 'What I can never understand, in a structure, is that by means of which it is not closed' (201). There is a rapport between this gap and the '*nothing*' or 'invisible difference that separates parallel things' and makes transcendental reduction possible (209). Also between the gap and the '*nothing*' that *logos* would be 'outside history and being [*être*]' (209/249). A metaphysical concern with *logos* as an essence, with the essence of reason or meaning would mean an abandonment of the genetic interest of phenomenology, which is for Derrida, a relation to opening. He affirms phenomenology's responsiveness to questioning: the transcendental ego 'is called upon to ask itself about everything', particularly 'the possibility of the unformed and naked factuality of the nonmeaning . . . of its own death' (211). Derrida doesn't say so, but that possibility is writing, in and as phenomenology, which would live on while questioning itself about its own death, among other things. At this point in *Writing and Difference*, references to Husserl begin to disappear.

Study Question

What are the implications of thinking about your own life in terms of beginning and becoming, or of seeing your life as a structure or complete form?

'LA PAROLE SOUFFLÉE'

> I found in Artaud's fundamental gesture something that could put to the test what I had been trying to work out elsewhere in various texts for example, to begin with, in *Of Grammatology* . . . Speech [*parole*] is stolen from me, said Artaud, and this experience of dispossession, of expropriation, is an *ambiguous* protest . . . at once a torment, and at the same time, in the process of writing, it is what makes Artaud's voice, his clamour.[58]

As a young man reading Antonin Artaud's extraordinary correspondence with Jacques Rivière, editor of the *Nouvelle Revue Français*, about his writing, life and madness, Derrida had identified with Artaud's conviction that when he wrote, he had nothing to say. This essay is the result of a more systematic reading of Artaud, but it keeps a sense of identification with, and sympathy towards, a man 'to whom nothing had been *dictated*' but who was nonetheless haunted by 'the passion, the pulsion of writing'.[59] Paule Thévenin, the dedicatee of '*La Parole soufflée*,' explains the importance of breath to Artaud, who

> wanted 'with the hieroglyph of a breath to find again the idea of a sacred theatre'; who for long years thought that breath had to accompany every effort, that it 'relights life', and that, nourishing life, breathing 'permits us to climb back up the stages by the steps'; so he now knows 'the visual, objective value of the breath'.[60]

La parole soufflée emphasizes Artaud's sense of powerlessness as essential, not incidental, to his writing and thinking. Derrida quotes the correspondence with Rivière: 'it is not a matter of the higher or lower existence involved in what is known as inspiration [*inspiration*], but of a total absence, a veritable dwindling away' (222/263). Something 'furtive', Artaud explains 'takes away from me the words *which I have found.*' The word 'furtive', Derrida explains, is a furtive reference to theft, from Latin 'in the manner of a thief'. Artaud thought about his writing and his life in terms of theft and substitution. His sense of loss included, or rather precluded, his relation to his own body. Derrida ventriloquizes Artaud, saying: 'ever since my birth I no longer am my body. Ever since I have had a body I am not this body, hence I do not possess it' (226). A *parole soufflée* would be a stolen word and Derrida's epigraph speaks of a 'stolen [*volé*, also 'flying'] verb' that Artaud will destroy in order to replace it with something else. This emptying out of speech happens very fleetingly. Derrida recognizes that Artaud's madness is both absolutely his own and at the same time an advanced, courageous and imperfect acknowledgement of a universal condition.

Souffle, Psukhe, Psychologism

As well as meaning 'stolen', the French adjective *soufflée* means 'whispered', as a stage prompt reminds an actor of a forgotten bit of script, and 'inspired'. Paule Thévenin glosses the title of Derrida's essay:

> The word that is *stolen/breathed* is a word *robbed* as well as *inspired*. But it can also be a word, which precisely because it is *soufflée*, because it is organic, succeeds, by the work of the breath, in finding once more on the inside of the body what had been taken away from it.[61]

Finally, *souffler* also means to blow up like a bomb. A *parole soufflée* would be, among other things, an exploded word or utterance. The essay is punctuated by references to explosion. Rather than being considered as the seat and guarantee of presence, voice and language scatter from inside, their appearance transformed by a violent energy. The Greek root of *souffler* is *psukhe*, which means not only 'breath' but 'spirit' and gives us 'psyche' and its cognate words. One of these is 'psychologism'. In the context of Husserl's philosophy, psychologism consists of a dogmatic adherence to the primacy of the self and its workings. It relates to everyday assumptions about the self, our ingrained sense that life in general is as we imagine ourselves to be. Life makes sense on the basis of my presence and awareness.

The things around me have the status of tools or instruments that I use to enact my wishes. This tendency goes back to the beginning of Western philosophy and remains so deeply ingrained in our culture that challenges to it, such as those presented by Derrida, by phenomenology, or very differently by Artaud, can seem quite strange. Artaud's notion of 'Unpower' (221) and Husserl's concept of 'transcendental life' cannot be properly understood from within these assumptions. What 'La parole soufflée' calls the *clinical* perspective on writers of the 'mad genius' kind, would be an example of psychologism. Blanchot calls Artaud's life story 'a pathetic error' (214). Jean Laplanche appeals to the idea of uniqueness, but at the end of his book on Hölderlin, Derrida wryly comments: 'we are still out of breath searching for the unique [*on s'essouffle encore devant la unique*]' (217/258).

Artaud

Artaud was not a critic or an academic but not simply a creative practitioner either. Madness, from his early correspondence on, was inextricable from his thinking of life and writing. Derrida's opening declaration of innocence and inexperience suggest his respect for the man whose work he is reading: 'Naïveté of the discourse we begin here, speaking toward Antonin Artaud' (212). The movement to and fro of discourse (from Latin *discurrere*, 'to discourse, to run to and fro') is blocked by Artaud, the poet–thinker who wrote from Rodez asylum in 1946:

> When I write there is nothing other than what I write. Whatever else I felt I have not been able to say, and whatever else has escaped me are ideas of a stolen verb which I will destroy, to replace them with something else. (212)

Under these conditions how could a discourse *on* Artaud be said to exist? And yet if he wants to read Artaud, Derrida cannot abandon language, discourse and reason. The opening pages of the essay refer to a kind of infinite closeness, a unity, continuity, a presence, proximity, a drawing near, an approach, perhaps within whispering distance of Artaud – but without a shared horizon. Derrida connected Artaud's sense that what there is to be said did not pre-exist the act of speaking with his interest in the theatre. Artaud wanted a theatre in which nothing would pre-exist the act, in the form of bodily movements that would not obey a pre-decided text or meaning. He called these acts hieroglyphs, a writing without dictation, prompting or author–god. This extreme desire for presence without a trace of repetition, for a unique, spontaneous and essentially non-verbal, living writing, dominated his thought and brought it close to Derrida's own impossible desire for a writing that would be equal to the multiplicities, substitutions, expropriations and divisions of life.

Husserl and Artaud in Parallel

Derrida's thinking of beginning and his resistance to clinical and critical appropriations of Artaud resonate with Husserlian phenomenology's energetic resistance to psychologism. Husserl explicitly sought to break with any notion that the origins of temporality and meaning are psychological. His thinking of consciousness is not psychological but it seeks, having discovered its true basis, to take psychology into account. In *Speech and Phenomena*, Derrida describes Husserl's notion of *transcendental consciousness* and his investigation of consciousness and meaning. Husserl wanted to establish a general notion of 'the living present, the self-presence of transcendental life' in its ideality and repeatability.[62] 'Ideality' remains something of a specialist phenomenological term: it was defined in opposition to the existence of actual, non-ideal, empirical, historical, objects and yet, at the same time, it depended on the existence of those objects. More exactly, ideality depends on the possibility of being experienced *as if* the ideal object were phenomenal and possessed appearance.

Derrida's dissertation on Husserl asked the question of the preconditions of genesis itself, of the beginning of beginning, before the transcendental subject has been constituted. *Speech and Phenomena* identifies phenomenology as a 'philosophy of life'.[63] Life must come first and be the condition of the operations of phenomenological thinking. Phenomenology entails an idealization, a notion of 'transcendental life' yet to be related to psychological or worldly life, which is thereby revealed to itself as a topic for thought within the context of another unity, incorporating the transcendental *and* the psychological. Husserl's movement out of psychologism to a more rigorous and revelatory way of thinking continues to need what it leaves behind.

There is some kind of unity between these two notions of living. But they do not inhabit the homogenous space of some kind of life-in-general. Phenomenology needs psychology, even if only to think about its underlying presuppositions. Husserl outlines the need for a phenomenological psychology which 'has the task of fixing the sense of concepts derived from psychology, and first of all the sense of what is called the *psyche*'.[64]

So there are two ways to understand the word 'life'. There is life, which is discovered by phenomenology to be a kind of regional sense of life that comes before the transcendental life. But transcendental life turns out to need this limited understanding of life, with its exaggerated idea of itself, that starts off by thinking it is everything. And indeed, Derrida points out that 'the domain of pure psychological experience incorporates the total domain of what Husserl calls transcendental experience.' No linear movement out of this situation is possible. Like life itself, it is an experience of the nonlinear and the inescapable. Life starts before you know it and you live it while it relates to itself in a different way from your experience of your relation to it. Life is not the same as my living presence. In the discussion of the relation between psychological and 'what Husserl calls transcendental experience' in *Speech and Phenomena*, Derrida highlights a difference in a way that helps us to understand the title of *Writing and Difference* a little differently. Despite the 'perfect' incorporation of Husserl's philosophically modified sense of experience as transcendental within 'pure psychological experience':

> a radical difference remains, one having nothing in common with any other difference, a difference in fact distinguishing nothing, a difference separating no state, no experience, no determined signification – but a difference which, without altering anything, changes all the signs, and in which alone the possibility of a transcendental question is contained. That is to say, freedom itself.

Difference does not depend on distinctions between actual states or positively identifiable existent elements. Language has no way of marking this difference, which is *nothing*. After this detour we can perhaps understand better why '*La parole soufflée*' begins as it does, by marking certain inevitable entanglements and obstacles besetting any attempt to write about Artaud. Derrida's work on Artaud negotiates with his work on life in Husserl, and the work on Husserl helps explain why Artaud cannot be an example of a certain kind of writing for Derrida, as he became at times for Blanchot and Laplanche.

Parole

More can be said about the untranslatable title of the essay and the singular freedom it offers by not indicating a single goal or direction for the text that follows it. We have begun to read the word *soufflée*. But what about parole? A *parole* is a word, from Greek *parabole* meaning a comparison or parable, literally 'a throwing beside', from *para-* 'alongside' + *ballein* 'to throw'. Later, Latin *parabola* took on the meaning 'word', hence French *parole*, which also means the faculty of speech, the use of that faculty, the action or fact of speaking, a particular manner of speaking, and an element of spoken language. This furtive or non-obvious connection with parable, a discourse avowedly parallel to or different from itself, suggests that a *parole* may be separated from itself by something like the unique, radical, invisible difference between phenomenological psychology and transcendental phenomenology', the *'nothing* that distinguishes . . . parallels'.[65]

Unique Artaud

> Artaud had a voice and a concept of voice . . . that was absolutely unique. Once you have heard that voice . . . you can no longer read his texts . . . in the same way. To read him must imply that you resuscitate his voice, that you read him by imagining him in the process of uttering his texts.[66]

Part of what Derrida wants to do is to read Artaud without becoming clinical, without diagnosing, *but also* to read Artaud without making his text into a neutralized critical example of a way of thinking. For Artaud is a thinker of writing with an extraordinary sense of what writing will do, but he is not, as Derrida wants to be, responsible to philosophy. Essays earlier in the collection have approached criticism, and madness, with caution. To engage with Artaud is to insist that there is more to mad writing and to those who have written it than either the embodiment of certain truths about literature on the one hand or the articulation of symptoms on the other. Derrida is not satisfied with the characterization of writing implied by a tendency to speak of 'madness *and* the work', driving, primarily, at their enigmatic conjunction (213).

That phrase 'madness *and* the work' reminds us of the argument with Foucault. But '*La parole soufflée*', unlike 'Cogito and the History of Madness', is not preoccupied by the questions Derrida sees as unresolved in critical work on Artaud, but with 'speaking toward' him, '*en direction de Antonin Artaud*' (212/253). 'Direction' comes from Latin *dirigere,* 'to straighten', 'set straight', 'direct', 'guide', and in French *diriger* recalls the direction that is given to a group of actors by the *metteur en scene*, the director. The word suggests a naïve wish for presence or to follow Artaud. It maintains an element of risk and uncertainty about who or what 'Antonin Artaud' might be and how best to try to throw your voice his way or speak alongside him. Derrida's reading is not an exercise in intellectual curiosity, because the proper name of a unique individual is involved. Derrida is not aiming to have understood Artaud. And he begins by taking seriously the possibility that it won't be possible to be faithful to Artaud. If *parole* means not just word but also promise (as in giving one's word) and furthermore denotes the power of speech and speech itself, then how can a *parole soufflée*, a whisper from the prompt box, reinforcing the dominance of the author and his words over the actor, also be a restoration of breath, body and magical gesture that Artaud wanted? Again, the notion of an invisible difference comes into play. The *soufflée*-effect acknowledges the loss incurred in speech. And yet, in the gesture of acknowledging and accepting that necessary state of affairs, breath opens a realm in which life relights. What might sound like a very primitive and unthought appeal to lived experience returns on the other side of an acceptance of the cruel and painful fact of the non-immediacy of presence. Derrida is speaking in the direction of what is necessary and has not yet happened.

Artaud is neither mistake, nor example, nor model, nor guide. He is necessary and yet to come – a living Artaud who gives us the possibility of a new understanding of life. He understood his own life in terms of radical dispossession. Artaud is not an 'author' embedded in a culture that gives us the meaning of the particular, historically determined concepts of 'author', 'life' and 'work', then, but a singularity to be encountered by reading. Reading must be transformed. And it is not a matter of the death of the author and the birth of the reader as it has been described by Roland Barthes but of the life of the writing that comes to us as an existential challenge. Derrida patiently loosens the cultural ties and assumptions that prevent us from reading Artaud. He frees himself from opposition to Blanchot's and Laplanche's readings of Artaud and Hölderlin. It is a negative movement. Derrida can do little more at this moment than say what his intention is *not*: 'not to refute or criticise the principle of these readings' (218). He does not appeal to law, critical productivity or truth, except to affirm and accept what Blanchot and Laplanche have done as 'legitimate, fruitful, true'. It's not that he feels called upon to protect 'subjective existence, the originality of the work or the singularity of the beautiful . . . against the violence of the concept by means of moral or aesthetic precautions'. For Derrida, the violence of the concept is already at work. He affirms it, as well as affirming the reduction, analysis, decomposition and shattering of the text. Faith is at work here. Reduce, analyse, decompose as much as possible: one can only reduce the irreducible, analyse the unanalysable and decompose the undecomposable – a unity which will no longer be an object of thought but an elusive experience of reading.

Commentary and the Unique

Derrida moves on to the notion of commentary. We recall that Derrida describes it as a respectful doubling, based on the author's conscious, voluntary, intentional relation to the history to which he belongs thanks to the element of language. But reading must also double the text, betray it and be defeated by destroying what it sets out to understand and reproduce. Reading must be violent: even if it thinks all it wants to do is double or repeat the work in commentary, it cannot help but be new. Artaud spoke of the theatre's double and desired 'a theatre within which repetition is impossible' (223). Derrida insists that the violence of primal doubling is necessary. He goes on to speak of a 'unity' and an 'archaic ground' commentary cannot unbury without ceasing to be commentary (218, 219). The unique must be shattered by reading in order to go beyond the polarities, Derrida calls them 'differences' that currently dominate our response to the unique. Those differences are madness and the work, psyche and text, example and essence. The shattering would let us move towards common ground which is not simply *there* but which can be approached by a 'negative route'. Its unity has to be *read* into being. The metaphysical notion of history as the context within which the text and the author belong gives way to another notion of genesis. Derrida describes this unity as 'tumultuous presence' and speaks of fields of force and magnetic pulls, and of the ground and of the resonant cries of Artaud (219). Summoned by that resonance, discourse will be pulled but also given its own magnetic charge by that presence which is not, Derrida implies, present in the sense of directly apprehensible. It has to be inferred by its effects which exert themselves in a non-simple way.

Derrida reinstates a distance between tumultuous presence and subjective existence: 'And if we say, to begin, that Artaud teaches us this unity, we do not say so in order to construe Artaud as an example of what he teaches. If we understand him, we expect no instruction from him' (219). Instruction would be too direct and too directive. We are not to expect Derrida to instruct us either, as if the beginning of his essay were only a set of precautions and protocols. Method and generalization must fail before the unprecedented 'howls' that promise 'the existence of a speech that is a body, of a body that is a theatre, of a theatre that is a text because it is no longer enslaved to a writing more ancient than itself'. The inseparable unity of Artaud's life and work is an adventure that opens only on adventures in reading. Artaud's refusal to respect differences enshrined in metaphysics by his 'existence refusing to signify', his 'art without works' and his 'language without a trace' attacks the metaphysical dualities of body and soul, speech and existence, text and body.

Theft

Derrida spends some time reading the word *soufflée*, which names a separation not only between speech and body but between reader and text. Once the reader sees the text as a sort of public spectacle, according to Derrida and Artaud, a theft has taken place: 'all speech fallen from the body, offering itself to understanding or reception, immediately becomes stolen speech' (220). We have the strange notion of writing against readability, against accessibility. The objectivity and instrumentality inherent in the idea of a comprehensible discourse, from which the meaning can be readily separated, is analysed here as itself a theft of speech. Such a theft is 'not a theft among others' but defines 'the fundamental structure of theft', as theft is always the theft of the speech, text or trace because possession acquires meaning and value through discourse. Artaud is not only against expropriation but against property itself as a way of understanding life. Derrida's notion of reading 'from afar' and his sense that the desire to appropriate Artaud's text is naïve are in sympathy with Artaud's questioning of ownership as a supreme cultural value.

The Proper

Hélène Cixous describes 'the general cultural heterosocial establishment' in terms of the proper:

> Etymologically, the 'proper' is 'property', that which is not separable from me. Property is proximity, nearness: we must love our neighbours, those close to us, as ourselves: we must draw close to the other so that we may love him/her, because we love ourselves most of all. The realm of the proper, culture, functions by the appropriation articulated, set into play, by man's classic fear of seeing himself expropriated, seeing himself deprived . . . by his refusal to be deprived, in a state of separation, by his fear of losing the prerogative, fear whose response is all of History.[67]

The strength of Cixous' interest in sexual difference allows us to recognize the traces of a masculine economy still at work in Artaud, alongside the challenge he presents to the realm of the proper. Artaud failed to accept a 'total and original loss of being itself' (222). However, his insistence that a malign god had deprived him of himself suggests a mitigated loss in which *his* loss must, he imagines, be *someone else's* gain. What Derrida's essay reveals is that the 'unpower' of speech is not anyone's exclusive property or individual curse but a shared state always nonetheless experienced by each of us in a singular way.

Unpower

If Derrida is conscious that the possibility of speaking towards Antonin Artaud arises in terms of personal communication within values of property, proximity and propriety that Artaud wants to explode, he does not abandon the notion of dialogue and communication altogether. For example, Artaud's notion of speech as stolen 'establishes communication between the essence of theft and the origin of discourse in general' (220). Derrida focuses on the *souffleur*, the offstage prompt ready to whisper the right lines to the actor who has forgotten what he or she ought to want to say. But of course a *souffleur* is also the exploder and inspirer, what Derrida calls the '*other* voice that itself reads a text older than the text of my body and the theatre of my gestures'. Derrida is nonetheless prepared to follow Artaud's 'intention', which is not on the side of the author–god, avatar of property, but on the side of negative inspiration that sucks my breath and speech away: 'the breath of a prompter [*souffleur*] who draws his breath in and thereby robs me of that which he first allowed to approach me and which I believed I could say *in my own name*' (221). Unpower would not be disempowerment but an experience of 'the radical irresponsibility of speech' which explodes the possibility of dialogue between named subjects who are responding to each other. This is why it would be shortsighted to see '*La parole soufflée*' as Derrida's response to Artaud.

Derrida will work through the exappropriating effect of speech elsewhere, for example in 'Envois'. '*La parole soufflée*' helps to explain a familiar difficulty approaching Derrida in a Derrida text. Where is he? What does he really think? Which voice is his? He is not simply there, or he is there in a diffuse, irregular, aneconomic way. His commentary does not distinguish itself finally from what it is reading. It is a destroyed commentary, in fact, and to read him well is in a sense to let go of him. 'I am in relation to myself within the ether of a speech which is always spirited away [*soufflée*] from me, and which steals from me the very thing that it puts me in relation to' (221). Furthermore, consciousness of speech, 'that is to say consciousness in general, is not knowing who speaks at the moment when, and in the place where, I proffer my speech'. Hearing-oneself-speak is something Derrida will return to as a source of the shattering discovery that

I am not the source of my own speech, which nonetheless cannot be located outside me. Cixous argues that the search for origin is masculine: 'Rather it's the beginning, or beginnings, the manner of beginning, not promptly with the phallus in order to close with the phallus, but starting on all sides at once, that makes a feminine writing.'[68] Derrida keeps beginning, he is the absolute beginner par excellence and this is why it's so important to read him in a spirit of beginning and re-beginning, with a kind of second-order naivety.[69]

Study Question
Can something valuable really be made out of the conviction that you have nothing to say? What would distinguish this conviction from indifference?

'FREUD AND THE SCENE OF WRITING'

> Up until 1965, I had not yet realized the necessity of psychoanalysis in my philosophical work. Beginning with *Of Grammatology*, I sensed the properly *deconstructive* necessity of again calling into question the primacy of the present, of full presence, as well as self-presence and consciousness, and therefore of putting the resources of psychoanalysis to work.[70]

Necessity strikes the keynote of Derrida's systematic but surprising reading of Freud. 'Freud and the Scene of Writing' elaborates the notions of trace, *différance*, supplement and spacing that emerged in the first section of *Of Grammatology*. Derrida wastes no time in saying that despite appearances: 'deconstruction is not a psychoanalysis of philosophy' (246). Freudian thought is complicit with metaphysics, and Derrida is aware of the need to question some of its conceptions and resist certain of its tendencies. Freud, throughout his work, understood writing in the limited and conventional sense of script. However, the 'circuitous path' of Freud's research is indispensable to deconstruction (430n.32). He did more than invent a new theoretical language. He tried to grasp living experience in language, including experiences that escape individual consciousness, such as forgetting and unconscious memory. He recognized that we do not live in a unified present, and wanted to describe effects that escape discourse.

Freud thought of himself as a scientist but 'Freud and the Scene of Writing' more than once refers to Freud's enterprise as fiction, as if there were something about it that was closer to the non-philosophical researches of Jabès, Artaud and Bataille than to philosophy or theory. Freud called his concepts 'theoretical fictions': what Derrida later called his 'subversive virtue' did not lie in metapyschological theorizing nor in the distinctive vocabulary of psychoanalysis.[71] 'Freud and the Scene of Writing' never simply breaks with that vocabulary but puts psychoanalytic concepts in quotation marks to emphasize their provisional and strategic value. It stresses Freud's daring and courage. Derrida thought of Freud in terms of what he made possible. After Freud 'one can, for example, renew the question of responsibility.' What does it mean to be answerable before, to or for another, once one has recognized that there is more to psychic life than 'conscious, egological intentionality'? 'Freud and the Scene of Writing' approaches these questions in terms of reading and writing. We must, Derrida says 'be several in order to write' (284).

Derrida's reading demonstrates that the phenomena that provoked Freud's curiosity and theoretical creativity (memory, intervals of forgetting, the relation between conscious and unconscious aspects of the mind) can be explained in terms of writing and difference. Freud's language does more than found psychoanalysis as an institution devoted to the investigation of the psyche. It is caught up in writing as world and as history. Derrida wants to go beyond the language Freud used and to sustain something in Freud's discourse that 'opens itself to the theme of writing' and thereby becomes something other than simply psychoanalysis (288). Writing was something *technical* for Freud who, for purposes of explication, also considered the psyche as an apparatus or machine. But beyond these theoretical fictions, Derrida emphasizes, Freud knew how to write. That is, how to let the scene of writing 'duplicate, repeat and betray itself within the scene'. Knowing how to write (or read) is not a technique. It entails letting things happen as well as a kind of vigilant awareness that is not necessarily fully conscious. For Derrida, to write is always to let one scene dissimulate another, something that also applies to the operations of what Freud, not Derrida, would call 'the unconscious'. Because of this duplicity of writing, the players are not identifiable in familiar terms: Freud the author, Derrida the reader of Freud and so on. The sometimes mechanical grind of 'Freud and the Scene of Writing' has a remarkable effect on the conceptual apparatus of traditional reading.

Derrida's approach is pedagogical, chronological and systematic, moving off from Freud's early work on memory traces in the *Project for a Scientific Psychology* (1895) through the notion of 'psychic writing' in the *Interpretation of Dreams* (1900) and the essay on 'The Unconscious' (1915) to the short 'Note on the Mystic Writing Pad' (1925), which takes a novelty writing toy as a model of psychical functioning. The 'Note' is a good example of Derrida's preference for 'Freud's partial, regional, and minor analyses'.[72] In the process Derrida acknowledges that Freud was no stranger to the thought of the trace as well as distinguishing some metaphysical aspects of Freudian thought. The overall effect is unsettling. Our psychic life remains lodged between two notions of writing, so that Derrida can say: 'if there is neither machine nor text without psychical origin, there is no domain of the psychic without text' (250). We write and we are written: therefore we must read.

The Scene

For Derrida, writing has no proper scene. It opens scenes and is nothing less than the 'stage of history and the play of the world' (287). The notion of a scene combines duration and space. It also introduces the theatrical dimension of experience: pretence, dissimulation. *Of Grammatology* describes the experience of a trace whose movement is hidden from us and which only becomes describable as a kind of drifting-off. It is not just the individual subject who drifts but subjectivity itself.[73] The scene of writing hides writing. The trace is 'necessarily occulted' and 'produces itself as self-occultation'.[74] Should it announce itself as such, it can only be in pretence or by a feint. Never given to direct perception, 'it presents itself in the dissimulation of itself'. The trace never appears to me, therefore reading remains indispensable. No vocabulary, not even the speculative concepts of metapsychology, can do the work of reading for me and reading must go beyond language and knowledge.

Psychoanalytic interpretation comes up against a similar effect. It constantly finds itself reckoning with something unknown to psychology and other than language. Freud's metapsychology responded to the insight that the psyche would be unthinkable and impossible without language, which initiates the possibility of the psyche becoming aware of its own inner processes. However, language is part of psychic functioning and can never provide direct access to the psyche to describe it. Our acts of consciousness, Freud believed, 'are immediate data and cannot be further explained by any sort of description'.[75] Freud understood he had to work with metaphors and that even scientific language was, for psychoanalysis, metaphorical. The question of metaphor interests Derrida very much (see 249–50, 287). Freud's figurative language, like that of Bataille, extends the realm of the unknown and generates new questions. Freud's gamble was that his discoveries, which exceeded the domain of reason, nonetheless had a grammar of structures and mechanisms that could be understood scientifically and passed on in an institution. His 'Outline of Psychoanalysis' acknowledges at the outset that the object of psychoanalytic research could not be localized and that the psyche had to be understood in terms of its effects. He knew that psychic life was everywhere: inward but also worldly. He also recognized the necessarily unpredictable emergence of unconscious effects. The anatomical brain was the *Schauplatz* or 'scene of action', a stage for psychic life, where its forces could be seen to play.[76] But like players in the theatre, those forces appeared in disguise. What was shown was a *text*: something to be analysed without recourse to further empirical data. And analysis was a clinical experience lived by analyst and patient, rather than a decoding that aimed only to make meaning explicit.

The dramatic term '*scène*', which also translates as 'stage', connects Freud's discoveries with Artaud, who called for a theatre without text, author, code or precedent, its language invented anew with each gesture. Such a theatre must 'restore "existence" and "flesh" in each of their aspects' (293). Pleasure would not be the least of these. There is no deconstruction without 'the liberation of forbidden jouissance'.[77] What is missing from psychoanalysis, if not from Freud's writing, is the kind of theatre Artaud dreamed of.

READING THE TEXT

The Failed Repression of Writing

The first Freudian term to be provoked is 'repression'. Derrida uses it to describe the attempt, throughout the history of Western thought, to contain and suppress writing. There has been a 'general censorship of the text in general' (247). Derrida is a new kind of historian, describing this 'necessary' and 'finite' censorship, which has only been successful up to a point. Derrida's notion of 'logocentric repression' is what 'permits an understanding of how an original and individual repression became possible within the horizon of a culture and a historical structure of belonging' (248). His historical understanding does not take the form of narrative but of a patient, inventive reading of texts. Freud's terminology belongs to the era of the repression of writing. And yet Freud's text is original, capable of 'a movement unknown to classical philosophy . . . somewhere between the explicit and the implicit' (250). His metaphors do not produce new knowledge, rather they make 'what we believe we know in the name of writing enigmatic' (250).

Repression has spatial effects. It 'contains an interior representation, laying out within itself a space of repression' (247). It is the construction of a stage and makes the scene of writing possible. Derrida's history uncovers the 'system of logocentric repression' organized 'to exclude or to lower . . . the body of the written trace' (248). His account of this system as it works and fails to work in particular texts by Freud finds possibilities of detour, delay, difference, deferral and interruption. Writing undoes repression by means of these indirect effects.

For Freud psychic life is not a formal or material continuity but an effect of 'difference within the exertion of forces' (253). *Différance* already moves in us. Freud recognized that 'a main characteristic of nervous tissue is memory' (251). Bodies remember and Derrida's essay pursues this thought in terms of the trace. Freud's account of memory develops a theory of breaching, *frayage*, from Latin *fragare*, to break. Breaching is a kind of writing. It presupposes 'a certain violence and a certain resistance to effraction' (252). Because 'breaching breaks open', Freud 'accords a privilege to pain', but (here *différance* comes in) beyond a certain quantity, pain, 'the threatening origin of the psyche, must be deferred' (254). Life 'protects itself by repetition, trace, *différance*' (254). *Différance* is vital to life: Derrida says it 'constitutes the essence of life', but as it is not presence, substance or subject, 'it is *not* life.' The life/death opposition which Freud explicitly questions in *Beyond the Pleasure Principle* (1920), is already, Derrida discerns, in play in the Project's notion of breaching. There is 'death at the origin of a life which can defend itself against death only through an economy of death' (253–4).

Psychical Writing and the Bodies of Words

Cixous has written about dreams as 'theatres' thus:

> [they] put on the appearance of a play in order to slip other unavowable plays between the lines of the avowal scenes: you reader–spectator are aware of this but you forget what you know so you can be charmed and taken in.[78]

Our dreams are more original than we are. They teach us to forget rectitude. What looks like a story told in images is saying something else. For Freud also the dream is a kind of 'psychical writing' that 'cannot be read in terms of any code' (262). It is 'originary' and illegible: its private theatre cannot be reduced to the model of 'script which is coded and visible "in the world"'. A dream, Derrida recognizes, 'puts words on stage without becoming subservient to them'. Unconscious experience affects the very notion of signification. Ignoring the dictionary, it 'produces its own signifiers' (263). If Freud thought that dreams were the royal road to the unconscious, Derrida insists that the unconscious is not a destination. It cannot be a text in the positive, metaphysical sense: 'already there, immobile, the serene presence of a statue, of a written stone or archive whose signified might be harmlessly transported into the milieu of a different language' (265). It is undeniable that Freud at times assumed the possibility of 'the generality and the fixity of a specific code for dream writing', but he nonetheless respected the absolute inventiveness of dreaming. This originality has to do with the dream's relation to the materiality of language, to the bodies (*corps*) of words, their sounds and letters which 'cannot be translated . . . into another language' (264/312). Psychoanalysis is full of interpretations but its insights cannot be reduced to those of a theory of translation or translatability. Translation, as paraphrase within a single language or as a carrying of meaning from one national language to another, seeks to 'relinquish materiality [*laisser tomber le corps*]'. The 'grammar' of a dream or of a dreamer is a kind of body. Its signified content is not the key to its meaning. Therefore the interpretation of dreams, like any other kind of real reading, cannot be a technique. And within the psyche there is a similarly irreducible otherness that differentiates the unconscious from consciousness. Unconscious thoughts cannot be simply translated into conscious ones: their 'signified content . . . harmlessly transported into the milieu of a different language, that of the preconscious or the conscious' (265).

Freud, Artaud and Acting Out

Derrida's insistence that there is 'no text *present elsewhere* as an unconscious one' and the emphasis on the body of dream writing are again reminiscent of Artaud. Artaud wanted to modify a 'general structure' that had 'never been modified' within which an 'infinite chain of representations' had always 'dissimulated or dissolved, suppressed or deported' the 'irrepresentability of a living present' (297). Against the notion of an 'author–creator who, absent and from afar, is armed with a text and keeps watch over, assembles, regulates the time or the meaning of representation', Artaud's theatre of cruelty wanted to restitute the body so that it cannot be replaced nor can it act as a cipher. He 'promises the existence of a speech that is a body, of a body that is a theatre, of a theatre that is a text because it is no longer enslaved to the writing more ancient than itself' (219). And in Artaud's vision of the theatre, speech, like verbal expression in dreams, will not be reducible to meaning and will have a body. Speech becomes gesture: 'the *logical* and discursive intentions which speech ordinarily uses to ensure its rational transparency, and in order to purloin its body in the direction of meaning, will be reduced or subordinated' (302). This process, Artaud believes, 'lays bare the flesh of the word, lays bare the word's sonority, intonation, intensity'. Derrida sees a similar tendency in psychical writing.

Correspondingly, he does not read Freud as a cipher for deconstruction. Towards the end of his essay, Derrida refers to Freud as a performer. He is not the (disembodied) origin of writing, an author, but its actor and character: 'Freud performs for us the scene of writing [*nous fait la scène d'écriture*]. Like all those who write. And like all who know how to write, he let the scene duplicate, repeat and betray itself within the scene' (288/338).

What psychoanalysis calls unconscious 'acting-out', is a kind of failed repression. According to Freud this kind of spontaneous theatre is the action of a subject 'in the grip of his unconscious wishes and fantasies'.[79] He 'relives' these wishes and fantasies 'in the present' with an intense feeling of immediacy, 'heightened by his refusal to recognise their source and repetitive character'. After Derrida, acting-out deserves to be recognized as a general phenomenon, one that could be said to underpin all phenomenal experiences of being as presence. We are inevitably actors, for whom in Derrida's words there is 'no present text in general, and there is not even a past present text, a text which is past as having been present. The text is not conceivable as an originary or modified form of presence' (265).

The unconscious text is 'a weave of pure traces'. It therefore has no essence. These traces are differences 'in which meaning and force are united' in a 'text nowhere present, consisting of archives which are *always already* transcriptions' (265–6). A memory trace is already a transcription received via perception, and living experience is unthinkable without recourse to the fact of memory. Derrida's notions of *trace* and *supplement*, apparently additions to or after-effects of presence, are necessary to understand how something happens for *the first time*.

Deferred Action and Supplementarity

Nachträglichkeit, Freud's notion of deferred action, suggests that the structure of experience is such that events can, in effect, happen for the first time some time after having taken place. Laplanche and Pontalis explain that experiences, events and memory-traces:

> may be revised at a later date to fit in with fresh experiences or with the attainment of a fresh stage of development. They may in that event be endowed not only with a new meaning but also with psychical effectiveness.[80]

Nachträglich means *supplementary*. According to its ordinary meaning and to the logic developed in *Of Grammatology*, the supplement is what 'seems to be added as a plenitude to a plenitude' and is equally 'that which compensates for a lack' (266). Derrida also notes that a *Nachtrag* in German is specifically a textual afterthought, meaning 'appendix, codicil, postscript' – a writing that comes after writing to transform its meaning or effect. Derrida's text performs the 'strange logic' of the supplement that he describes: the 'call of the supplement is primary', but it makes itself heard here by way of Freud's chronologically prior notion of *Nachträglichkeit*. 'Experience' is not constituted by 'the purity of the living present'. Freud calls us to think this theme using a conceptual scheme unequal to the task. The as yet uncompleted task of thinking that Freud invites us to undertake is, according to Derrida, the only one that belongs neither to metaphysics nor science.

Freshness of Surface and Depth of Retention

In *The Interpretation of Dreams* Freud speculatively projects the psyche's energetic processes into the workings of an *'optical machine'* (270). We have seen that the psyche is not actually locatable. However, citing Freud at length, Derrida notes that 'a certain spatiality' is irreducible and inseparable from the notion of the psyche as a system. The psyche is not simply being identified with its spatial locality; it consists of forces and runs like a machine. Since the *Project* Freud had been aware that psychical experience encompasses two systems: combining 'freshness of surface' for new impressions and 'depth of retention' so that events not immediately present can be repeated as memory, dream or symptom (272). At the same time, as we have noted, Freud thought in terms of psychical writing. The notion of spacing as a 'fundamental property of writing' allows Derrida to articulate these models (272). Spacing articulates space and time; it is 'the becoming-space of time and the becoming-time of space'.[81] Derrida's notion of spacing lets him speak openly of what Freud's metapyschological metaphors, models, apparatuses and analogies slip 'between the explicit and the implicit'.

The *Project*'s account of memory and perception had called for a way to account for the psyche's 'potential for indefinite preservation' and 'unlimited capacity for reception' (279). Twenty years later the Mystic Writing Pad allowed Freud to bring together a writing apparatus and the psyche's perceptual mechanisms. It offered the desired combination of, in Freud's words, 'an ever-ready receptive surface and permanent traces of the inscriptions that have been made on it' (280). Derrida emphasizes the existential significance of what Freud initially describes in its mechanical aspect. The Mystic Pad's combination of a wax slab covered by a double-layered sheet (protective celluloid on top, receptive waxed paper beneath) 'joins the two empirical certainties by which we are constituted: infinite depth in the implication of meaning, in the unlimited envelopment of the present, and, simultaneously, the pellicular [skin-like] essence of being, the absolute absence of any foundation' (281). Freud sees the apparatus in its explanatory power; Derrida reads memory, or writing, as 'the opening of [the] process of perception itself. The "perceived" may be read only in the past, beneath perception and after it' (282). There is a *'time of writing'* (283). The 'Note on the Mystic Writing Pad' relates Freud's understanding of time as discontinuity to his understanding of the structure of the psyche. The notion of scene is necessary to account for psychical workings that have 'neither the continuity of a line, nor the homogeneity of a volume'.

The Sociality of Writing as Drama

The opening of presence is complex. It opens to the other: 'its maintenance is not simple. The ideal virginity of the present [*maintenant*] is constituted by the work of memory. At least two hands [*mains*] are needed to make the apparatus function' (284/334). The Mystic Pad is part of a larger scene in which hands and therefore bodies are needed. Including, the insistence of *main* reminds us here, the bodies of words. Where Freud's focus can be taken as a cue to narrow the perspective of our thinking, 'writing' in Derrida's sense requires us to think of the scene of writing 'in other terms than those of individual or collective psychology, or even of anthropology. It must be thought in the horizon of the scene/stage of the world, as the history of that scene/stage. Freud's language is *caught up* [*pris*] in it' (288). There is no pure Freudian idiom. There are what *Of Grammatology* calls 'supplementary mediations that produce the sense of the very thing they defer: the mirage of the thing itself, of immediate presence, of originary perception'. Language is one of these. Consequently, we must be several to write, 'and even to perceive' (284). The origin of the work cannot be thought on the basis of the individual, nor in terms of some sociologically defined collectivity. Neither can the '*system* of relations between strata' that make up the 'subject of writing' be thought in terms of classical reception theories based on 'the oppositions sender–receiver, code-message' (285). This of course should affect how books like the present guide are written and read. Derrida calls for an 'entirely different discipline' to respond to what he calls the '*sociality* of writing as *drama*'. It would be aware that reading and writing do not have the linear sequence or the self-identical *dramatis personae* prescribed by common sense.

The Machine as Death

Freud opposed living memory, as Plato did, to the exteriority of writing as a memory aid. The thought of the trace involves an acceptance of death at work within life:

> The trace is the erasure of selfhood, of one's own presence, and is constituted by the threat or anguish of its irremediable disappearance, of the disappearance of its disappearance. An unerasable trace is not a trace, it is a full presence . . . This erasure is death itself . . . (289)

The thought of the trace, with the accompanying possibility of erasure, has made repression possible. This radical thought of writing as the erasure of selfhood and presence also opens the way to future thinking, allowing various fields of research to work 'at the point of articulation' where 'writing in the current sense' interacts with what Derrida calls 'the trace in general'.

This has the effect of making writing enigmatic. Derrida notes Freud's interpretation of 'all complicated machinery' in dreams, as 'genitals (and as a rule male ones)' (288), also his understanding that writing and walking [*la marche*, also the word for the working of a machine] can unconsciously be given the meaning of 'the performance of a forbidden sexual act' (289). There is desire at work in and as writing. The body and writing also work automatically like machines. Sexuality and sexual difference are part of the system of relations between strata that the scene of writing is. This awareness runs throughout Derrida's work, to the most extraordinary effect in *The Post Card*. 'Freud and the Scene of Writing' puts a series of challenges or suggestions to psychoanalysis: how will it relate itself to the problem of responsibility; to the history of writing; to the generative power of the letter and the *'originality of the literary signifier'* (290)? Derrida indicates the importance of Melanie Klein as an analyst of 'good and bad objects' and of the infantile origins of morality, for the illumination of the 'valuation and devaluation' of writing (291). If psychoanalysis is necessary for Derrida, it is not enough. It must be articulated with the history of the repression of writing and with its inventive capacities. This work begins with that history and that invention in the text of Freud but does not end there.

Study Question

If you accept the notion of unconscious impulses and the multiplicity of the self, how can you possibly take responsibility for what you say, do or write?

'THE THEATRE OF CRUELTY AND THE CLOSURE OF REPRESENTATION'

In comparison with the detailed commentary of 'Freud and the Scene of Writing', this essay moves fast and gets to work straight away. The epigraphs from Mallarmé and Artaud say things about presence and the supplement that Derrida might have said himself: 'A unique time in the world, because of an event I still will [am yet to] explain, it is not of the Present – a present does not exist' (292). And Artaud writes '. . . as for my forces,/they are nothing but a supplement,/the supplement of a state of fact,/it is that the origin never took place'. These first person poetic statements are unargued and unarguable: they watch over the genesis of the history Derrida is writing. The opening quotation, also from Artaud, takes us back to the Nietzschean dance-writing at the end of 'Force and Signification', where Derrida cited *Twilight of the Idols* (1889). There, in a chapter called 'What the Germans Lack', Nietzsche insists that 'thinking needs to be learned just as dancing needs to be learned, *as* a kind of dancing'.[82] The end of 'Force and Signification' follows Nietzsche in affirming writing by means of writing. Derrida does not outline 'a technique, a teaching plan, a will to mastery in thinking' other than learning to dance 'with the feet, with concepts, with words'. And here Artaud like Nietzsche affirms what is not or what is yet to be, saying that '*dance/and consequently the theatre/have not yet begun to exist*' (292/273). Despite the connotations of its name, the theatre of cruelty is what Nietzsche calls himself: '*yea-saying*'.[83] And Derrida repeatedly said that deconstruction was affirmative.[84] It is by means of affirmation that we can continue to think about thinking as what Derrida calls, towards the end of 'Freud and the Scene of Writing', 'the *thought of the trace* (a thought because it escapes binarism and makes binarism possible on the basis of *nothing*)'. Binarism is a logic that defines A oppositionally on the basis of not-A; it is a way of thinking that depends on forbidding logical contradiction and that can only allude to the unknown by means of the known. Binarism is a form of closure, and what Derrida calls 'the thought of the trace' opens it up.

The thought recurs in *Of Grammatology* where Derrida, reflecting on the generative properties of his reading of Rousseau, explains that the movement of opening the closed and therefore apparently unassailable system of metaphysical thinking, is always going to look odd, and from the point of view of the system it challenges, even unnecessary. What he calls the 'opening of the question, the departure from the closure of self-evidence, the putting into doubt of a system of oppositions' must 'necessarily have the form of empiricism and of errancy'.[85] Simply describing those movements in terms of 'past norms' will impose this form on them.

> We must begin *wherever we are* and the thought of the trace, which cannot not take the scent into account, has already taught us that it was impossible to justify a point of departure absolutely. *Wherever we are*: in a text where we already believe ourselves to be.

Necessity and Affirmation

It will be helpful to bear this in mind as we read. The first pages of the essay frequently refer to 'implacable [*inéluctable* – from

Latin *ex*, out and *luctari*, to struggle] necessity' (292/341). Artaud has a very strong sense of necessity as something which imposes itself in an irresistible way, but is not simply present. What Artaud calls 'the theatre of cruelty' is absolutely impossible to wriggle out of and yet – Derrida quotes Artaud – it is an affirmation that has 'not yet begun to exist' (293). This combination of necessity and non-presence is a very strong form of the imperative to begin. It is the experience of the tension of a divided present that allows us, in a sense that Derrida and Artaud make unfamiliar, to *act*. That is, to write, in the most expansive sense imaginable. Derrida is interested in how to invent, how to act inventively. And theatre, which according to Artaud 'was never made to describe man and what he does', would be one way of playing what *Of Grammatology* calls 'the game of the world'.[86]

Affirmation is not just about words. It even goes beyond what the philosophy of language calls speech acts, in which saying 'I swear', or 'I do', can, in the right context, be a legally binding deed. So when Derrida invokes the kind of verbal repetition known to rhetoric and linguistics as *anaphora* (literally, 'carrying back', or reference) and associates this verbal gesture with the birth of affirmation, there seems to be a crossing between something within language and something outside it. Affirmation entails repetition that is not based on anything having been present. Thus, a 'necessary affirmation can be born only by being reborn to itself'. As with Freud's account of memory traces, repetition and difference are the basis on which what is understood as existence becomes possible. The theatre of cruelty would be an affirmation of this kind. Derrida speaks of birth here, as he will at the end of 'Structure, Sign and Play'. This is not only because Artaud thinks of theatre in terms of birth, life and death: Derrida is himself a thinker of life and a dance-writer for whom bodies are vital for writing and thinking. But the body does not precede writing.

Artaud saw the relation between life and death as non-linear and understood it in terms of repetition and substitution at the origin. Before affirmation can be born, 'existence' and 'flesh' must be repeated, on the understanding that these words do not refer to actual entities which the theatre would represent but to what Derrida will call traces. The body comes after writing. Artaud believed that his body had been 'stolen from him at birth' by a 'thieving god' born, Artaud said, 'to pass himself off/as me'. What might look like Artaud's idiosyncrasy, the magical thinking and creative illogicality of a crazy surrealist, makes sense in terms of Derrida's generalization of the notion of writing. This generalization goes beyond the classical notions of language and text to which it has been traditionally assigned. For Derrida, Artaud's theatre of cruelty is not a cultural practice, a sociopolitical programme or an idea belonging to a particular period of history but a shaking of the notion of representation that Western thought has held on to since the days of Greek theatre and philosophy. If, as 'Freud and the Scene of Writing' puts it, Freudian repression 'contains an interior representation, laying out within itself a space of repression' then the theatre has been made to function as just such a repression of writing in general. The theatre has been believed to represent life, the world and history outside the theatre. The theatre has therefore been destined to efface itself before what it represents – 'born in its own disappearance'. The theatre of cruelty announces the existence of that repression and therefore makes known 'the limit of representation' (294). That is why Derrida finds it capable of a 'system of critiques *shaking the entirety*' of Western history (296). Artaud's anguished personal sense that his 'proper body, the property and propriety of his body' had been stolen at birth and that he might therefore work towards 'access to a life before birth and after death' can be understood in terms of a condition and an opportunity shared by our entire epoch (293).

Cixous has recognized a similar non-self-containment in Derrida's autobiographical writing and in his life. For him too it is a little as if he had not yet been born; he is able to be other than himself and even at moments of suffering there is an intrinsic sense of theatre. For example, he writes in *Circumfessions* about being 'sorry *for myself*'.[87] In the process he illuminates a general structure of self-pity as a game of substitutions: 'I'm crying *over myself* . . . but like *another*, another wept over by another weeper. . . . I weep from my mother over the child whose *substitute I am*'. Cixous comments: 'That's the key: this *like* or *as if*. I am *as if* I were another. He is as if, like (as if he were) another. True, we are all substitutes but he is a substitute truly like no-one.'[88] Identity comes into being by detour, thanks to difference. What we do and experience takes place for us *as if* it were being done or happening to someone else. Self-consciousness occurs as an erasure of the self. In 'Freud and the Scene of Writing', 'the very idea of the first time' became enigmatic, that is, something to think about. Coming into being was associated with the trace, that is, with 'the erasure of selfhood' (289). By this logic, erasure offers the possibility of a future: the 'theatre of cruelty is to be born by separating death from birth and by erasing the name of man' (293). Derrida recognizes that this is not a destructive project.

Différance and Cruelty

Cruelty is an opening, it is a spacing. It has to do with the 'strange distance' separating us from the necessary work of affirmation. *Différance* is cruel. We are cruelly separated from the present and from ourselves. This isn't anyone's fault. Representation has claimed to restore presence by means of imitation, as if the audience were able to see itself on stage. It is this attempt to redeem presence by imitating it that Artaud wants to abandon in favour of affirmation. He understands that presence and 'contemporary, *active*' affirmation have not yet happened and that they are necessary. Life *is* this contretemps and the 'theatre of cruelty is not a *representation*. It is life itself, in the extent to which life is unrepresentable. Life is the nonrepresentable origin of representation' (294). The notion of 'man' is only a limited and historically determined representation of life. According to Artaud, the theatre 'must make itself the equal of life . . . the sort of liberated life which sweeps away human individuality and in which man is only a reflection' (295).

We could call this tragic, if the notion of tragedy were not so closely identified with man and his problems. Derrida identifies a kinship between Artaud and Nietzsche, who wanted to rethink the birth of tragedy in a way that did not rely on the idea of representation but conceived of it as something generated by the interaction of irreconcilable tendencies. The erasure of the self can always be experienced as a loss: it wouldn't be doing much to affirm that erasure if its broken immediacy were not capable of causing us a kind of classical sadness. Derrida's thought is neither serene nor afraid of pathos. His thinking of the movement of the trace, its play, refuses to choose between the mood of Rousseau and that of Nietzsche. That is, between what 'Structure,

Sign and Play' will call 'the saddened, *negative*, nostalgic, guilty, Rousseauistic side of the thinking of play whose other side would be the Nietzschean *affirmation*, that is the joyous affirmation of the play of the world and of the innocence of becoming' (369). Nietzschean affirmation is itself an affirmation of the tragic, which *Twilight of the Idols* describes not as an individual predicament but as 'saying yes to life, even in its strangest and hardest problems'.[89] Derrida emphasizes that there is no *choice* between these irreconcilable alternatives. And yet one has to choose, and that is cruel.

Theatre as Representation

For Artaud and for Derrida the theatre 'more than any other art' has been 'marked by the labour of total representation in which the affirmation of life lets itself be doubled and emptied by negation' (295). And it is this that makes the theatre more than the theatre. Artaud's writings on theatre are 'more *solicitations* than a sum of precepts, more a system of critiques *shaking the entirety* of Occidental history than a treatise on theatrical practice' (296). This language recalls the trembling and shaking in 'Force and Signification'. The theatre of cruelty would be an experience of force. In what follows Derrida clarifies the way that theatre-as-representation limits our understanding of creation and text. The text in classical Western theatre is in thrall to representation and in it 'the irrepresentability of the living present is dissimulated or dissolved, suppressed or deported, within the infinite chain of representations' (297).

A theory of interpretation accompanies this state of affairs. Derrida patiently explores the implications of Artaud's refusal to accept classical theatre – it's everywhere; the alternative has not yet come into being, but the theatre as it is, is not cruel enough, not necessary enough, not in touch enough with the severe protocols of its very existence. What *is*, is not *necessary*: a disturbing and liberating thought that *Writing and Difference* often provokes, if we let it. Derrida describes Western theatre as a closed system of interpretation without creativity at any point. The author–god is interpreted by directors and actors who represent characters who represent what the creator thinks. But the author–god in fact 'creates nothing . . . only transcribes and makes available for reading' a text that is itself representative of another reality elsewhere, which is then presented to a 'passive, seated public' (296).

The Stage and Spacing

Creativity is, Artaud and Derrida suggest, possible by means of the stage, in French *la scène*, as in 'Freud and the *Scene* of Writing'. It's there, in the scene of writing, which is unlocatable. It is necessary first to work through all the places on earth that it isn't, where its possibilities are held back, too clearly foreseen or restricted to a finite space by those unable to believe in the spacing of writing. Derrida's absolute generalization of the notion of text corresponds to Artaud's hope 'to put on stage [*scène*] and to overthrow the tyranny of the text' (298). Artaud and Derrida work by spacing, by putting onstage but not in order to display, make evident, or present. 'Spacing', it says in *Of Grammatology*, in a sentence interrupted by parenthesis, an after- or before-thought, a between-thought interrupting the uninterruptible unfolding of writing: 'Spacing (notice that this word speaks the articulation of space and time, the becoming-space of time and the becoming-time of space) is always the unperceived, the nonpresent and the nonconscious.'[90] Spacing is not compatible with presence and furthermore: 'Writing can never be thought under the category of the subject.' Artaud's theatre of cruelty, which deposes 'man' in favour of 'life' cannot be thought under that category either.

And just as spacing can't be thought in a purely linear and one-thing-after-another way, so it would be wrong to think of the theatre in an out-with-the-old-in-with-the-new-way. Derrida affirms, in spite of all he has said and quoted Artaud as saying, that the theatre and its arts 'have lived richly for twenty-five centuries' (298). And theatre has not failed to betray itself in that time – a betrayal that Derrida understands affirmatively, rather in the way that he understood the 'failed repression' of writing at the beginning of 'Freud and the Scene of Writing'. Theatre has betrayed itself, 'if to betray is at once to denature through infidelity, but also to let oneself be evinced despite oneself, and to manifest the foundation of force' (298). This betrayal or perversion has been brought about by the dominance of the text and the author–god. Released from those, it may return to its 'creative and founding freedom' (299). At this point Derrida does some paleonymic work on the word 'representation'.

Representation and Cruel Reading

Paleonymy is defined in *Dissemination*, where Derrida insists on

> the necessity, today, of working out at every turn, with redoubled effort, the question of the preservation of names: of *paleonymy*. Why should an old name, for a determinate time, be retained? Why should the effects of a new meaning, concept, or object be damped by memory?[91]

He goes on to explain what paleonymy does. The word (for us, 'representation') has the structure of a *'double mark'*. It is

> *caught* – both seized and entangled – in a binary opposition, one of the terms retains its old name so as to destroy the opposition to which it no longer quite belongs, to which in *any* event it has *never* quite yielded, the history of this opposition being one of incessant struggles generative of hierarchical configurations.[92]

This affects how we read and write. Our reading and writing are inevitably *spacings*, divisions and doublings, according to the structure by which 'every concept necessarily receives two similar marks – a repetition without identity – one mark inside and the other outside the deconstructed system should give rise to a double reading and a double writing'. This helps us understand why a kind of second-guessing reading doesn't work for Derrida's texts. No author–god will tell us what to think. The text is where the boundary of the deconstructed system takes place and where the unperceived effects of spacing can begin to be felt and thought. We could think of our reading as an experience of Artaudian 'cruelty'. It isn't held up in front of us, something outside us that we could perceive, and it isn't a matter of suffering bloody violence, but when we read we perhaps undergo an experience that is both necessary and yet to be. This kind of reading would be a thoroughgoing experience in which we would undergo the unrepresentable: 'Cruel representation must permeate me. And nonrepresentation is, thus, original representation, if representation signifies, also, the unfolding of a volume, a multi-dimensional milieu, an experience that produces its own space' (299).

Closure

The liberation of theatre as staging is to be brought about not by doing away with all boundaries but by means of a closed space: 'that is to say, a space produced from within itself and no longer organised from the vantage of another absent site, an illocality, an alibi or invisible utopia' (300). This different kind of representation would be, Artaud says: 'spectacle . . . acting not as reflection, but as force'. This closure would not be an end and it helps us understand better the sentence at the opening of the essay: 'A necessary affirmation can be born only by being reborn to itself' (293). One name Artaud gave to this force is 'poetry'. Not literary or written poetry but poetry as what Derrida calls 'scenic representation'. Artaud insists that 'the kind of diffuse poetry which we identify with natural and spontaneous energy' must find its 'purest, sharpest and most truly separated expression, in the theatre' (301). This closure, this rebirth and the possibility of birth that attends it, depends on killing off the author–god, so that the theatres is no longer 'organised from . . . another absent site'. For the author–god is an 'abusive wielder of logos', a 'father' and 'the God of a stage subjugated to the power of speech and text'. His murder would be at the origin of cruelty understood not as violence but as *'necessity* and *rigour'*. It is not only desirable or possible or preferable that the author is no longer in control: it is already so. What Artaud wants is an acknowledgement of what is already the case. Authorial intention, for example, should no longer be a guiding principle even if 'difficult to know' nor should it be dismissed as irrelevant, in favour of some other controlling principle. Knowing or realizing authorial intention would cease to be the goal of the theatre, because the person controlling the direct handling of the stage would have killed off the fantasy of the process being controlled or dictated from elsewhere.

The Flesh of the Word

Speech and writing will 'once more become *gestures'* (302). They will no longer aim at 'rational transparency'. The body would no longer be required to make sense, in a process that affects speech and writing. Speech would no longer be about diaphanousness (from the Greek, through-showing or through-appearing), as if the body were supposed to efface itself, become transparent, erase, steal or manifest itself and as if language were only the privileged means of doing this. Think about the implications of this kind of acceptance of bodies as things that don't have to be explained or interpreted. This kind of body would have another kind of inside – one that does not say itself as if it were revealing its inner truth through the medium of words. What Derrida calls the 'deconstitution of diaphanousness' has an effect on words. It

> lays bare the flesh of the word, lays bare the word's sonority, intonation, intensity – the shout that the articulations of language and logic have not yet entirely frozen, that is, the aspect of oppressed gesture which remains in all speech, the unique and irreplaceable movement which the generalities of concept and repetition have never finished rejecting. (302)

For the theatre of cruelty, speech will no longer reject itself or be enslaved by a concept of language that makes of the word merely a conceptual or communicative tool. In the terminology developed by Nietzsche, Artaud and Derrida are imagining a Dionysian language over which the values of figurative representation and articulate form no longer hold sway. Derrida details the separations that articulated language brings in its wake and which Artaudian theatrical language would anticipate by returning to 'the borderline of the moment when the word has not yet been born' (302–3). The theatre of cruelty would go back before the separation of 'concept and sound, of signified and signifier, of the pneumatical and the grammatical', before 'the freedom of translation and tradition, the movement of interpretation, the difference between the soul and the body, the master and the slave, God and man, author and actor' to 'the very eve of the origin of languages' (303).

Artaud and Psychoanalysis

Theatrical writing will cover the 'entire range' of a 'new language' including vocal sound, vision, pictures and three-dimensional movements that will make a kind of hieroglyphic writing. What Artaud wanted to bring about corresponds to the generalization of the concept of writing at the heart of Derrida's own project. The lengthy quotations from Artaud throughout the essay appear without the kind of reservations Derrida showed about Freud's metaphysical presuppositions in the previous one. (Derrida returns to Freud for a page or so to explore the links between his notion of the dream as a kind of writing not dominated by spoken language and Artaud's conception of speech as one theatrical gesture among others.) This is not to say that deconstruction is a form of surrealism: Derrida is interested in something unique to Artaud. Furthermore, the theatre of cruelty cannot act as a precedent for some Derridean utopia, because it is itself a necessary anticipation and not a blueprint or a programme. Artaud's writings do not depend on future presence as their alibi: their power has no guarantee and Derrida's conception of necessity is severe enough not to be restricted to what is possible or predictable. And yet Artaud's notions of what he calls 'language in space' are iron in the bloodstream of Derrida's writing. There is a sense that Artaud's stage, like psychoanalysis, possesses an 'initiative and powers of initiation' that no one 'can wield' (305).

Artaud's is a 'theatre of dreams'. However, what Derrida calls '*cruel* dreams' are not random or spontaneous productions of the unconscious. Artaud is a rigorous thinker and cruel dreams are 'necessary', 'determined', 'calculated and given direction'. For Artaud, psychoanalysis is a means of learning the law of dreams; he 'rejects the psychoanalyst as 'interpreter, second-remove commentator, hermeneut or theoretician' (306). To adopt a psychoanalytic perspective would be another attempt to subordinate the theatre to offstage domination. Neither the unconscious nor analysis should dominate. Consciousness should take the lead, beginning with the consciousness of the deliberate murder of the author–god. Derrida quotes Artaud: 'It is consciousness that gives to the exercise of every act of life its blood-red colour, its cruel nuance, since it is understood that life is always someone's death.' And as the erasure of man permits life itself to be reborn, so the death of God permits the divine and the sacred to return among us.

Fidelity

In the section that follows Derrida enumerates the 'themes of infidelity' to Artaud in modern theatre. If modern theatre cannot fulfil his writings, Derrida can at least be precise about the cases in which it is 'surely unfaithful to him'. Derrida will insist a couple of pages on 'fidelity is impossible' (313). This approach uses negation to shape by exclusion the distinctive space or opening of the theatre of cruelty. As Derrida excludes various more or less familiar or imaginable types of theatre we again see the cruelty of cruelty, its incommensurability with any kind of positivism and its strange relation to time and space. Cruelty, or necessity, belongs only 'in the *act and present tense* of the stage' (313).

Study Question
Why should we be interested in impossible or failed projects like the Theatre of Cruelty?

'FROM A RESTRICTED TO A GENERAL ECONOMY: A HEGELIANISM WITHOUT RESERVE'

The essay wants to find a way to write, to express the relation between Bataille and Hegel. Once more, it is a question of what writing can do. The strange and specific qualities of that relationship expose something already at work in Hegel's philosophy that cannot be reduced to the workings of dialectic. Hegel called the dialectic 'the very nature of thinking'.[93] It followed from this, that 'as understanding', thinking 'must fall into the negative of itself, into contradictions'. Contradictions will form, according to Hegel, part of the progress of thought. As Stuart Barnett puts it, Hegel's philosophy 'absolutely requires the work of the negative' and this means that 'to be anti-Hegelian is to be profoundly Hegelian'.[94] Hegel set out to provide a philosophical account of all forms of reality (biological, cultural, political, psychical and so on) on the basis of a single principle: Reason. Bataille is not Hegelian, nor is he non-Hegelian. He is *ultra-Hegelian*. To say this is already to begin to think of Hegel in terms that cannot be reduced to dialectics, not related into a system of propositions, axioms and concepts, privileging the philosophical notions of consciousness, mastery and knowledge. Hegel is the thinker of systems, of difference as a moment in a movement that assimilates it to a system in the form of contradiction or negation.

For Derrida, existing readings of Bataille have failed to recognize the peculiar quality of his relation to Hegel, which Derrida calls 'Hegelianism without reserve'. One of the things that is wrong with the reception of Bataille as a Hegelian thinker is that it takes Hegel as read, takes his thought and writing for granted and in doing so assumes that Hegel, brought to bear on Bataille in a closer or more attentive way, would dominate and annihilate the later writer. For Derrida, the practice of assuming Hegel's power and skipping over his interaction with Bataille, as if to spare Bataille the might of reason, is itself the extending and unfolding of Hegelianism as a dominant and enveloping mode of thought. Reading itself, it would seem, poses a threat to the system advanced by Hegel. So Derrida's essay does not take Hegel as obvious, self-evident, therefore unbearable and unbeatable. It sticks with Hegel and reason which becomes, for Bataille and Derrida, and thanks to the French language which makes reason a feminine noun, a woman. The relation with her is nocturnal and somewhat erotic.

To Spend the Night with Reason

There is a relation with reason that is dialectical, that would consist of moving into sleep and dreaming in order to affirm and confirm reason. Under this regime reason and knowledge would assimilate sleep, dream and monstrosity, which would only be moments in the progression of reason and knowledge. All phenomena would be destined to be known and subordinated to the totalizing principle of reason. Derrida, coming off Bataille, imagines a different sleep that would accompany reason through the night, staying as close as possible to her sleep, dream and waking, the better to recognize it as *hers*. Difference is here in the mode of sexual difference. Bataille and Derrida want to see reason, the philosophical animal, open its eyes. In his *Elements of the Philosophy of Right* (1820) Hegel wrote that philosophy was too late to teach the world or rejuvenate it: 'The owl of Minerva begins its flight only with the onset of dusk.'[95] He associated reason with light and the day, as does Goya's etching 'The Sleep of Reason Produces Monsters' (1796–1797) in which a man fallen asleep over a writing or drawing table is approached by eager, wakeful owls, bats and cats. The notion of traversing this sleep, going through it, crossing over it, intersecting with it, being immersed in it and living through it but not so as to make it one's own moment (can we say 'my sleep,' any more than we could say 'my unconscious'?) corresponds to various possibilities of reading. Some types of reading can be spatially configured in terms of separate reading projects, others involving a more confused and indistinct type of sharing. To 'have spent the night with reason, to have kept watch and slept with her [*veillé, dormi avec elle*]' – where it is not clear who woke and who slept when, during the course of an entire night, in the depths of which Hegel came up with a discourse

> by means of which philosophy, in completing itself, could both include within itself and anticipate all the figures of its beyond, all the forms and resources of its exterior; and could do so in order to keep these forms and resources close to itself by simply taking hold of their enunciation. (318–19).

It is the night before this dawn that interests Derrida, a night that does not serve the day but is where 'something was contrived, blindly. I mean in a discourse' (318). Bataille and Derrida are awake enough, asleep enough, dreaming enough to recognize this and to take their bearings not from reason, discourse, sense and philosophy alone but also from the night that makes all these possible and that cannot be reduced to them.

Laughter

Night and day is just one of the hierarchical couples that the essay plays with. Derrida values what Western culture and philosophy would take to be the negative or inferior term. Another is laughter and seriousness. Laughter cannot be included in or anticipated by philosophy. It cannot even be kept close to philosophy. (And it is not necessarily just. Cixous' essay 'Sorties' notes that Hegel's dialectical thinking is 'commonly at work in our everyday banality'.[96] That the Hegelian schema of recognition has no room for 'the *other* alive and different'.[97] And she finds Bataille's laughter complicit in the economy that appropriates women as subordinate, night to man's day. That economy works for the disappearance of the woman, who exists as a function of the male partner, he who desires not the other, but to return to the same by taking her as an object. She asks

> Why did this comedy, whose final act is the master's flirtation with death, make Bataille laugh so hard, as he amused himself by pushing Hegel to the edge of the abyss that a civilised man keeps himself from falling into? This abyss that functions as a metaphor both of death and of the feminine sex.[98]

Derrida's next paragraph glosses spending the night with reason in terms of laughter. Laughter, like eroticism, would be a way of going along with reason, then awakening from, with and without reason, having lived the same experience but in a different way. It is not the sign of chaotic misrule. It calls for a *discipline* that observes and understands what it laughs at, acknowledges the philosopher's byways, 'understands his techniques, makes use of his ruses, lets him deploy his strategy, appropriates his texts' (319). The figure is still of an interpersonal relationship but now with a man. The figure of the philosopher in Derrida is masculine. After this relation, laughter 'quickly, furtively and unforeseeably' breaks with philosophy by laughing at it. Not from on high. Many classical theories of laughter are theories of hierarchy. Bataille on the other hand gives us 'rapidly sketched movements of experience; rare, discreet and light movements, without triumphant stupidity': private, almost anguished. Bataille's discourse moves between this kind of movement and the language of philosophy. There is 'extreme point of "experience" which makes Hegelian discourse dislocate itself' (319). In a perfectly Hegelian way, this empirical phenomenon is inscribed in a Hegelian language. But Hegel is not Bataille's script. Bataille understands that Hegel cannot be read bit by bit, lemmatically, but must be approached as a chain of linked concepts forming a system. Bataille put this chain into question precisely by 'thinking the chain as such, in its totality, without ignoring its internal rigour' (320). We might pause here to note that in this respect Hegel could not be more different from Derrida. The separate bits of Derrida's writing have a kind of coherence without formal totality that invites us to give close attention at the level of the paragraph, the sentence and the word – confident that this will yield a better understanding of the scope and force of his thought than any attempt at a general survey or reduction to basic concepts. The language Bataille uses to describe his relation to Hegel is dramatic, anthropomorphic and draws on biography, but Derrida insists that the dramatic metaphor and the characters Hegel and Bataille arise from texts. 'The drama is first of all textual.' It is an effect of writing and of reading, even though Bataille cannot claim to have pored over the letter of Hegel's writings. Intellectual history bears this out. Bataille received Hegel initially via Alexandre Kojève's influential lectures on Hegel at the *Ecole pratique des hautes études* in Paris (1933–1939). Kojève's reading of the Master–Slave dialectic in the *Phenomenology of Spirit*, a key text for Bataille and for Derrida's essay, took the form of a dramatic encounter between human subjects, and a sense of drama marks Bataille's appropriations of Kojève and Hegel. This is, however deceptive. Something strictly philosophical is at stake: a 'formal law' that has 'constrained the relationship of all his concepts to those of Hegel, and through Hegel's concepts to the concepts of the entire history of metaphysics'. Bataille's strange writings are capable of making the concepts he takes from Hegel 'tremble'. Given Hegel's place in the history and development of philosophy as the *ne plus ultra* of systematic thinking in the service of meaning, knowledge and consciousness – this makes what Bataille does indispensable to Derrida's exploration of the effects of writing and difference in and on philosophy in general and especially with regard to phenomenology.

Sovereignty

This is going to be an important notion in later work by Derrida, where it may be read initially as a concept operating in international law and politics, denoting supreme and independent authority, self-government and the territory of a sovereign state. The word is derived from Latin *super*, 'over' and refers us to questions of hierarchy and power. 'From a Restricted to a General Economy' indicates Derrida's abiding interest in political questions. For readers of Bataille, 'sovereignty' seems to mean Hegel's *Herrschaft*, which English translators of the *Phenomenology* render as the rather archaic-sounding 'lordship' and which Derrida's French text gives us as *maîtrise* or self-control, mastery, skill. Bataillean sovereignty will engage all these notions. According to Derrida's reading of Hegel, this mastery would not be linked to any determinate or specific existence but to the whole of life in which life loses its customary sense of the life of particular determinate living beings. (There is a 'not' missing from the English version of Derrida's citation of Hegel here. The text, which re-marks a certain reception of Hegel via Jean Hyppolite's translation of the *Phenomenology*, can be translated as 'The operation of mastery consists, writes Hegel, in "showing that it is not attached to any determinate *being-there*, any more than to the universal singularity of being-there in general, in showing that one is not attached to life"' (321/373). Derrida also notes Bataille's adoption of the term 'operation' from Hegel's use of the German word *Tun*, doing, action, activity, in the chapter on the master–slave dialectic. Bataille often speaks of a 'sovereign operation.')

Hegel is propounding a certain way of thinking about life and death. Mastery or lordship is not tied up with life in its particularity; it raises itself above life. It 'amounts to risking, putting at stake . . . the whole of one's own life' (321/373). 'Putting at stake' or more literally 'putting into play', *mettre en jeu*, a favourite phrase of Bataille's. The lordly man or master is prepared to put his life at stake, where the servant or slave wants to conserve life. To contemplate death itself, as lordship does, gives access to the for-itself (that which is not appropriated as a means to an end) namely freedom and recognition. Death would seem to be outside life and above it, and to act as a kind of guarantee of authentic risk-taking. In what follows, this relation between life and death, as instances related within a progression and a system, will be questioned.

Derrida does not proceed to compare the notions or show how the one develops out of the other. Hegel is the consummate thinker of the meaning of relations. Derrida is interested in how one might read the difference between lordship or mastery and sovereignty *given that this difference cannot be understood within reason or meaning*. It is a '*difference of sense*' or of meaning (321). For Hegel, the putting at stake of life is a moment in the constitution of meaning, a moment, when for the lord or master, experience and truth coincide, consciously, in a way that is not limited to any empirical particularity. However, servitude does not cease to exist at that point. Given that the master must stay alive 'to enjoy what he has won by risking his life', the truth of the free, independent consciousness remains the economical, conservative consciousness of the slave (322). 'To stay alive, to maintain oneself in life, to work, to defer pleasure, to limit the stakes, to have *respect* for death at the very moment when one looks *directly* at it – such is the servile condition of mastery.' Such also is the condition of meaning, the history of discourse and of philosophy. The servile condition of mastery is the kind of ruse of reason Bataille laughs at, and thinks about.

Life is not one category among others but for reason it still is a category, set within the system, set to work on behalf of self-consciousness, truth and meaning. The paragraph that starts with a '[b]urst of laughter from Bataille' develops at excessive length and closes with a long quotation from Bataille's *Hegel* (323). It opens up the process whereby another concept of life, essential, one that survives, works, defers, limits life, welded to biological life but not the same as it, comes to 'surreptitiously' take the place of life. This would be a restricted economy, an 'economy of life' that restricts itself to conservation, to circulation and self-reproduction as the reproduction of meaning'. So powerful the moment you take it seriously, the masterful 'independence of self-consciousness becomes laughable at the moment when it liberates itself by enslaving itself, when it starts to work, that is, when it enters into dialectics'. This movement can be read. It is possible to read Hegel and laugh. This laughter is an excess. Laughter doesn't work; it exceeds philosophy and bursts out only on the basis of giving up, and giving up on meaning. It is this that gives it a relation to death; it is an 'absolute risking of death, what Hegel calls abstract negativity'. This laughter never resumes work, never rejoins the dialectic because it is a negativity 'that never takes place, that never *presents* itself'. It 'exceeds phenomenality in general'. How, then, do we know this laughter? It is not known through a process, rather through reading and through something in reading that does not limit itself to the reproduction of meaning. What opens a reading is not dialectical, even if what protects reading is the restricted economy of commentary. Reading cannot be reduced to a dialectical movement of independent self-consciousness, nor to work, process, mourning, the re-assimilation of the other.

No: one reads and reads laughter in a sudden magical *éclat*, a burst, a lightning strike, the flash of an instant. Derrida says that the word 'laughter' itself must be read in a burst, as its nucleus of sense bursts in the direction of the *system* of the sovereign operation. As if something of laughter scattered itself towards what will never gather it up. The examples Bataille gives of sovereign operations, acts or privileged moments are unsystematic, passionate and Dionysian in the extreme: 'drunkenness, erotic effusion, sacrificial effusion, poetic effusion, heroic behaviour, anger, absurdity'. Difference cannot be shown, neither served nor mastered: it takes writing to let it leap out. That is what Derrida's book does; it makes difference shine, as he describes Bataille doing in the burst of laughter that 'makes the difference between lordship and sovereignty shine [*briller*], without *showing* it however and, above all, without saying it' (323/376). That is not done by manoeuvring concepts or by the showing and saying that aim to present meaning.

Laughter and Freedom

Derrida links sovereignty to the freedom that is the prerogative of the Hegelian lord. Sovereignty is more and less than freedom; it is more and less free than philosophical freedom. Derrida and Bataille connect Hegel's philosophical language with everyday language, without attempting to normalize or explain what cannot be reduced to common sense: 'sovereignty is totally other' (323). It is not comprehended by the philosophical system or dialectics, but it is also unpresentable in terms of a quick definition in everyday English or French. Sovereignty comes free. It is 'no longer a figure in the continuous chain of phenomenology' that preoccupies Hegel. Hegel would call sovereignty 'abstract negativity' and make it part of his system, but for Bataille and Derrida sovereignty puts everything into play and makes the 'seriousness of meaning appear as an abstraction inscribed in play' (324). A thought we will find again, for example inscribed in 'Structure, Sign and Play'. Play confounds meaning and sinks into it. And the laughter here is on the side of play. It 'constitutes sovereignty in relation to death' and 'laughs at itself'. So it is not, for example the kind of laughter Hobbes writes about in *Leviathan* (1651) the 'sudden glory' that triumphs over the laughed-at.[99] Bataillean laughter is on the side of a life that exceeds any philosophical project and indissolubly joins the minor laughter, the instance of laughter, to a major laughter the effects of which scatter everywhere. Laughter 'needs life . . . in order to be in relation to itself in the pleasurable corruption of itself'. Philosophy cannot work on or work out the 'burst of laughter', for it is the 'almost nothing into which meaning sinks, absolutely'. Derrida details what is risible: '*submission* to the self-evidence of meaning', to the demand that there must be meaning, that nothing must definitely be lost in death', that work must always be possible. We are reminded of the essay's refusal, right from the start, to accept the self-evidence of Hegelian thought and of Derrida's refusal to stop reading.

To submit to the self-evidence of meaning and the demand that nothing be definitely lost in death is to enter into an economy of deferral – an absurd attempt to master death and get the best out of it. Not to submit to this is to be unable to avoid suffering. 'Absolute comicalness is the anguish experienced when confronted by expenditure on lost funds, by the absolute sacrifice of meaning: a sacrifice without return and without reserves.' One can think of sacrifice as a placatory gesture, giving up some life in order to receive benefit or in the service of some higher end such as consciousness. Hegelian thinking 'works the "putting at stake" into an *investment*'. It is blind to death as the death of meaning and blinds itself to 'the baselessness of nonmeaning from which the basis of meaning is drawn, and in which this basis of meaning is exhausted' (324–5). This blindness is a kind of 'indifference to the comedy of the *Aufhebung*', where *Aufhebung* refers to the movement of setting aside and raising, as we saw earlier when the slave was preserved and changed in the dialectical relation with the master.

Phenomenology cannot cope with laughter that laughs at philosophy. Bataillean laughter raises questions about experience, as laughter is for no-one and cannot be recuperated dialectically. The expression 'figure of experience' will hardly serve to describe laughter. The expression 'figure of experience' implies a stable rhetorical framework through which an unknown, namely experience, becomes known through the phenomenon of laughter. But laughter shakes that framework. Laughter laughs at the process that would take it seriously, reduce it to a form of knowledge and bring it back within meaning. If laughter is indeed a 'sacrifice without return and without reserves', then it is not a figure of anything. A little later on we will hear how Bataille's 'expenditure and negativity *without reserve*' exposes a 'blind spot of Hegelianism' caused by Hegel's setting negativity to work in a system that takes negativity to be 'the underside and accomplice of positivity' (327). Bataille's sovereign operation takes negativity to a point where it can 'no longer be determined as negativity in a process or a system'. The sovereign operation scars discourse, inscribing itself there by crossing out the predicates that might define it (it is neither this, nor that) or practising what

Derrida describes as a 'contradictory superimpression' – a phrase that suggests a different relation to contradiction than the one that Hegel so powerfully and successfully assimilates into the progress of understanding, where it appears as the negative of thinking. Derrida glosses 'contradictory superimpression' with another curious phrase from Foucault: 'nonpositive affirmation' – an affirmation that posits nothing and is without meaningful content.

Laughter and Poetry

We might pause here to ask a more general question about Bataille. Is he propounding poetry? Can his reading and writing rightly be seen as a poetic riposte to the language of philosophy? Derrida says no. There is no generic language proper to sovereignty (any more, one might add, than there is a working language of deconstruction). And although Bataille asserts that only 'sacred, poetic speech, limited to the level of impotent beauty, manifests full sovereignty', Derrida insists that, still, 'there is only one discourse' and 'it is significative' (330). Even poetic language cannot avoid language's capacity to signify and mean: it cannot mark itself apart from meaning and logic. It must risk itself being read, brought back within the system that it exceeds. (The deliberate production of nonmeaning, in a writing or a reading, would be determined from the outset as a project within meaning, destined to mean by meaning nothing.) 'The poetic or ecstatic is that *in every discourse* which can open itself up to the absolute loss of its sense, to the (non-)base of the sacred, of nonmeaning [*non-sens*], of un-knowledge or of play.'

How do we read such an opening-up? Poetry, as Derrida points out, can be dismissed easily enough as 'play without rules', and to avoid this risk, Bataille recommends that poetry should be 'accompanied by an affirmation of sovereignty' which provides 'the commentary on its absence of meaning' (330–1). This formulation, which Derrida both admires and finds 'untenable', helps us with the difficult notion of a 'contradictory superimpresssion that exceeds the logic of philosophy'. The tension of Bataille's writing provokes similar tension in Derrida's response, which marks a limit of understanding ('untenable') and affirms it unconditionally ('admirable'). The 'affirmation of sovereignty ... which provides the commentary on its absence of meaning' could, Derrida suggests, 'serve as a heading for everything we are attempting to reassemble here as the form and torment of [Bataille's] writing'. And we might ask – how can there be commentary, which reproduces a signifying structure, in the absence of meaning? How can poetry possibly offer a reading of its own lack of grounding in meaning? But without that gesture, poetry will be either *'subordinated'* or will, in Bataille's words 'subsist autonomously, in a reserve, *inserted* into a sphere', along with laughter, drunkenness, sacrifice and eroticism, *'like children in a house*. Within their limits they are minor sovereigns who cannot contest the *empire* of activity' (331). Only ruined metaphors can give access to the unknown that is the realm of major play.

Sliding

Sovereignty operates in the sliding of words. Bataille encourages us to find words and objects that slide and that make us slide. This glissade is major play and is related to various tricks (ruses, stratagems, simulacra) that reintroduce what Bataille calls 'the sovereign silence that interrupts articulated language' (332). We might note that the French *glisser* carries within it *lire*, 'to read' and silently takes up the letters of *silence*. This sovereign silence is 'foreign' to the difference that is the source of signification. We need a lot of negatives to come near it. It is undifferentiated and seems to erase discontinuity, losing the differences without positive terms and deferrals of meaning that make discourse possible. However, the Bataillean *'continuum'* is not a continuity of meaning or presence. 'The experience of the continuum is also the experience of absolute difference.' It is not, like difference in Hegel, 'difference in the service of presence, at work for (the) history of meaning' (333). *Continuum* and *communication* in Bataille are sovereign operations that disturb the concepts that would usually go under these names. The *instant* in Bataille affirmatively eludes presence. The operations of reading and writing by which these words become capable of exceeding meaning are curious and difficult, when compared with positive recommendations of the how-to-read kind. In a French word taken up by Artaud, Genet and Cixous, the instant is *stolen* and *flies* (*se vole*): its movement furtively absents itself and escapes. Nothing happens in the open, none of these notions – continuum, communication, the instant – appears or can be shown. And yet one must find words capable of sliding sovereign silence back into articulated language. There will be a point at which a word, drawn from discursive language, will start, 'by virtue of having been place there and by virtue of having received such an impulsion, to slide and make the entire discourse slide'. A 'violent and sliding, furtive movement must inflect the old corpus in order to relate its syntax and its lexicon to major silence' (334).

'Minor' and 'Major'

Derrida does not offer definitions of these Bataillean categories but we could say that minor laughter is the laughter of relief. It is not without reserve, and the 'gaiety' that Bataille opposes to minor laughter is 'tied to the work of death', anguished to the point that it can 'no longer be determined as negativity as a process or a system'. The 'writing of lordship' would be a minor writing. It attempts to exploit the possibilities of the trace without exposing itself to the possibility of erasure that the trace also implies. Willed, it '*projects* the trace', and 'the will seeks to maintain itself within the trace, seeks to be recognized within it and to reconstitute the presence of itself' (335). It serves a 'phantom of life'. The phantom becomes a clearly apparent theme in later Derrida, starting with *Specters of Marx*, where Derrida says that ghosts haunt all couples. Sovereign or 'major' writing eludes presence and constitutes itself on the basis of 'the possibility of absolute erasure'. Its super-fidelity to the trace generates a paradoxical effect. Poetry will go unrecognized. Bataille says a poet must erase himself, 'undergo solitude, suffer harshly from it, renounce being recognized: one must be there as if absent, deranged, and submit without will or hope, being elsewhere. Thought . . . must be buried alive' (336). Writing is also able to 'interrupt the servile complicity of speech and meaning'. Writing that exceeds mastery and puts will itself and consciousness itself into play without the form of reserve called 'hope' is major. The milieu of continuum is the 'night of secret difference'. Difference that appears openly by day can be brought back into relation with the Same. Sovereignty itself could be treated like that and would remain 'inside a classical philosophy of the subject' and of the will (338).

The movement from minor to major does not take place in space. It is a matter of reading and writing, no longer of conceptual operations projected into an area of knowledge. Derrida's reading of Bataille discovers that 'there is no nucleus of meaning, no conceptual atom, but that the concept is produced within the tissue of differences'. What is woven into the text cannot be observed separately from it, nor can concepts be separated from a reading, questioning and judgement of Bataille or of Hegel that is not comprehended by significative discourse. For example, the distinction 'form/content' does not hold good for Bataille's writing as major writing. Sliding ruins concepts, which appear to be unchanged but are 'struck by the loss of sense towards which they slide'. Bataille's writing may take on philosophical features and relate them to 'the moment of sovereignty, to the absolute loss of meaning' (339). But such a writing is not governed by sovereignty: the relation of major writing to the operation of sovereignty brings together relation and non-relation and places 'the chain of discursive knowledge in relation to an unknowledge that is not a moment of knowledge'.

And yet the writing of sovereignty is a science, therefore a restricted economy, but the particular kind of science it is, relates its object to the destruction, without measure, of meaning.

General Economy and Reading

Bataille identified general economy as 'the science of relating the object of thought to sovereign moments'. General economy 'envisages the meaning of these objects in relation to each other and finally in relation to the loss of meaning' (342). It is visionary and encompasses the Hegelian phenomenology of mind, which is restricted to the 'horizon of absolute knowledge' and the 'circularity of the logos' (343). Phenomenology is 'a restricted economy'. It is interested in wealth rather than expenditure and in circulation and consumption rather than the 'absolute production and consumption of value' or the 'exceeding energy' that is lost without aim or meaning (344). The last pages of the essay are devoted to affirming the unprecedented effects Bataille's concepts have on meaning. These effects are not there 'in order to *mean* [*vouloir-dire*, intend, want to say] something' (344/400). They are there 'to make sense slide, to denounce it or deviate from it'. These slidings can't be assembled into a new system of knowledge: the 'play of difference is indispensable for the correct reading of the general economy's concepts' (345).

To know how to read Bataille would mean submitting 'contextual attentiveness and differences of signification to a *system of meaning*'. One could generalize this further perhaps: to know how to read, to reduce reading to the 'promise of absolute formal mastery' is no longer to read. Bataille's writing must be recognized in its unprecedentedness. And it must 'assure us of nothing, must give us no certitude, no result, no profit. It is absolutely adventurous, is a chance and not a technique' (346). Such a writing and such a reading *do not work*. Hegelian dialectic always works and is always right but remains within 'the system or the work of signification' (348). Bataille aligns his own concept of 'transgression' with the Hegelian *Aufhebung*, which is an untranslatable word that Bataille translates as 'to surpass while maintaining'. As we have seen, this transcendence which conserves constitutes meaning. Derrida demonstrates that the work of *Aufhebung* differs from the effect of transgression in a very important way. While *Aufhebung* belongs within law, discourse and meaning and serves them, Bataille's transgression transgresses law, discourse and meaning. Bataille's analogy empties the *Aufhebung*, which operates within philosophy, and uses it to describe a movement which 'properly constitutes the excess' of every possible philosophical concept or statement (349). This is a different kind of displacement from the *Aufhebung*, which cannot escape the restricted economy of the dialectical progress of consciousness. Bataille's analogy exposes philosophy's dependence on naïve consciousness. Philosophy

> develops the sense, or the desire for sense, of natural consciousness, the consciousness that encloses itself in the circle in order to *know sense*; which is always where it comes from and where it is going to. It does not see the nonbasis of play upon which (the) history (of meaning) is launched. (349)

Play would be a way out of this very sophisticated form of naivety and non-freedom. Derrida's last paragraph describes Bataillean general economy as a kind of unthinkable vision which is also reading itself. Not reading as the gathering of meaning but reading as a sovereign encounter with what cannot be read. It describes a certain text: silent, active, producing the eye that perceives and tearing itself away from the knowledge that it also produces. This text is not there, neither solid nor servile. It remains to be read. When it is read it becomes part of a restricted economy. Derrida affirms that which cannot be reduced to knowledge: writing.

Study Question
What does Derrida's focus on laughter and play do to the idea of 'serious' thought or of the 'weakness' or 'strength' of an argument?

'STRUCTURE, SIGN AND PLAY IN THE DISCOURSE OF THE HUMAN SCIENCES'

The title of this most anthologized essay of Derrida's is noticeably more *academic* than any other in the collection. 'Structure, Sign and Play' identifies and analyses certain elements and forces at work in the language of a group of academic disciplines and began public life as a conference paper delivered at a conference on 'Critical Languages and the Sciences of Man' at Baltimore on the Eastern seaboard of the United States in October 1966. The human sciences are of course defined by their object, humanity, and would include psychology, sociology, ethnology, political science, economics, philosophy and linguistics. On the French scene, Michel Foucault had recently chosen *The Order of Things: The Archaeology of the Human Sciences*, for the title of his latest book (1966). Although the contemporary thinker Derrida engages with directly in 'Structure, Sign and Play' is the ethnologist Claude Lévi-Strauss, whose work is also discussed at length in *Of Grammatology*, Derrida's implicit questioning of Foucault's inventive historicism in 'Cogito and the History of Madness' continues here. The engagement is signalled by the presence of the terms 'discourse,' 'event' and *'episteme'* on the first page of 'Structure, Sign and Play'. As a historian of concepts, Foucault's notion of what an event might be is inevitably very different from Derrida's, and the opening of 'Structure, Sign and Play' begins by marking an interest in the event. 'Perhaps,' Derrida begins, keeping determination at bay from the outset:

> Perhaps something has occurred in the history of the concept of structure that could be called an "event" if this loaded word did not entail a meaning which it is precisely the function of

structural – or structuralist – thought to reduce or suspect. Let us speak of an 'event', nevertheless. (351)

Derrida is speaking cautiously but clearly against the ownership of the word 'event' by structural thinkers and also against a certain reduction of the event that would take place by a mode of thought set on accounting for events, determining their place within what 'Cogito and the History of Madness' called 'the totality of beings and determined meanings' or within what 'Structure, Sign and Play' calls 'presence' or 'total form' (352). An event, then, does not take place within the continuity of presence. We are not yet told what the content of the event Derrida is thinking of is, but that its outward form is that of a *'rupture and redoubling'* (351). It would seem that it appears to be at the same time a breakthrough *and* the repetition of or reflection upon something that is already the case.

Epistēmē

I have spent some moments on the context of Derrida's essay, national and international, but as always in his work, the context is ancient and still to be determined. He uses a Greek term strongly associated with Foucault, *epistēmē*, (literally, 'knowledge' or 'science') to indicate that the concept and the word 'structure' are by no means recent inventions and that they are rooted not in any particular academic or philosophical discourse but in ordinary language. Foucault used the notion of *epistēmē* to elaborate a historical theory of the conditions of what may be recognized as knowledge. There is, according to Foucault 'an historical a priori' on the basis of which ideas appear, sciences are established, experience reflected in philosophies and rationalities formed.[100] The account of the human sciences in *The Order of Things* works with a notion of 'modern episteme' that starts at the beginning of the nineteenth century. In an interview in 1977, Foucault described *The Order of Things* as an attempt to write the history of modern *epistēmē*, defined as

> the strategic apparatus which permits of separating out from among all the statements which are possible those that will be acceptable within, I won't say a scientific theory, but a field of

scientificity, and which it is possible to say are true or false. The *epistēmē* is the 'apparatus' which makes possible the separation, not of the true from the false, but of what may from what may not be characterized as scientific.[101]

Derrida's notion of *epistēmē* in 'Structure, Sign and Play' describes something 'as old as Western science and Western philosophy' and rather than being approached in terms of historical periods is a metaphorical displacement of the depths of ordinary language. A discourse such as philosophy gains rigour, the power to articulate distinctions and wield knowledge, at the expense of what a note to 'Cogito and the History of Madness' calls 'the original and essential equivocality of the signifier . . . in the language of everyday life' (390n.3). That everyday shifting of the signifier is crucial to Derrida's thinking. As a writer he never really leaves what 'Structure, Sign and Play' calls 'the soil [*sol*] of ordinary language' (351/409). The essay closes with an invitation to think the 'common ground [*sol*]' and the *différance* that generate conflicting possibilities of interpretation (370/428). Derrida also wants to think history on the basis of a conception of the event that is not historically determined.

To return to the opening of the essay, Derrida argues that since the beginning of Western philosophy, the force of 'structurality of structure' has been neutralized or reduced by being oriented in relation to a fixed point or centre that limits its play. Centre and totality structurally complement each other. (For example, the eighteenth-century German philosopher Johann Gottfried Herder formulated the philosophical quest for knowledge as the search for an immobile centre: 'We wander over the Earth in a labyrinth of human fancies: the question is; where is the central point of the labyrinth, to which all our wanderings may be traced, as refracted rays to the Sun?')[102] Derrida says it has been 'forbidden [*interdite*]' (351/410) for there to be substitution of elements at the centre. Derrida emphasizes this as a discursive intervention, a prohibition rather than an impossibility, and links the prohibition to desire and to anxiety. Classically, the centre holds a structure together by being exempt from the play that it makes possible. If structurality implies the possibility of substituting elements in the structure, then the centre is both '*within* the structure' as its principle of coherence, 'and *outside* it' as the one element that is not permitted to remain open to the possibilities of substitution (352). Derrida detects desire behind this contradictory coherence. Its fixity actually expresses a force. Derrida's logic suggests that we perhaps have never understood play and that the history of meaning is a series of failures to understand it. 'The concept of centred structure is in fact the concept of a play based on a fundamental ground, a play constituted on the basis of a fundamental immobility and a reassuring certitude, which itself is beyond the reach of play.' The purpose of the certitude is to master the anxiety provoked by being alive, being already in the text: 'for anxiety is invariably the result of a certain mode of being implicated in the game, of being caught in the game, of being as it were at stake in the game from the outset.' The metaphor of archaeology that Foucault used in his book on madness, in *The Order of Things*, subtitled *An Archaeology of the Human Sciences*, and will continue to deploy in *The Archaeology of Knowledge* (1969) presupposes the *presence* of the structure to be investigated and that all

> repetitions, substitutions, transformations, and permutations are always taken from a history of meaning – that is, in a word, a history – whose origin may always be reawakened or whose end may be anticipated in the form of presence. This is why one perhaps could say that the movement of any archaeology, like that of any eschatology, is an accomplice of this reduction of the structurality of structure and always attempts to conceive of the structurality of structure on the basis of a full presence that is beyond play. (353)

Such changes as have occurred are only a series of substitutions of centre for centre going under different names. Derrida lists some of the Greek and French terms for the determination of being as presence: '*eidos, archē, telos, energeia, ousia* (essence, existence, substance, subject), *alētheia*, transcendentality, consciousness, God, Man and so forth'.[103] The bound energy has, perhaps, begun to be released from these terms belonging to philosophical discourse and the history of metaphysics. A certain deregulation has begun to be possible.

The Event?

But what is this event Derrida has been talking about? What has made it possible? He sounds as if he might be making a calculated guess when he says that it 'presumably would have come about when the structure of structurality had to begin to be thought' (353). According to the logic of what he is saying about a disruption befalling regulated play, things may be reaching a point where it is no longer inevitable to talk about structure on the basis of presence and its many pseudonyms. Certitude and the denial of both anxiety and desire discussed in his argument about the centre are no longer necessary to thought. So there isn't going to be a first cause in this essay. The argument has to proceed in another way. The disruption is, as Derrida said earlier, repetition. From it arises the possibility and necessity of thinking 'both the law which somehow governed the desire for a centre in the constitution of structure, and the process of signification which orders the displacements and substitutions for this law of central presence'. This central presence 'has never been itself'. And it has been a quick step from acknowledging that law of substitution right from the start and at the start to 'thinking that there was no centre' but a sort of function or no-place where 'an infinite number of sign-substitutions came into play'. Negation of the centre made it possible to believe that 'everything became discourse', where no 'central' or 'transcendental' signified stood outside the system of differences that language is. Derrida is talking about how structuralism became necessary, with its privileging of language as signification in the understanding of all sorts of phenomenon and knowledge. It was a way of beginning to think play. But for Derrida, what is interesting about structuralism is not the structures it looks for and expounds but the fact of structuralism as a reflection and disruption of metaphysics. If, as Derrida claims in 'Edmond Jabès and the Question of the Book', history is 'the only thing that begins by reflecting itself', then the reflection of and upon structure would be an event that initiates history.

So, if Derrida cannot tell us when or where the event is, without annulling its effect on our awareness of time and space, how are we to think about it? *Of Grammatology* suggests that we 'begin wherever we are' and where we are is 'in a text where we already believe ourselves to be'.[104] We don't go in search of a starting point; it calls to us. It is stronger than we are and gets us sniffing about, reading, finding out where we are. To say anything useful about the centre, it is necessary to abandon the neutrality and remoteness of expertise.

'Structure, Sign and Play' cites a number of kinds of de-centring modern thought as characteristic of the 'event' in the history of the concept of structure that has prompted Derrida's own essay. He notes that these re-thinkings of the centre are *destructive* interventions. They aim to keep up philosophical assurance by amending the language of thought: getting rid of some terms, adding new ones, re-defining others. But as attempts to destroy metaphysics, the very conceptual framework within which they articulate themselves, they deprive themselves of what they attack and remain naïve about their complicity with it. Metaphysics remains inevitable. It's the indispensable branch of philosophy that deals with 'first principles of things or reality, including questions about being, substance, time and space, causation, change, and identity' and is 'the ultimate science of being and knowing' (OED). The scene is not simple. A naivety about the possibility of destroying the part of philosophy that deals with the first principles of things persists alongside an immense sophistication and ingenuity in the analysis of metaphysics. These discourses remain attached to the history of metaphysics as its destruction and therefore can't help but prolong what they hope to cut off. Derrida specifies some of these highly purposeful but necessarily inadequate attempts to think 'the structurality of structure':

> the Nietzschean critique of metaphysics, the critique of the concepts of being and truth for which were substituted the concepts of play, interpretation and sign (sign without present truth); the Freudian critique of self-presence, that is, the critique of consciousness, of the subject, of self-identity and of self-proximity or self-possession; and, more radically, the Heideggerian destruction of metaphysics, of onto-theology, of the determination of being as presence. But all these destructive discourses and all their analogues are trapped in a kind of circle. (354/412)

Derrida, committed to the belief that there is something other than language, is not concerned with making one more verbal clean-up job. 'Structure, Sign and Play' identifies a widespread tendency to destructiveness that is circular and continues metaphysics. He insists:

> *There is no sense* in doing without the concepts of metaphysics in order to shake metaphysics. We have no language – no syntax and no lexicon – which is foreign to this history; we can pronounce not a single destructive proposition which has not had already to slip into the form, the logic, and the implicit postulations of precisely what it seeks to contest.

If the critique of metaphysical thinking is necessary and just, then it must take a form other than critique. That is, it must remain complicit with what it is trying to give up, and not give it up, in order to give it up. Nothing must be forbidden. This logic is totally incompatible with the notion of Derrida as the inheritor of a Nietzschean, Freudian or Heideggerian tradition. Derrida's reading of the philosophical tradition is revolutionary but not polemical.

Why Lévi-Strauss?

Within this general situation, which Derrida recognizes is not confined to 'philosophical and scientific discourse' but is 'political, economic, technical, and so forth', deconstruction is confronted by a problem of *economy* and *strategy* (356). Derrida chooses to write about the texts of the ethnologist Claude Lévi-Strauss because Lévi-Strauss has developed an explicit doctrine relating to 'the problem of the status of a discourse which borrows from a heritage the resources necessary for the deconstruction of that heritage itself' (357). For Lévi-Strauss this problem can be pinpointed in the opposition between nature and culture, which he is aware that he has found it necessary to use but that he also finds impossible to accept. No sooner has he distinguished the natural as spontaneous and universal, and the cultural as concerned with variable norms, than he comes up against a phenomenon that is both universal and a 'system of norms and interdicts' – therefore has essential features of both nature and culture: *incest prohibition*. (We note here the recurrence of the word *interdit*, here in the form of a noun, that Derrida earlier applied to the permutation or transformation of elements at the centre of a structure.) The incest prohibition is an accepted and consequential fact for Lévi-Strauss's work but it is not able to take on the immobility of a centre because its status is equivocal with regard to the traditional nature–culture opposition, and furthermore it is not reducible to a scandalous exception. It 'escapes' traditional concepts 'and certainly precedes them, probably as their condition of possibility' (358). The possibility of the 'whole of philosophical conceptualization' depends on something (the origin of the incest prohibition) that philosophical conceptualization is 'designed', Derrida claims, to keep unthinkable.

Scandalous Supplementarity

The notion of scandal returns towards the end of the essay, where it is associated with 'a word whose scandalous signification is always obliterated in French': *supplementarity* (365). The supplement has come up earlier in the book, in 'Freud and the Scene of Writing', where 'supplementary' translates the German word *nachträglich*, used by Freud to describe the absolute deferral and belatedness of meaning in the supposed movement between the unconscious and consciousness. From the evidence surrounding this psychical effect, Derrida made the more general argument that presence does not come first. He commented that 'the call of the supplement is primary, here, and it hollows out that which will be reconstituted by deferral as the present' (266). The supplement decisively affects the notion of life as a kind of simple being-there, here and now. Neither the unconscious, nor consciousness, can properly be understood as presences underlying or completing psychic life. Rather, psychic life is the invention or 'reconstitution' of living presence or experience out of a logic that relates missing meaning to a surplus of meaning, a 'not enough' to a 'too much', and acknowledges a 'too late' at the heart of the feeling and the meaning of 'now'. Derrida quotes the authoritative French dictionary Littré: '*Suppléer*: 1. To add what is missing, to supply a necessary surplus.' With presence, there's never enough, there is always a desire for *absolute* presence and there's always also an anxiety because presence is untimely and excessive; it isn't possible to fix or contain its meaning in one place or at one time. Derrida's work on and with the word 'supplement' is a powerful example of something that Cixous has identified as follows:

> I cannot emphasise enough that his whole philosophy is a consequence of the displacement of everyday language, a modern mocking of French as cliché. The writing surarrives and puts time out of joint, derails it, it makes its entry as the past-already while holding out the promise of the already-future that it is, that it will be. It makes your head spin.[105]

It is as if Derrida was the first to read and write the word *suppléer* awake to what it really says, has been saying and could say.

To return to 'Structure, Sign and Play' and its reading of Lévi-Strauss: the 'scandalous signification' of supplementarity describes the play of substitutions without centre, as in music, discovered by Lévi-Strauss in his researches into what he called 'the syntax of South American mythology'. This research has philosophical implications that cannot, Derrida insists, be assimilated within philosophy. Philosophy requires that structures of knowledge have a centre. Myth and the structural analysis of myth do not. Lévi-Strauss's work implies that 'the philosophical or epistemological requirement of a centre' is itself 'mythological, that is to say . . . a historical illusion' (363). Derrida quotes Lévi-Strauss describing the science of myths in terms of angled and broken light. The science of myths includes 'the study of both reflected rays and broken rays' (362). He also emphasizes that structural ethnology, for all its refusal to stick with a single analytical discourse, is not simply an empirical exercise: Lévi-Strauss is not merely gathering new evidence of or about myths but has developed a discourse that has itself the uncentredness of myth. Derrida underlines here that 'the passage beyond philosophy does not consist in turning the page of philosophy (which usually amounts to philosophising badly) but in continuing to read philosophers *in a certain way*' (364).

Lévi-Strauss's work gives us a clue to the sort of thing Derrida *won't* be advocating. The way of reading philosophers that interests him will not rely on organising their efforts into a single system, a set of propositions to be knocked down or adopted, nor will it apply a fixed vocabulary of concepts to their work. Lévi-Strauss's model is language itself, understood as a movement of signification without fixed centre. But where Lévi-Strauss leaves his syntax of mythology open for fresh data, Derrida wants to clarify two possible approaches to totalization implied by the ethnologist's refusal to 'accept the arbitrary demand for a total mythological pattern' (365). There is the empirical incompleteness brought about by the limits of what a single subject can do or by a 'finite richness' that can't be mastered. This Derrida acknowledges, but sets aside, as it has no transformative implications for philosophy. But totalization is also impossible for an altogether different kind of reason: 'because the nature of the field – that is, language and a finite language – excludes totalization'. Instead of being 'too large', the field has intrinsically 'something missing from it'. What is missing from language is 'a centre which arrests and grounds the play of substitutions'. Derrida describes how the absence of a centre, a signified around which signification could orient itself, gives rise to an unstoppable and unsettling movement of signs:

> One cannot determine the centre and exhaust totalization because the sign which replaces the centre, which *supplements* it, taking the centre's place in its absence – this sign is added, occurs as a surplus, as a *supplement*. The movement of signification adds something, which results in the fact that there is always more, but this addition is a floating one because it comes to . . . supplement a lack on the part of the signified. (365–6/423)

To use the terms of the essay on Bataille in *Writing and Difference*, the supplement is an excess in relation to the processes of signification that produce meaning. Derrida recognizes the use of 'supplement' by Lévi-Strauss to describe a 'surplus of signification', a supplementary ration [*ration supplémentaire*] of signifiers, in relation to the signifieds (the concepts) to which they refer. Furthermore, Derrida detects supplementarity at the origin of *ratio* itself. *Ratio* signifies a relationship of proportion, as well as an allowance of something; the word comes from Latin *ratio*, reason, from the verb *rari*, to think. Derrida finds an account of the origins of thought in a variability of the relation between signifiers and signifieds.

To recap, Derrida is still interested in being and presence but no longer accepts that whatever is, is there, or that whatever is not, is not there. Shades of presence become conceivable. It is time to reconsider life and death. Later, in the 1990s, ontology, the philosophy of being, will learn how to become *hauntology*, a science of ghosts that can transform knowledge itself. The second discussion of supplementarity in 'Structure, Sign and Play' has radical implications for our understanding of what thought is. We may have assumed that thought took place on the basis of something there to be thought about – content, substance, subject matter. Thought would aim to come nearer to what truly is, but remains hidden. But Derrida's reading of Lévi-Strauss intimates something different. Lévi-Strauss observes symbolic thought as an ethnologist considering social phenomena and reading those phenomena as forms of language. Ethnology is unencumbered by what philosophy has thought about itself. According to Lévi-Strauss, symbolic thought does not originate in relation to being as presence but becomes possible thanks to language, which is a centreless process of signification. Thought has to be thought as a syntax, taking into account the play of what Ferdinand de Saussure called the 'relations and differences with respect to the other terms of language' that produce its conceptual and phonic values.[106]

We could cite as an example the equivocal term 'totalization' in Lévi-Strauss. As we have seen, there are two ways of conceiving the limit of totalization: as empirical finitude or as an a priori characteristic of language as the play of a finite system. Derrida's reading finds both 'implicitly in Lévi-Strauss's discourse' (365). We could, of course, point to 'supplement', too: it means both a surplus, and that which completes by adding what is missing. Both these examples show a play between different meanings that is decisive for thought. It is impossible to determine, one way or the other, a unified concept of totalization or of supplementarity.

Lévi-Strauss has noticed that the signifier produces more signification than can be attached to any one signified. There is an 'overabundance of signifier, in relation to the signifieds to which this overabundance can refer' (366). (His observation contradicts the implied symmetry in the Saussurean formula that the sign consists of the dual unity of a signifier and a signified, an acoustic mage and a concept.) So that is why it is so difficult to make sense of everything. There is, according to the ethnologist, 'a surplus of signification', and it is this supplement that provokes symbolic thought. Thought works to redistribute the excess (or if you prefer, lack) of meaning, so as to maintain the 'relation of complementarity' between signifier and signified 'which is the very condition of the use of symbolic thought'. Signification plays against the organization of signifiers in relation to signifieds that thought is – and that same play provokes thought to try to bind signifiers into conceptual systems and maintain itself. If we flash back briefly to the incest taboo, that primary attempt to subject desire to meaning, and decide a border between nature and culture, we can perhaps see better now why Derrida places it at the origin of conceptual thought.

The Trouble with Play

Lévi-Strauss focuses on a number of words such as *mana* that have 'apparently insoluble antinomies attached to them'. *Mana* is 'force and action, quality and state, noun and verb; abstract and concrete, omnipresent and localised'. It is 'in effect all these things'. But Lévi-Strauss sees that it can be all these things because it is none of them, but a 'zero symbolic value . . . a sign marking the necessity of a symbolic content *supplementary* [Derrida's italics] to that with which the signified is already loaded, but which can take on any value required' (366–7). These zero signifiers can be invoked by thought to master the anxiety caused by the overabundance of signs in relation to meanings. Play is not exactly fun: it is characterized by tension, therefore by desire and anxiety.

Derrida indicates two things in particular that are troubled by play. One is history and a historicism yet to acknowledge its complicity with 'that philosophy of presence to which it was believed history could be opposed' (367). Derrida values structuralism for its consequential invocation of 'the concepts of chance and discontinuity'. At the same time he acknowledges that 'ahistoricism of the classical type', indifference to history, won't do either. Play is problematic for history. It's also a trial for presence and Derrida outlines two interpretations, two moods or styles of response to play, as incompatible with the simplicity of presence. Neither is his own. One focuses on loss, the other on possibility – in interpretation and in structure, sign and play. One 'seeks to decipher, dreams of deciphering a truth or an origin which escapes play and the order of the sign, and . . . lives the necessity of interpretation as exile' (369). The other 'affirms play and tries to pass beyond man and humanism' – where man is the one who has dreamed of 'full presence, the reassuring foundation, the origin and end of play' (370). These two interpretations are 'absolutely irreconcilable even if we live them simultaneously and reconcile them in an obscure economy'. We can't master these two possibilities by choosing between them.

Derrida doesn't end with a prediction, a summary or a programme. We have yet to conceive of the common ground of the two interpretations. We have yet to research their detours and temporal formations. Derrida says 'conceive', not 'conceptualize'; he invokes the feminine bodily processes of childbearing and the arrival of an unheard-of living being to those who don't want to know what is coming and who want to relegate its historical actuality to the realm of what one can choose to ignore.

Study Question

Can traditional history really tell us whether an event has taken place? Is it dangerous and irresponsible to ask this question? Or is it dangerous and irresponsible not to?

'ELLIPSIS'

The word *supplement* brings together what is missing from a totality and what is surplus to it. By calling the last chapter of *Writing and Difference*, 'Ellipse', Derrida has given the piece of the book that completes it the name of a hinting figure of syntax that works by leaving words out. With a more conventional writer one would expect a conclusion here. The essay which ends *Writing and Difference* is brief and aphoristic. We could even call it 'poematic', a word used by Artaud. Derrida used the term to emphasize the value of extricating poems from the 'merry-go-round or circus' that would bring them back to a 'poetic source' or 'to the act or experience' of their 'setting-to-work in poetry or a poetics'.[107] Poetry does not work. 'Ellipsis' continues the analysis of circularity that began in 'Edmond

Jabès and the Question of the Book' and 'Structure, Sign and Play', where Derrida emphasizes its closure and endlessness. Geometrically, what is elliptical escapes circularity; it's an oval and its more technical mathematical description depends on a failure to meet.[108] 'Poematic' refers to the errant, playful and risky aspects of the poem and of 'Ellipsis', as writing that risks not making sense and abandoning responsibility. 'Ellipsis' cites Jabès's 'The Return to the Book' (1965), the third volume in *The Book of Questions*, but it is even less an interpretation of Jabès than 'Edmond Jabès and the Question of the Book'. Derrida's citations from *The Return to the Book* act as commentary on his own writing and on the discoveries of *Writing and Difference* as a whole, as if Jabès had read the book in advance. According to the argument Derrida puts forward, it is as if writing had been watching over the book.

One might add that this elli*ps*e is also a p. s. or postscript to *Writing and Difference*. The only essay written as a chapter for the book, it begins with an example of the deferred action of supplementarity as Derrida introduced it in 'Freud and the Scene of Writing': 'Here and there we have discerned writing: a nonsymmetrical division designated [*dessinait*, drew, delineated], on the one hand the closure of the book, and on the other the opening of the text' (371/429). These references to closure and opening should keep us on the threshold of the essay a moment longer, to notice its dedication to the writer and Jabès critic Gabriel Bounoure, a reader and supporter of French, Middle-Eastern and North African poetry, who was a civil servant in the French colonies of Syria and Lebanon and came across Jabès's work while working in Cairo. After the war, Bounoure resigned as a civil servant over his disagreement with the policies of the de Gaulle government in North Africa. His love of poetry and his political awareness connected the Middle East and the Western tradition in a way that resonates with Derrida's interest in the relation between Greek and Jewish approaches to writing. Jabès and Bounoure were close friends and Jabès acknowledged the value of such a reader.

The opening of 'Ellipsis' sketches a reading of *Writing and Difference* rather like the 'two interpretations of interpretation' mentioned in the 'Structure, Sign and Play' and the earlier essay on Jabès. Here we have two interpretations of writing. On one side the nostalgic: focusing on decipherment, figuring out the truth of an origin which escapes play and the order of the sign. It conceptualizes the book as a 'theological encyclopaedia' or its secular but no less logocentric equivalent, 'the book of man'. The book would be what gives the equivocality of writing to be understood. On the other hand, there would be an interpretation that turns its back on the origin, that affirms play, that attempts to pass beyond man and humanism, and that would not mourn the book. For this latter interpretation of writing, the classical notion of the book as the location of writing would be no more. Instead, reading would encounter 'a fabric of traces marking the disappearance of an exceeded God or of an erased man'. A 'joyous wandering' that would be 'without return'. Rather than starting out with a sense of being exiled from meaning, this reading would welcome, more blithely than Derrida felt prepared to do himself, the adventure of a text that is not enclosed within books.

Closure and the Book

Derrida proceeds to complicate the notion of the closure of the book. He works at the limit. In her reading of 'Force and Signification' Cixous sees Derrida making his way, up high on a tightrope or a ridge. Her visualization of his thinking suggests that to choose either side would mean a descent. He moves forward where two interpretations meet. There is no transcendence in that. For Derrida reading must be traditional, classical and respectful, but what opens a reading cannot be reduced to the faithful reproduction of what already exists. The book will remain crucial to our understanding of its limits. There is no simple passage beyond the book. Reading books will remain essential. For 'only in the book, coming back to it unceasingly, drawing all our resources from it, could we indefinitely designate [*désigner*] the writing beyond the book.' The book, like the dream, is capable of containing what exceeds it and exceeding what contains it.

In 'Ellipsis', there's no question of a recapitulation of preceding arguments. If the opening sentence of the essay suggests an elliptical writing, something that we make out 'here and there', this furtive creature or phenomenon writing turns out to have been keeping an eye on everything. Writing is awake and even alive with a life that is not the simple opposite of death. The notion of the *veille*, the vigil, relates watching and wakefulness to vigour and liveliness. As the book *is* writing and the possibility of repetition, even if it is also a delusory metaphysical representation of writing, return to the book does not shut us up in a library or in words. Writing has perhaps been playing, for a time, at being a book. And as there is no truth of writing, only differences and detours, to return to the book is to return to that play.

The Epoch of the Book

Reading is not a programme for finding writing as much as a wandering that happens on it. A line from Jabès suggests an endless succession as 'God succeeds God and the Book succeeds the Book' (371). Where a totality completes itself, it does so on the condition that another totality can be substituted for it. It's like the succession of centres that 'Structure, Sign and Play' described as making up the 'entire history of the concept of structure', where structure is thought of in terms of a full presence (353). If the book were such a structure, a full presence beyond play, then reading and writing would move from one book to another, with each book functioning as a metaphor or metonymy for writing itself. Instead 'Ellipse' offers us something far more strange: a furtive, fugitive writing that escapes observation and figuration, and watches over the movement from book to book. As that movement is endless, whatever we do, whether we 'protest' against the determination of the book as presence or whether we 'deconstruct' that determination, we are powerless to close the movement of history that 'Structure, Sign and Play' characterizes as a 'series of substitutions of centre for centre'. We remain in the '*epoch* of the book' as 'Ellipsis' calls it. An epoch is a period of time but it also connotes a fixing or a stopping, from the Greek word *epochē*, which was taken up by Husserl to describe the 'bracketing' of belief in the existence of perceived objects that was essential to phenomenological analysis. An epoch is a form of closure. 'Edmond Jabès and the Question of the Book' presents us with a series of what-ifs beginning: 'what if the Book was only, in all senses of the word, an *epoch* of being (an epoch coming to an end which would permit us to see Being in the glow of its agony or the relaxation of its grasp?)'(94/112). The end of such an epoch would not, finally, offer a proper understanding of being, an understanding freed from the dissimulation of writing that the book had been, but awareness of the 'original illegibility' that is 'the very possibility of the book' (95). In 'Ellipsis', the return to the book is possible because the book, as a form of writing, is less than present, requiring interpretation, and more than present, containing a hidden excess, something 'reserved within it' (372). Writing does not belong to the book: it 'feigns, by repeating the book, inclusion within the book'. The logic of originary repetition worked out in 'Freud and the Scene of Writing' applies here too: 'repetition is the first writing.' To read is to watch the origin of the book disappear.

Interfacings
What is the status of the quotations from Jabès? Derrida is barely reading them, if to read means to pursue the intended meaning of an author. Jabès's word *'entretoile'* or 'interfacing' describes the relation better. As Derrida says in 'Freud and the Scene of Writing', the 'sovereign solitude of the author' does not exist (285). 'The subject of writing is a *system* of relations between strata . . . Within that scene, on that stage, the punctual simplicity of a classical subject is not to be found.' Jabès refers to a book as 'the interfacing of a risk'. The term comes from sewing: an *entretoile* is an insert between pieces of cloth that stiffens or decorates them. Suspended between writing's withdrawal and its inner reserves, the book acts as a support for the risk involved in engaging with writing. In a sentence that is itself impossible to paraphrase because it is so mobile; Jabès speaks of a life as writing, as a vigil and as the rhythm that becomes perceptible thanks to the vigil's attention. Writing sees out the book, and writing is there in the combination of boundaries and spacing that closure is. And this can be lived: '. . . My life, from the book on, will have been a vigil of writing in the interval of limits'. In the amphibology of the line, writing is linked with the continuity of vigil and with the discontinuity of the interval which belongs on the side of limits but is still watched over by writing that works across all forms of closure. The line also fluidly and poetically associates life, book, vigil and interval by means of letters and sounds: *vie, livre, veille, intervalle.*

Bookle
Once we begin to notice that kind of thing, we can hear English 'book' in the French word *boucle*, meaning 'ring' or 'fastener',

along the lines of 'buckle'. *Boucler* also means to finish something off. 'Ellipsis' is Derrida's way of rounding off or finishing up or closing *Writing and Difference*. But he refuses to be pacified. The book lives on a belief, given to us by the book, that passion, 'having originally be impassioned by *something*, could in the end be appeased by the return of that something'. Has Derrida finished with that belief in appeasement? Escape, according to Cixous, is the province of poetic rather than philosophical writing: 'To work on what escapes can only be done poetically.'[109] Philosophical work on the book is vulnerable to the reappropriation of writing by concepts. The 'exit from the identical into the same remains very slight, weighs nothing itself, thinks and weighs the book as such' (373). One is reminded of the 'very little, almost nothing' that opens thought in 'Violence and Metaphysics'. Return can never be a linear return to the same; it engages not things but spaces and openings. 'Writing, passion of the origin, must also be understood through the subjective genitive. It is the origin itself that is impassioned.' 'Understood' here is '*s'entendre*', also meaning 'be heard' and the way through, the '*voie*', is a homophone for '*voix*', voice. One thinks of this or that subject having a passion for origins, but here the passion of the origin is something that moves the origin, plays it, unfixes the centre and lets it enter history.

Signing Off

'In order to sign, one has to stop one's text.'[110] The last words of *Writing and Difference* are not by Derrida. They cite a name, a fictional attribution to an imaginary rabbi from Jabès's *Book of Questions*: Reb Derissa. Derissa could be a signature, the proper name 'Derrida' with a difference or a dissonance that marks, as a signature would, the contingent distortion of a proper name so as to appropriate it more completely and unmistakeably and offer it to be read in the absence of whoever signs. Jabès would not be the fall guy or the straw man here. Rather, 'Ellipsis' *sets off The Book of Questions*, his writing acts as a foil and a spark igniting Jabès's researches into the book. Derrida is not looking for an opening to make a polemical point. Love animates his thinking. The key poles of affect in *Writing and Difference* are desire and anxiety. Anxiety is not only trembling for oneself but a solicitude for the other and a being-solicited by the other. In one way or another, Derrida is impassioned by the texts he reads.

The curls, spiralling helixes, curves and curbed movements of 'Force and Signification' reappear in 'Ellipsis' as rings and circles. One of Jabès's rabbis is anxious that he will see his life 'curve itself to form a ring' (372). An apparently immobile or timeless circular structure becomes a movement. However, such a movement cannot be located in linear time because it is a closed form and a repetition. It combines closure and difference, stillness and whirling.

The pace of Derrida's text can be measured in the return of its letters across words that deny letters and look away from them in order to mean. Jabès writes in a meditation on Derrida in *The Book of Margins*: 'You are against all repression and especially, on behalf of the book, against that of the letter; because the letter is perhaps an origin diverted from the origin by its tie to a signified whose weight it must help carry.'[111] Considered at the level of decipherment, the ramifications of Derrida's thought move infinitely fast. If the measure of a book is as Jabès suggests, how well it has been read by its author, Derrida has read himself better than anyone except perhaps Cixous, whose own writing is, as he says, 'most calculating'. But the letters remain. The interval between limits that life is, is also the vigil of writing. The vigil is marked for readers by the insistent presence of the letter. There's a sense that in the last part of this non-book, Derrida is recognizing something about 'the book *as such*', as the theatre of spacing, as what can't be upstaged by the philosophical genius for formulae that wastes itself heading for the signified through book after book. Derrida notices the letter and between letters 'the neutral space of succession . . . the suspense of the interval' (373). Return is not appropriation. The ellipsis is a form that has more space, more gap, more almost-nothing than a circle. It is a faulty form.

And within it 'the book *as such*' can be thought as repetition: 'redoubling of the route, the solicitation of closure, the jointing of the line' where 'solicitation' carries the sense of 'trembling' introduced in 'Force and Signification' and 'jointing' is *'brisure'* a word that means both breaking and joining. The French version of this sentence gives the word *'ellipsis'* in Greek letters here for the only time in the essay, marking the word's history. Derrida is still the Greekjew and the Jewgreek, giving the widest possible arc of reference for a word and all its subsequent references, still faithful to what is most archaic in the archive, in order to prolong its life and salute its diversity. Pure repetition, this simplest structural possibility, opens everything to whatever. Nietzsche's 'eternal return' is happening here, freed from existential bravado (373). There is also an echo of Husserl, as repetition makes the presence-to-itself of 'so-called living speech' disappear (374).

In 'Ellipsis' Derrida gives way to Jabès, opening the two oeuvres into each other so that the 'other is in the same'.

Desire

If Derrida affirms play, he also affirms the desire for a centre. If he quotes Jabès's Reb Madies: '*The scorned water permits the falcon to pursue his prey*', suggesting that we soar and hunt the skies rather than hanging about at the watering-hole, he also recognizes the thirst implied by the question 'Where is the centre?' The grapheme, that is, the unit of writing, letter or pair of letters, character, numeral or punctuation mark never had a centre. As a sign, it 'begins by repeating itself'. The centre was never there. To mourn it would be like mourning death. Like death, the centre 'reassures and appeases, but also . . . creates anguish and puts at stake (*en jeu*)?' (374/432). It seems that we thirst for death with the vitality of an indestructible desire. Jabès's lines '*Where is the centre?/ - Under ashes* [Où est le centre?/Sous la cendre]' evoke a less metaphysical kind of mourning, for the dead of the Holocaust (375/432). One would not dig through them to reach some kind of appeasement. The play *centre/cendre* makes the signifier elliptical, stretching it to accommodate death and life together, honouring the inextricability of the two. Writing hesitates between decentring and the affirmation of play. Derrida and Jabès insist on accommodating life and death, negation and affirmation: *seuil*, threshold, rhymes with *deuil*, mourning.

Once we begin to name the unnameable thing we desire, fantasy comes into play. Jabès calls the desired thing a well and in passages of the *Return to the Book* not quoted by Derrida, a hole. The fantasy is specifically masculine and phallic. It relates to what Derrida calls the 'name of man' as what utters 'the force of that which has been raised up' [the French has, more straightforwardly, 'erected', '*érigé*']. What follows plays with that fantasy, enters it and lets contingency change it. Jabès's text alludes to sex: '*this position on your belly. You are crawling. You are boring a hole through the wall at its base. You hope to escape, like a rat...*'. There's a play on the signifier linking *livre*, book; *troupieuvre*, hole-octopus (famous for being able to escape through tiny holes) and *oeuvre*, work. Derrida will later argue that the work of mourning is the model for all work. The book has been somewhat phallic, historically speaking. It has obeyed the logic and the economy of a masculine fantasy. But the octopus thing takes it to the point of monstrosity. It's there in Jabès but in Derrida even more weirdly so, in a passage coming before the quotation that both analyses and participates in its phantasmatic identification of book and phallus. The little suckers on an octopus's tentacles are like lips, leaving little sucker-imprints on our skin. The octopus is a polyp, *polys* many + *pous*, feet, but we also hear the English word 'lip' in the French *polype*. It's as if, rather than describe the book as a fantasy-penis, Jabès and Derrida have asked what does a penis want. In relation to the nameless, it wants to *rampe*, to creep like ivy, like a hole-octopus or a rat. Any one form would be a trap. Jabès describes the octopus (caught, presumably) and become a bizarrely attractive chandelier: '*hung from the ceiling... his tentacles began to sparkle*' (376). Finally the hole is too small for the octopus to hide itself in. Flight is impossible. One cannot inhabit metaphors, constructed out of a wish to escape the condition of desire, which is to desire the unnameable. The dwelling [*demeure*] is metaphor, another detour. The whole book is a doomed attempt to make reality phantasmatically into a sexual possession or refuge. But having cited Jabès, Derrida insists on the *serenity* of the return to the book and on writing as the strange assemblage of hole and book, hopelessness and joy.

Repetition, Repetition, Repetition

The Return to the Book is the third book of the *Book of Questions*. *Writing and Difference* is the third volume Derrida published in 1967. He reflects on the value of the third time as the first opportunity to think repetition. Philosophically, threes are associated with dialectical progression which reconciles difference in a movement from a thesis to its antithesis to a synthesis uniting the two.

Derrida puts forward the third volume of *The Book of Questions* as another kind of completion that works by doubling. There is a technical doubling, say that of an object reflected in a mirror, but Derrida chooses forms of doubling that have a conscious dimension. An eye reflects on itself, a commentary doubles the book that must be, and can't be, written. It becomes possible to *know* what one cannot simply summarize, even if that knowing has to take the form of failure. The book is the place where the impossibility of the book can be announced and where writing bears witness to the failed fantasies of the book. The third volume is where *The Book of Questions* manages to remain open in a complex way, by means of labyrinthine self-reflection, multiple surfaces and walls that prolong the book while keeping it from closing on itself. As we know, the labyrinth allows those who enter it to relate to the centre only by way of detours, delays and numerous possibilities requiring decisions that have to be at least partly guesses. Jabès's strategies are plural. His text pronounces non-closure (Derrida uses the verb *dire*, to say.) The content of this saying affirms openness, but so does its form, for literature 'allows one to *say everything*, in *every way*'.[112] *The Return to the Book* is

> simultaneously infinitely open and infinitely reflecting on itself, '*an eye in an eye*', a commentary infinitely accompanying the '*book of the rejected and called for book*', the book ceaselessly begun and taken up again on a site which is neither in the book nor outside it . . . (376–7)

Jabès's figure of the book as a labyrinth affirms what Derrida calls a 'desperate economy' capable of closing itself by 'thinking its own opening'.[113] The notion of economy suggests a degree of stabilization: the book has become liveable. It's not reassuring or comfortable: one does not set up house in a book, and its opening is not a spatial phenomenon but takes the form of 'reflection without exit' and the experiences of 'referral, return and detour' induced by the labyrinth. Derrida refers to a 'rhythm' that brings time and space into contact with the infinite and the unknown by way of the number three: the centre begins by repeating itself, there is a 'double origin plus its repetition', which makes three (378).

The closing sentence of 'Ellipsis' concerns tomorrow [*demain*] as it relates to the hand [*main*] that writes and the 'now' [*maintenant*] of writing. Reb Derissa comments: 'Tomorrow is the shadow and the reflexibility of our hands.' That reflexibility means there is a 'third party between the hands holding the book', dividing and supplementing the hand that writes the book, which is another hand. Would that be yours?

Study Question
Kafka argued for books that would 'take an axe to the frozen sea within us'. Should books resolve problems?

CHAPTER 4

RECEPTION AND INFLUENCE

In 2004, Derrida spoke of a strange *'double feeling'* about the future of his writing and described a reading not yet begun and at the same time, abandoned:

> to put it playfully and with a certain immodesty, one has not yet begun to read me, . . . even though there are, to be sure, many very good readers (a few dozen in the world perhaps, people who are also writer–thinkers, poets), in the end it is later on this all has a chance of appearing, but also, on the other hand, and thus simultaneously, I have the feeling that two weeks or a month after my death *there will be nothing left*. Nothing except what has been copyrighted and deposited in libraries.[1]

Not yet started and about to be forgotten. Too soon to judge and practically over. What kind of a legacy is that? How can the study of the reception and influence of *Writing and Difference* respond to the radical absence of writer and reader that the book insists on? 'Freud and the Scene of Writing' warns that we would 'search the "public" in vain for the first reader: i.e. the first author of a work' (285). *Writing and Difference* is a profoundly theatrical experience, rocked by movements that Derrida allows to appear but does not control. Each essay uses more than one voice and, the force of his arguments notwithstanding, Derrida has no authoritative voice. Samuel Weber, a writer and thinker profoundly influenced by Derrida, suggests that the notion of 'dying before you were born' is better articulated by 'theatrical staging' than by literary monologue.[2] If deconstruction were, as sometimes Derrida imagined, a 'dead-born individual' then we would see it become:

> a staging area for different tendencies and forces which themselves cannot be unified in any one individual and which

therefore cannot speak properly in their own name. Therefore, any one set of statements will always call for others that displace it. The impossibility of speaking or writing in one's own name is always at the bottom of what I would call the theatrics of writing.[3]

That impossibility of writing in one's own name is constantly in play in *Writing and Difference*. It is not only a matter of the variety of topics and authors treated but of readings that stage forces which 'cannot be unified in any one individual'. As Derrida puts it, the 'subject of writing' is not 'some sovereign solitude of the author' but a 'system of relations between strata'. That gives rise to new readings.

The initial reception of *Writing and Difference* in France and elsewhere associated it closely with *Speech and Phenomena* and *Of Grammatology*. Reviewers were concerned with the philosophical implications of Derrida's work and its effects on metaphysics and on contemporary structuralism. But they also registered that something unprecedented had happened. Along with the attempts to understand and to put into context was a sense of absolute surprise and excitement. Gerard Granel wrote in *Critique*: 'this year for the first time someone has *written on the origin*.'[4] Granel gave a careful exposition of Derrida's notion of writing and its philosophical import but acknowledged that Derrida's texts were to be greeted with 'a certain comprehension' mixed with 'total incomprehension of their meaning [*sens*] and their true place'.[5] The real difficulty Granel found in Derrida's work was not, he said, to do with the energy that it takes to read a 'difficult author' but with something Derrida runs into. Something 'that at once refuses him passage and yet, by that refusal assures him of his foothold, and of his foothold's grip, his path'.[6] This new kind of difficulty he associated less with a 'theoretical matrix' than with 'the force (of penetration, of clarification and finally of disruption)' to which each of Derrida's readings bore witness.[7] The notion of force was also taken up in a review of *Writing and Difference* by François Wahl in the fortnightly *Quinzaine Littéraire*.[8] Wahl picked out the notion of 'deconstruction' and foregrounded what Derrida had to say about French thinkers of the moment (Foucault, Artaud, Levinas and Bataille) over his book's engagement with philosophy from the pre-Socratics to Hegel and Husserl. He saw Derrida less as a patient and disturbing reader than as a thinker of otherness and a bold forcer-open of limits. The year before, *Quinzaine Littéraire* had prefaced Wahl's review of the parts *Of Grammatology* published in *Critique* with a note to its readers. If Wahl wasn't the kind of writer you would read 'on the train', the journal was publishing his review in order to 'break with certain habits of laziness and comfort' in French intellectual life and because it recognized that 'specialists, in a closed circle' were debating notions of wide relevance: literature, language and thought.[9] Wahl did not discuss reading as such but the journal registered the impact of Derrida's books even at one remove, recommending its readers to cut the essay out and come back to it if it rebuffed them at the first try.

Another immediate context was the United States. Derrida, David Carroll recollects, had been a very late addition to the programme of the *Languages of Criticism and the Sciences of Man* conference at Johns Hopkins in 1966, but his paper struck Carroll as '*the event* of the colloquium. Right away I knew that something was happening in his presentation that wasn't happening in any of the other papers'.[10] This conference was where Derrida met Paul de Man, who was also working on Rousseau at the time. They became friends and later, colleagues. De Man's deconstructive research into the rhetorical and ideological aspects of literary and philosophical language is exemplary in its rigour, inventiveness and care for reading. His work and that of his students became powerful enough by the early 1980s to attract the (often hostile and impatient) notice of senior academic figures in US literary studies. Derrida devoted a number of essays to his writings.[11] After the conference, from being France's most promising phenomenologist, Derrida became an international figure. He returned to give seminars at John Hopkins on Mallarmé and Plato in the autumn of 1968. He visited Berlin to give seminars in the same year. Meanwhile in Slovenia, the young philosophy student Slavoj Žižek began reading Derrida in early 1968. 'It was like a magic year when the three books appeared at practically the same time . . . the immediate insight was, "My God, this is the real thing".'[12] A translation of two chapters from *Of Grammatology* appeared in the Slovenian journal *Problemi* in the winter of 1967–1968: very likely the first translation of Derrida into a foreign language.

Derrida travelled worldwide but his most regular and sustained visits were to the United States. At first he gave seminars at Johns Hopkins, New York University and the University of California at Berkeley. There was his direct influence as a colleague and teacher: he was a visiting professor at Yale from 1975 until 1987 when he joined the faculty at the University of California, Irvine. There was a more diffuse influence via a number of journals founded by American academics who read, translated and wrote about Derrida. In 1971, *Diacritics* was started in the department of Romance Studies at Cornell by Jonathan Culler and others and became an important publishing venue for translations of Derrida's essays and related work. Peggy Kamuf, one of Derrida's foremost translators, and a vital intellectual link between US academia and contemporary French thought and writing, took her PhD at Cornell. In 1975, at Johns Hopkins, Samuel Weber, Jeffrey Mehlman and others set up *Glyph*. At the University of California at Berkeley, a reading group worked on Derrida, including Leo Bersani. Bersani's work barely mentions Derrida but his rigorous, original and powerful readings of literary, psychoanalytic and cultural texts have learned a lot from him. (In Britain at that time a group formed at Oxford, including Ann Wordsworth, Geoffrey Bennington, Timothy Clark, Nicholas Royle and Robert Young. They founded the *Oxford Literary Review* in 1977.) Then there was the 'Yale school', which perhaps dominates popular renown because it gave rise to a book.

Deconstruction and Criticism came out in 1979 and contained essays on Shelley's 'Triumph of Life' by five established male scholars: Derrida (whose contribution was more about Blanchot than Shelley), Paul de Man, Hillis Miller, Harold Bloom and Geoffrey Hartman. Among these de Man and Miller remained intellectually closest to Derrida. Barbara Johnson and Shoshana Felman did not contribute to the book but were part of the small collegial group teaching English, French or Comparative Literature at Yale. Johnson was de Man's PhD student. She went on to do a zestful translation of Derrida's *Dissemination*. Her work on literature, politics, race and sexual difference is a fine example of the multiple directions that interaction with Derrida's work has helped academic work to take. She has pointed out that Derrida, unlike the other four 'Yale critics', consistently and explicitly foregrounded the question of gender.[13] Gayatri Chakravorty Spivak, another student of de Man's, missed the Johns Hopkins conference but got hold of a copy of *De la grammatologie* when it came out and set to work on a translation and a remarkable preface. Her subsequent work has combined interests in deconstruction, Marxism and the politics of sexual difference and has helped to establish post-colonial theory. Johnson, Felman and Spivak became powerful academics in the United States and internationally. All are highly sensitive to the political and historical stakes and possibilities of reading. The figure whose work is perhaps closest to Derrida's is also a woman: Hélène Cixous, former Director of the University of Paris VIII, the reader Derrida describes as 'incomparable' from 'a certain point of view, that of writing itself'.[14] He felt that Cixous, best known in France for her literary writing, found 'at a stroke the best access, the most secret, to the workshop and the form, to the meaning and the unconscious body of my writing'. Her work has ceaselessly engaged with his since they met in the early 1960s. A number of students of Derrida's are important thinkers in their own right. Perhaps foremost of these is the philosopher Jean-Luc Nancy, often writing with Philippe Lacoue-Labarthe. Nancy's most recent book, *A plus d'un titre: Jacques Derrida*, is precisely a tribute to the multiplicity of Derrida.

The literary authors treated in *Writing and Difference* were not especially important to the first American and English readers of Derrida. They do not rival say Mallarmé and Blanchot in terms of critical attention in the English-speaking world today. It is possible to be a philosopher working in the field of phenomenology and not engage directly with Derrida's readings of Husserl. There are analysts in France and the United States who read Derrida: René Major has worked on the practical and theoretical connections first sketched in 'Freud and the Scene of Writing', and Alan Bass, the book's translator, has been practising as a psychoanalyst for more than twenty-five years. For him the 'day-to-day practice of psychoanalysis is inevitably deconstructive'.[15] For readers of Levinas, the dialogue with Derrida is crucial: it precipitated a further intensification of Levinas's thought. The two thinkers are still frequently read together, especially by students of ethics.[16] Being read by Derrida was important for Jabès: Rosmarie Waldrop notes how after the essays in *Writing and Difference* the poet emphasized a troubled awareness of the radical illegibility underpinning his books.[17] The exchange between Derrida and Foucault continues to attract critical attention. Foucault objected strongly to 'Cogito and the History of Madness' and riposted with a detailed essay on Derrida's reading of Descartes that called deconstruction a 'historically well-determined little pedagogy'.[18] A second essay, 'Reply to Derrida', reasserts the value of history against philosophy.

The diversity of texts Derrida reads in *Writing and Difference* and the plurality of his writing styles and reading approaches should be read in terms of engagement rather than affiliation. The connections of the book are too many, too nuanced, too concerned with opening up reading and thought, to be reduced to a programme. The conception of *Writing and Difference* owes little to the routines of modern scholarship: the packaging of books as commodities in an academic marketplace, their presentation as polemical interventions in recognized debates or as developments in existing traditions. For all their patient attention to classic texts, for all the times they have been cited, after decades of being read and taught, these essays remain untamed.

NOTES

1. CONTEXT

1. Jacques Derrida, 'Afterword: Toward an Ethic of Discussion', trans. Samuel Weber, in *Limited Inc* (Evanston, IL: Northwestern University Press, 1988) 137.
2. Jacques Derrida, 'Violence and Metaphysics', trans. Alan Bass, in *Writing and Difference* (London: Routledge, 2002) 98. I have worked with Alan Bass's pioneering translation and with *L'écriture et la différence* (Paris: Seuil, 1967). All references to *Writing and Difference* give the page number following the citation. Where I cite the French or slightly modify the translation, I add the page number in the French edition.
3. Derrida, 'Afterword', *Limited Inc*, 137.
4. Jacques Derrida and Maurizio Ferraris, *A Taste for the Secret*, trans. Giacomo Donis (Cambridge: Polity, 2002) 29.
5. Derrida, 'Afterword', *Limited Inc*, 137.
6. Ibid., 136.
7. Geoffrey Bennington, 'Derridabase', in Geoffrey Bennington and Jacques Derrida, *Jacques Derrida* (Chicago: University of Chicago Press, 1993) 118.
8. Jacques Derrida, '"This Strange Institution Called Literature": An Interview with Jacques Derrida', trans. Geoffrey Bennington and Rachel Bowlby, in *Acts of Literature*, ed. Derek Attridge (London: Routledge, 1992) 34.
9. The myth revives in Hélène Cixous' 'Jacques Derrida as a Proteus Unbound', trans. Peggy Kamuf, *Critical Inquiry*, 33 (Winter 2007) 389–423.
10. Jacques Derrida, 'Les voix d'Artaud (la force, la forme, la forge)', interview with Evelyn Grossman, *Magazine littéraire*, 434, *Antonin Artaud* (September 2004) 35.
11. Jacques Derrida, 'Dialanguages', trans. Peggy Kamuf, in *Points . . . Interviews, 1974–1994*, ed. Elisabeth Weber (Stanford: Stanford University Press, 1995) 143–4.
12. Edmond Jabès, 'The Moment After', trans. Rosmarie Waldrop, in *The Book of Margins* (Chicago: University of Chicago Press, 1993) 46.
13. Derrida, 'This Strange Institution Called Literature', *Acts of Literature*, 34.
14. Jacques Derrida, 'Philosophie et littérature: Entretien avec Jacques Derrida', *Moscou aller-retour* (Paris: Editions de l'Aube, 1995) 147.
15. Jacques Derrida, 'Discussion' following 'Structure, Sign and Play in the Discourse of the Human Sciences', trans. Richard Macksey,

NOTES

in *The Structuralist Controversy: The Languages of Criticism and the Sciences of Man*, ed. Richard Macksey and Eugenio Donato (Baltimore, MD: Johns Hopkins University Press, 1970) 267.
16 Jacques Derrida, *The Post Card*, trans. Alan Bass (Chicago: University of Chicago Press, 1987) 4.
17 Jacques Derrida, 'The Spatial Arts: An Interview with Jacques Derrida', trans. David Wills, in *Deconstruction and the Visual Arts: Art, Media, Architecture*, ed. Peter Brunette and David Wills (Cambridge: Cambridge University Press, 1993) 21.
18 Derrida, 'Discussion', *Structuralist Controversy*, 266–7.
19 Jacques Derrida, 'Signature Event Context', trans. Alan Bass, in *Margins of Philosophy* (Brighton: Harvester Press, 1982) 320.
20 Hélène Cixous, 'Letter to Zohra Drif', trans. Eric Prenowitz, *College Literature*, 30.1 (2003) 85.
21 Jacques Derrida, *Monolingualism of the Other*, trans. Patrick Mensah (Stanford: Stanford University Press, 1998) 44.
22 Derrida, *The Post Card*, 87–8. See also 'Curriculum Vitae', Bennington and Derrida, *Jacques Derrida*, 326–7.
23 Derrida and Ferraris, *A Taste for the Secret*, 27.
24 Derrida, 'This Strange Institution Called Literature', *Acts of Literature*, 35.
25 Ibid., 35–6.
26 Derrida, *Monolingualism of the Other*, 45.
27 Derrida and Ferraris, *A Taste for the Secret*, 45.
28 Derrida, *Monolingualism of the Other*, 47.
29 Ibid., 57.
30 Jacques Derrida, 'The Time of a Thesis: Punctuations', trans. Kathleen McLaughlin in *Philosophy in France Today*, ed. Alan Montefiore (Cambridge: Cambridge University Press, 1983) 40.
31 On Immanuel Kant, see 'Economimesis' (1975), *Truth in Painting* (1978) and 'Of an Apocalyptic Tone Recently Adopted in Philosophy' (1981). On G. W. F. Hegel, see 'The Pit and the Pyramid: An Introduction to Hegel's Semiology' (1971) and the left-hand column of *Glas*.

2. OVERVIEW OF THEMES

1 Stéphane Mallarmé, *Collected Poems and Other Verse*, trans. E. H. and A. M. Blackmore (Oxford: Oxford University Press 2006) 262.
2 Jacques Derrrida, *Of Grammatology*, trans. Gayatri Chakravorty Spivak (Baltimore, MD: Johns Hopkins University Press, 1976) 93.
3 Ibid., 110.
4 Ibid., 112.
5 Geoffrey Bennington, 'Derridabase', in Geoffrey Bennington and Jacques Derrida, *Jacques Derrida* (Chicago: University of Chicago Press, 1993) 202.
6 Jacques Derrida, '*Confessions* and "Circumfession"', *Augustine and Postmodernism: Confessions and Circumfession*, ed. John Caputo

NOTES

and Michael Scanlon (Bloomington: Indiana University Press, 2005) 32.
7 See Maurice Blanchot, 'The Book To Come' [1959], *The Book to Come*, trans. Charlotte Mandell (Stanford: Stanford University Press, 2002) 224–44.
8 Jacques Derrida, *Dissemination*, trans. Barbara Johnson (Chicago: University of Chicago Press, 1981) 5.
9 Derrida, *Of Grammatology*, 159.
10 Samuel Weber, *Return to Freud: Jacques Lacan's Dislocations of Psychoanalysis*, (Cambridge: Cambridge University Press, 1991) 27.
11 See Rosmarie Waldrop, *Lavish Absence: Recalling and Rereading Edmond Jabès*, (Middletown, CT: Wesleyan University Press, 2002) 24.
12 Jacques Derrida, 'Semiology and Grammatology: Interview with Julia Kristeva', trans. Alan Bass, in *Positions*, 2nd English edn (London: Continuum, 2004) 19.
13 Derrida, *Of Grammatology*, 93.

3. READING THE TEXT

1 Hélène Cixous, *Portrait of Jacques Derrida as a Young Jewish Saint*, trans. Beverley Bie Brahic (New York: Columbia University Press, 2004) 9; orig. pub. as *Portrait de Jacques Derrida en Jeune Saint Juif* (Paris: Galilée, 2001) 18.
2 Jacques Derrida, *Of Grammatology*, trans. Gayatri Chakravorty Spivak (Baltimore, MD: Johns Hopkins University Press, 1976) 159.
3 Jacques Derrida, *Monolingualism of the Other*, trans. Patrick Mensah (Stanford: Stanford University Press, 1998)57.
4 The translation sometimes varies. See 'Violence and Metaphysics', 'dislodge', 101, 'making ...tremble', 109, 'tremor', 167; 'The Theatre of Cruelty', 'overturns and disturbs', 304.
5 Hélène Cixous, 'Le bouc lié', *Rue Descartes*, 48, *Salut à Jacques Derrida* (April 2005) 26, trans. Eric Prenowitz.
6 Jacques Derrida, 'Signature Event Context', trans. Alan Bass, in *Margins of Philosophy* (Brighton: Harvester Press, 1982) 316.
7 Jacques Derrida, 'Circumfessions', trans. Geoffrey Bennington, in Geoffrey Bennington and Jacques Derrida, *Jacques Derrida* (Chicago: University of Chicago Press, 1993) 266–7.
8 Jacques Derrida, 'Positions: Interview with Jean-Louis Houdebine and Guy Scarpetta', trans. Alan Bass, in *Positions*, 2nd English edn (London: Continuum, 2004) 76.
9 Samuel Beckett, *Proust and Three Dialogues with Georges Duthuit* (London: Calder, 1969) 8.
10 See Hélène Cixous, 'The Book as One of Its Own Characters', trans. Catherine Porter, *Critical Inquiry*, 33.3 (2002) 427.
11 Søren Kierkegaard, *Philosophical Fragments: Johannes Climacus*, trans. Howard V. Hong and Edna H. Hong (Princeton: Princeton

University Press, 1985) 52. The Princeton translation gives 'the moment of decision is *foolishness*'.
12 Kierkegaard, *Philosophical Fragments*, 1.
13 Jacques Derrida, 'The Villanova Roundtable: A Conversation with Jacques Derrida', *Deconstruction in a Nutshell: A Conversation with Jacques Derrida*, ed. John D. Caputo (New York: Fordham University Press, 1997) 25.
14 G. W. F. Hegel, *Phenomenology of Spirit*, trans. A. V. Miller (Oxford: Oxford University Press, 1977) 126.
15 *Derrida*, directors Amy Ziering Kofman and Kirby Dick, perf. Jacques Derrida, Marguerite Derrida, et al. (2002) DVD, Zeitgeist Video, 2004.
16 Jacques Derrida, 'A "Madness" Must Watch Over Thinking', trans. Peggy Kamuf, in *Points . . . Interviews, 1974–1994*, ed. Elisabeth Weber (Stanford: Stanford University Press, 1995) 363 and 'Une "folie" doit veillée sur la pensée', *Points de suspension: Entretiens*, ed. Elisabeth Weber (Paris: Galilée, 1992) 374.
17 Michel Foucault, 'My Body, This Paper, This Fire. Appendix of 1972 edition', *History of Madness*, trans. Jean Khalfa and Jonathan Murphy (London: Routledge, 2006) 550–74 and 'Reply to Derrida: "Michel Foucault: "Derrida e no kaino,"' *Paideia* (Tokyo) February 1972"', *History of Madness*, 575–90.
18 Geoffrey Bennington, 'Cogito Incognito: Foucault's "My Body, This Paper, This Fire"', *Oxford Literary Review*, 4.1 (1979) 6.
19 Edmund Husserl, *Cartesian Meditations: An Introduction to Phenomenology*, trans. Dorion Cairns (Dordrecht: Kluwer Academic Publishers, 1999) 2.
20 Derrida, *Of Grammatology*, 158.
21 Blaise Pascal, *Pensées*, trans. J. Warrington (London: J. M. Dent, 1940) 110.
22 Derrida, 'A "Madness" Must Watch Over Thinking', *Points . . . Interviews*, 363.
23 Derrida, *Of Grammatology*, 159.
24 Ibid., 158.
25 Hélène Cixous, 'Writing Blind,' trans. Eric Prenowitz, *Stigmata: Escaping Texts* (London: Routledge, 1998) 150.
26 Jacques Derrida and Maurizio Ferraris, *A Taste for the Secret*, trans. Giacomo Donis (Cambridge: Polity, 2002) 29.
27 Ibid., 29–30.
28 Derrida, *Of Grammatology*, 18.
29 See 'The Villanova Roundtable', *Deconstruction in a Nutshell*, 9–10.
30 Rosmarie Waldrop, *Lavish Absence: Recalling and Rereading Edmond Jabès* (Middletown, CT: Wesleyan University Press, 2002) 13.
31 Edmond Jabès, epigraph to *Le seuil et le sable: poésies complètes 1943–1988* (Paris: Gallimard, 1990).
32 Steven Jaron, *Edmond Jabès: The Hazard of Exile* (Oxford: Legenda/ EHRC, 2003) 7–8.

NOTES

33 Edmond Jabès and Philippe Boyer, 'Interview with Edmond Jabès', in *The Book, Spiritual Instrument*, ed. Jerome Rothenberg and David Guss (New York: Granary Books, 1996) 129.
34 Derrida emphasized the need for a carefully differentiated political sensibility on nationalism, racism and anti-semitism, speaking against the 'anti-Jewish confusions of those who cannot see any dividing line between criticising the Israeli State and anti-Israelism, anti-Zionism, anti-Semitism, and revisionism, etc. There are at least five possibilities here, and they must be kept absolutely distinct'. 'The Deconstruction of Actuality: An Interview with Jacques Derrida', trans. Jonathan Rée, *Radical Philosophy*, 68 (Autumn 1994) 33.
35 Edmond Jabès, 'The Moment After', trans. Rosmarie Waldrop, in *The Book of Margins* (Chicago: University of Chicago Press, 1993) 39.
36 A sentence is missing from the translation 86/107.
37 Jacques Derrida, 'White Mythology: Metaphor in the Text of Philosophy', trans. Alan Bass, in *Margins of Philosophy* (Brighton: Harvester Press, 1982) 270.
38 Jacques Derrida, *The Animal That I Therefore Am*, trans. David Wills (New York: Fordham University Press, 2008). For an account of the animals that he is, see Hélène Cixous, 'Jacques Derrida as a Proteus Unbound', trans. Peggy Kamuf, *Critical Inquiry*, 33 (Winter 2007) 389–423.
39 Translation repeats the last ten words.
40 Hélène Cixous, *Insister of Jacques Derrida*, trans. Peggy Kamuf (Stanford: Stanford University Press, 2007) 26–7.
41 Husserl, *Cartesian Meditations*, 92.
42 Ibid., 109.
43 Jacques Derrida, *Learning to Live Finally: An Interview with Jean Birnbaum*, trans. Pascale-Anne Brault and Michael Naas (Hoboken, NJ: Melville, 2007) 27–8.
44 Ibid., 28–9.
45 Jacques Derrida, 'Implications', trans. Alan Bass, *Positions*, 2nd English edn (London: Continuum, 2004) 4.
46 Husserl, *Cartesian Meditations*, 20.
47 Timothy Clark, *Martin Heidegger* (London: Routledge, 2002) 11.
48 See Plato, *Phaedo*, trans. David Gallop (Oxford: Clarendon Press, 1975).
49 Derrida, 'The Villanova Roundtable', *Deconstruction in a Nutshell*, 6.
50 G. W. F. Hegel, *Lectures on the History of Philosophy*, trans. E. S. Haldane (London: Routledge 1963) vol. 1, 254.
51 Husserl, *Cartesian Meditations*, 109.
52 Jacques Derrida, *Speech and Phenomena and Other Essays on Husserl's Theory of Signs*, trans. David Allison (Evanston, IL: Northwestern University Press, 1973) 79.
53 Jacques Derrida, *The Problem of Genesis in Husserl's Philosophy*, trans. Marian Hobson (Chicago: University of Chicago Press, 2003) xix.

NOTES

54 Jacques Derrida, *Edmund Husserl's Origin of Geometry: An Introduction*, trans. John P. Leavey (Lincoln: University of Nebraska, 1989) 88.
55 Derrida, *Speech and Phenomena*, 82.
56 Derrida, '*Différance*', *Margins of Philosophy*, 159.
57 Edmund Husserl, *The Crisis of European Sciences and Transcendental Phenomenology: An Introduction to Phenomenological Philosophy*, trans. David Carr (Evanston, IL: Northwestern University Press, 1970) 360–1.
58 Jacques Derrida, 'Les voix d'Artaud (la force, la forme, la forge)', interview with Evelyn Grossman, *Magazine littéraire*, 434, *Antonin Artaud* (September 2004) 35.
59 Ibid., 34–5.
60 Paule Thévenin, 'The Search for a Lost World', Jacques Derrida and Paule Thévenin, *The Secret Art of Antonin Artaud*, trans. Mary Ann Caws (Cambridge, MA: MIT Press, 1998) 44.
61 Ibid., 56n.116.
62 Derrida, *Speech and Phenomena*, 6.
63 Ibid., 10.
64 Ibid., 11.
65 Ibid., 12.
66 Derrida, 'Les voix d'Artaud', 36.
67 Hélène Cixous, '**Castration or Decapitation?**', trans. Annette Kuhn, *Signs*, 7.1 (Autumn 1981) 50.
68 Ibid., 53.
69 See Sarah Wood, 'Let's Start Again', *Diacritics*, 29.1 (1991) 4–19; Sean Gaston, *Starting With Derrida* (London and New York: Continuum 2007).
70 Jacques Derrida and Elisabeth Roudinesco, *For What Tomorrow . . . A Dialogue*, trans. Jeff Fort (Stanford: Stanford University Press, 2004) 170.
71 Ibid., 176.
72 Ibid., 172.
73 Derrida, *Of Grammatology*, 69.
74 Ibid., 47.
75 Sigmund Freud, 'An Outline of Psychoanalysis', *The Standard Edition of the Complete Psychological Works*, XXIII, trans. James Strachey (London: Hogarth Press and the Institute of Psychoanalysis, 1937–1939) 144.
76 Ibid., 144.
77 Jacques Derrida, '"This Strange Institution Called Literature": An Interview with Jacques Derrida', trans. Geoffrey Bennington and Rachel Bowlby, in *Acts of Literature*, ed. Derek Attridge (London: Routledge, 1992) 56.
78 Hélène Cixous, *Dream I Tell You*, trans. Beverley Bie Brahic (Edinburgh: Edinburgh University Press, 2006) 3.
79 Jean Laplanche and J. B. Pontalis, *The Language of Psychoanalysis*, trans. Donald Nicholson-Smith (London: Hogarth Press, 1983) 4.
80 Ibid., 111.

NOTES

81 Derrida, *Of Grammatology*, 68.
82 Friedrich Nietzsche, *Twilight of the Idols*, trans. Duncan Large (Oxford: Oxford University Press, 1998) 42.
83 Nietzsche, *Twilight of the Idols*, 41.
84 See for example 'The Villanova Roundtable', *Deconstruction in a Nutshell*, 5–6.
85 Derrida, *Of Grammatology*, 162.
86 Ibid., 50.
87 Derrida, 'Circumfessions', *Jacques Derrida*, 119.
88 Cixous, *Portrait of Jacques Derrida*, 53.
89 Nietzsche, *Twilight of the Idols*, 80.
90 Derrida, *Of Grammatology*, 68.
91 Jacques Derrida, *Dissemination*, trans. Barbara Johnson (Chicago: University of Chicago Press, 1981) 3.
92 Ibid., 4.
93 G. W. F. Hegel, *The Encylopaedia Logic*, trans. T. F. Geraets, W. A. Suchting and H. S. Harris (Cambridge: Hackett, 1991) 35.
94 Stuart Barnett, 'Introduction', in *Hegel After Derrida*, ed. Stuart Barnett (London: Routledge, 1998) 3.
95 G. W. F. Hegel, *Elements of the Philosophy of Right*, trans. H. B. Nisbet, ed. Allen Wood (Cambridge: Cambridge University Press, 1991) 23.
96 Hélène Cixous, 'Sorties: Out and Out: Attacks/Ways Out/Forays', in Hélène Cixous and Cathérine Clément, *The Newly-Born Woman*, trans. Betsy Wing (London: I. B. Tauris, 1996) 78.
97 Ibid., 79.
98 Ibid., 80.
99 Thomas Hobbes, *Leviathan*, ed. Richard Tuck (Cambridge: Cambridge University Press, 1991) 43.
100 Michel Foucault, *The Order of Things: An Archaeology of the Human Sciences* (London: Routledge, 2002) xxiii.
101 Michel Foucault, 'The Confession of the Flesh', trans. Colin Gordon, in *Power/Knowledge: Selected Interviews, and Other Writings 1972–1977*, ed. Colin Gordon (London: Longman, 1980) 197.
102 Johann Gottfried von Herder, *Reflections on the Philosophy of the History of Mankind*, trans. T. O. Churchill (Chicago: University of Chicago Press, 1968) 49.
103 *Eidos* means 'form'; *archē*, 'origin'; *telos*, 'end'; *energeia*, 'activity'; *ousia*, 'being'; *alētheia*, 'truth.'
104 Derrida, *Of Grammatology*, 162.
105 Cixous, *Portrait of Jacques Derrida*, 59.
106 Ferdinand de Saussure, *Course in General Linguistics*, trans. Wade Baskin (London: Peter Owen, 1974) 117.
107 Derrida, '*Istrice 2: Ick bünn all hier*', *Points . . . Interviews*, 304.
108 If a conical surface is cut with a plane which does not intersect the cone's base, the intersection of the cone and plane is called an ellipse.

NOTES

109 Hélène Cixous, *Readings: The Poetics of Blanchot, Joyce, Kafka, Kleist, Lispector, and Tsvetayeva*, trans. Verena Andermatt Conley (Minneapolis: University of Minnesota Press, 1991) 92.
110 Jacques Derrida, *Signéponge/Signsponge*, trans. Richard Rand (New York: Columbia University Press, 1984) 34.
111 Jabès, 'The Moment After', *The Book of Margins*, 46.
112 Derrida, 'This Strange Institution Called Literature', *Acts of Literature*, 36.
113 A sentence is missing from the translation 377/434.

4. RECEPTION AND INFLUENCE

1 Jacques Derrida, *Learning to Live Finally: An Interview with Jean Birnbaum*, trans. Pascale-Anne Brault and Michael Naas (Hoboken, NJ: Melville, 2007) 34.
2 Samuel Weber with Terry Smith, 'Repetition: Kierkegaard, Artaud, Pollock and the Theatre of the Image' (16 September 1996) Power Institute of Fine Arts, University of Sydney, available at www.stanford.edu/dept/HPS/WritingScience/etexts/Weber/Repetition.html, accessed 10 August 2008.
3 Ibid.
4 Gérard Granel, 'Jacques Derrida et la rature de l'origine', *Critique*, 22 (November 1967) 887.
5 Ibid., 889.
6 Ibid., 896.
7 Ibid., 897.
8 François Wahl, 'Forcer les limites', *La quinzaine littéraire*, 32 (15 July 1967) 14.
9 François Wahl, 'L'écriture avant la parole?', *La quinzaine littéraire*, 4 (1 May 1966) 14.
10 David Carroll, 'Jacques Derrida or the Gift of Writing – When Something Happens', *SubStance*, 106, 34.1 *Jacques Derrida: A Counter-Obituary* (2005) 61.
11 For example, *Memoires for Paul de Man*, trans. Cecile Lindsay, Jonathan Culler and Eduardo Cadava (New York: Columbia University Press, 1986); 'Like the Sound of the Sea Deep Within a Shell: Paul De Man's War', in *Responses: On Paul de Man's Wartime Journalism,* ed. Werner Hamacher, Neil Hertz and Thomas Keenan (Lincoln: University of Nebraska Press, 1989) 127–164; 'Psyche: Inventions of the Other', trans. Catherine Porter, in *Reading de Man Reading, ed.* Lindsay Waters and Wlad Godzich (Minneapolis: University of Minnesota Press, 1989) 25–65 and 'Typewriter Ribbon: Limited Ink (2)', *Without Alibi*, trans. Peggy Kamuf (Stanford: Stanford University Press, 2002) 71–160.
12 Slavoj Žižek and Glyn Daly, *Conversations with Žižek* (Cambridge: Polity Press, 2004) 29.

NOTES

13 See Barbara Johnson, 'Gender Theory and the Yale School', *A World of Difference* (Baltimore: Johns Hopkins University Press, 1987) 32–41.
14 Jacques Derrida, 'Du mot à la vie: un dialogue entre Jacques Derrida et Hélène Cixous', *Magazine littéraire*, 430 (April 2004) 24.
15 Alan Bass, *Difference and Disavowal: The Trauma of Eros* (Stanford: Stanford University Press, 2000) viii.
16 For example in John Llewellyn, *Appositions of Jacques Derrida and Emmanuel Levinas* (Bloomington: Indiana University Press, 2002).
17 Rosmarie Waldrop, Lavish Absence: Recalling and Rereading Edmond Jabès (Middletown, CT: Wesleyan University Press, 2002) 82.
18 Michel Foucault, 'My Body, This Paper, This Fire. Appendix of 1972 edition', *History of Madness*, trans. Jean Khalfa and Jonathan Murphy (London: Routledge, 2006) 573.

FURTHER READING

SECONDARY MATERIAL

Selected Works by Derrida Related to *Writing and Difference*

'*Différance*' [1968], in *Margins of Philosophy*, trans. Alan Bass (Brighton: Harvester Press, 1982) 1–27.

'Discussion' following 'Structure, Sign and Play in the Discourse of the Human Sciences' [1966], trans. Richard Macksey, in *The Structuralist Controversy: the Languages of Criticism and the Sciences of Man*, ed. Richard Macksey and Eugenio Donato (Baltimore, MD: Johns Hopkins University Press, 1970) 265–72.

Edmund Husserl's Origin of Geometry: An Introduction [1962], trans. John P. Leavey (Lincoln: University of Nebraska, 1989).

'Implications: Interview with Henri Ronse' [1967], in *Positions*, trans. Alan Bass, 2nd English edn (London: Continuum, 2004) 1–14.

Of Grammatology [1967], trans. Gayatri Chakravorty Spivak (Baltimore, MD: Johns Hopkins University Press, 1976).

'Positions: Interview with Jean-Louis Houdebine and Guy Scarpetta' [1971], in *Positions* 35–78.

The Problem of Genesis in Husserl's Philosophy [1990], trans. Marian Hobson (Chicago: University of Chicago Press, 2003).

'Semiology and Grammatology: Interview with Julia Kristeva [1968], in *Positions*, 15–33.

'Signature Event Context' [1971], in *Margins of Philosophy*, 307–30.

Speech and Phenomena and Other Essays on Husserl's Theory of Signs [1967], trans. David B. Allison (Evanston, IL: Northwestern University Press, 1973).

'Les voix d'Artaud (la force, la forme, la forge)', interview with Evelyn Grossman, *Magazine littéraire*, 434, *Antonin Artaud* (September 2004) 34–6.

Selected Secondary Material

This guide emphasizes that it isn't just what one reads but how one reads it that matters. I have not included works already cited by Derrida in *Writing and Difference*. Derrida tends to put *writing* ahead of philosophy and literature, and I have recommended books and essays on Derrida that, one way or another, do the same.

FURTHER READING

Secondary Material Relating to **Writing and Difference**

Attridge, Derek, Geoffrey Bennington and Robert Young (eds), *Post-Structuralism and the Question of History* (Cambridge: Cambridge University Press, 1989). An invaluable treatment of the subject.

Bennington, Geoffrey, 'Cogito Incognito: Foucault's "My Body, This Paper, This Fire,"' *Oxford Literary Review*, 4.1 (1979) 5–8. The argument and the stakes are put clearly and succinctly.

Cixous, Hélène, 'What is it o'clock or The door (we never enter)', in *Stigmata: Escaping Texts* (London: Routledge, 1998) 57–83. She can *see* and *feel* Derrida's writing; this essay starts off from 'Force and Signification'.

Foucault, Michel, 'My Body, This Paper, This Fire', and 'Reply to Derrida' [1972] in *History of Madness*, trans. Jean Khalfa and Jonathan Murphy (London: Routledge, 2006) 550–74 and 575–90. An angry, detailed response to 'Cogito and the History of Madness' and a more temperate reply that accuses Derrida of lacking historical sense and aligns his work with philosophy.

Granel, Gérard, 'Jacques Derrida et la rature de l'origine', *Critique*, 22 (November 1967) 887–905. A thoughtful, enthusiastic review of *Speech and Phenomena*, *Of Grammatology* and *Writing and Difference*.

Jabès, Edmond, 'The Moment After', in *The Book of Margins*, trans. Rosmarie Waldrop (Chicago: University of Chicago Press, 1993) 33–48. An insightful poetic meditation on Derrida and writing.

Wahl, François, 'L'écriture avant la parole?', *La quinzaine littéraire*, 4 (1 May 1966) 18–20. Perhaps the first attempt to explain Derrida to non-specialists.

— 'Forcer les limites', *La quinzaine littéraire*, 32 (15 July 1967) 14–15. A detailed early review.

General Introductory Works and Readers

Bennington, Geoffrey, 'Derridabase', in Geoffrey Bennington and Jacques Derrida, *Jacques Derrida* (Chicago: University of Chicago Press, 1993). Lucid and trustworthy.

Cixous, Hélène, 'Jacques Derrida as a Proteus Unbound', trans. Peggy Kamuf, in *Critical Inquiry*, 33 (Winter 2007) 389–423. Perhaps Derrida's best reader, beautifully attuned to his writing.

Kamuf, Peggy, *A Derrida Reader: Between the Blinds* (New York: Columbia University Press, 1991). First among Derrida's anthologies for the range and selection of pieces and for the concise, unerring introductory remarks to each of them.

McQuillan, Martin, *Deconstruction: A Reader* (Edinburgh: Edinburgh University Press, 2000). Goes before and beyond Derrida and includes some excellent recent commentators as well as the work of his contemporaries and those who influenced him.

Royle, Nicholas, *Jacques Derrida* (London: Routledge, 2002). A bold, engaging and committed introduction.

FURTHER READING

Introductory Works by Thinkers Important to Writing and Difference

Freud, Sigmund, 'An Outline of Psychoanalysis' (1938), in *The Standard Edition of the Complete Psychological Works*, XXIII, trans. James Strachey, Anna Freud, Alix Strachey and Alan Tyson (London: Hogarth Press and the Institute of Psychoanalysis, 1937–1939) 139–207. Gives all the major concepts straight from the horse's mouth.

Hegel, G. W. F., *The Encylopaedia Logic*, trans. T. F. Geraets, W. A. Suchting and H. S. Harris (Cambridge: Hackett, 1991). A good place to start to read Hegel.

Husserl, Edmund, *Cartesian Meditations: An Introduction to Phenomenology*, trans. Dorion Cairns (Dordrecht: Kluwer Academic Publishers, 1999). Invaluable in getting a sense of what is at stake in Husserl's phenomenology.

INDEX

absence 24, 42, 136–7
  of addressee 35, 49, 164
  of God 19, 76
  and language 37, 150
  and writing 68, 94, 114
affirmation 73, 92, 121, 136, 137, 160
  and necessity 117–20, 124
  of play of the world 67, 121
Algeria 8, 9, 10, 11
Althusser, Louis (Marxist thinker) 10, 11
animality 16, 69–70
anthropology 4, 23, 114
  see also Lévi-Strauss
anti-semitism 9
anxiety 27, 33–5, 40, 143, 148, 152, 158–9
  of language 35, 36, 44
  about life as play 144, 145, 152
  see also shaking; solicitation; trembling
L'Arc (journal) 13
Aristotle (philosopher) 6, 11, 19, 69
Artaud, Antonin (writer) 2, 5, 14, 38–9, 94–105, 116–27, 153
  and Freud 108, 111–12, 125–6
  and metaphysics 19, 21
Aufhebung (concept) 135, 140
Austin, J. L. (philosopher) 11
author 111–12, 164–5
  and intention 5, 28–9, 53, 124
  and reading 11, 100–2, 157, 159
author-god 97, 104, 111, 121, 122, 123, 124, 126
authority 48, 50, 51, 64, 131
autobiography 3, 14, 119

Barnett, Stuart (critic and theorist) 127
Bass, Alan (translator of *Writing and Difference*, psychoanalyst) 168
Bataille, Georges (writer) 1, 2, 5, 22, 127–41, 150, 165
Being 79, 84–5, 86, 156
  and being 38, 75
Bennington, Geoffrey (critic and theorist) 3, 14, 18, 49, 167
Bersani, Leo (critic and theorist) 167
Blanchot, Maurice (writer) 2, 14, 15, 19, 39, 167
  on Artaud 96, 99, 101
Bloom, Harold (critic and theorist) 167
body 3, 5, 19, 83, 88
  and Artaud, 95, 100, 102, 111
  as text 104, 126
  of words 110–11, 109, 125, 168
  and writing, 27, 40, 115, 124–5
book 1, 14, 43, 44–5, 58, 59–71, 153–63
  and *logos* 52, 89
  and poetic freedom 19–20, 39
  Writing and Difference not one 2, 4, 13
Bounoure, Gabriel (reader of Jabès) 154
breath 12, 40, 94, 95–6, 100, 104

INDEX

Carroll, David (critic and theorist) 166
Celan, Paul (poet) 14
centre 7–8, 143–6, 148, 149–51, 160, 162–3
Cixous, Hélène (writer) 9, 15, 43, 58, 103, 110, 129–30, 137, 158
 Derrida on 159, 168
 on Derrida 27, 30, 69, 72, 119, 149, 155
closure 13, 17, 20–2, 116–24, 154, 155–6, 157–8, 159
'Cogito and the History of Madness' 1, 19, 20, 24, 46–59, 67, 141, 142, 143, 169
commentary 5, 11, 23–4, 52–3, 72, 101–2, 104, 116, 136–7, 154, 162
 and the book 71, 162
 and literality 12, 69
Corneille, Pierre (playwright) 1, 28
Critique (journal) 1, 165, 166
cruelty 120–1, 123, 124
 theatre of 116–27
Culler, Jonathan (critic and theorist) 167
culture 5, 90, 96, 101, 103, 109, 129
 versus nature 147–8, 152
 and structuralism 36, 37

dance, writing as 27, 29, 116–17, 118
de Man, Paul (critic and theorist) 166, 167, 168
death 69, 76, 91, 93, 160
 and laughter 133, 134, 138
 and life 22, 110, 115, 118, 119, 126, 151, 155
 and mastery 129, 132, 135
 and meaning 17, 135
 and writing 35, 49, 68
 decision 25, 40, 47, 52, 55, 56, 162
 and *logos* 77, 99
deferred action 154
 see also Nachträglichkeit
Derrida, Jacques
 life 3–4, 9–12, 119–20
 reception and influence 164–9
 relation to words and language 10, 12, 28, 36
 works
 Archive Fever 13
 'Circumfessions' 3, 14, 36, 119
 'Cogito and the History of Madness' 1, 19, 20, 24, 46–59, 67, 141, 142, 143, 169
 'Différance' 23, 25, 92
 Dissemination 13, 22, 123, 176
 'Edmond Jabès and the Question of the Book' 19, 24, 39, 59–71, 145, 154, 156
 'Ellipsis' 20, 153–63
 'Force and Signification' 1, 8, 9, 24, 19, 27–46, 67, 116–17, 121, 155, 159
 'Force of Law,' 14
 'Freud and the Scene of Writing' 2, 13, 17, 19, 21, 25, 48, 105–16, 117, 119, 120, 122, 148, 154, 157, 164, 168
 'From a Restricted to a General Economy' 2, 22–3, 25, 127–41
 '"Genesis and Structure" and Phenomenology' 1, 6, 21, 87–91, 101
 Glas 3, 11, 31

INDEX

'Introduction to the *Origin of Geometry*' 91
La parole soufflée 2, 19, 21, 94–105
Learning to Live Finally 15
'Living On / Border Lines' 11
Monolingualism of the Other 28
Paper Machine 14
Politics of Friendship 15
The Post Card 3, 11, 13, 104, 116
The Problem of Genesis in Husserl's Philosophy 88–9
Specters of Marx 15, 138
Speech and Phenomena 2, 11, 13, 23, 60, 74, 91–2, 97–9, 165
'Structure, Sign and Play in the Discourse of the Human Sciences' 2, 7, 11, 19, 20, 22, 66, 67, 118, 120–1, 134, 141–53, 154, 156
'The Theatre of Cruelty and the Closure of Representation' 2, 21, 116–27
'Violence and Metaphysics: an Essay on the Thought of Emmanuel Levinas' 19, 20, 23, 25, 69, 72–87, 158
Voiles 15
Descartes, René (philosopher) 5, 12, 24, 49–54, 57–8, 59, 67, 86, 169
desire 27–8, 45, 128–9, 158, 160–1
and anxiety 143, 152, 158
for centre 140, 143–5, 160
for presence 73, 97
for sense 140, 152
dialectic 12, 23, 55, 128, 161–2
Hegelian 127, 129, 131–5, 140

différance 3, 13, 18, 22, 25, 84, 91–2, 105, 120–1, 143
cannot be historicized 55, 90
as life 71, 109–10
difference 16–17, 21, 22, 45, 55, 137–8, 139–40
and Artaud 21, 98–9
and being 70, 86
and language 30, 48, 68
and reason 89–90, 132
and Saussurean linguistics 23–4, 145, 151
and writing 28, 34, 43, 60
see also 'sexual difference'
drama 57, 108, 114–15, 130–1
see also theatre
dream 17, 27, 33, 44–5, 58, 87, 128–9, 155
and Freud 107, 113, 115, 128
of origin without play 67, 153
as theatre 110–11, 126

ébranlement see shaking
economy 2, 22–3, 44, 53, 58, 59, 83–4, 110, 127–41, 162
masculine 103, 129, 161
'Edmond Jabès and the Question of the Book' 19, 24, 39, 59–71, 145, 154, 156
Einstein, Albert (physicist) 7
'Ellipsis' 20, 153–63
empiricism 18, 86–7, 117
epistēmē (concept) 141, 142–4, 145–7
ethnography *see* anthropology
event 6, 56, 70, 79, 91–2, 141–3, 145–7
experience 2, 13, 16, 21, 27, 29, 46, 52, 54, 75, 97–9, 123, 135, 137
according to Bataille 130
according to Husserl 90–1
and Freud 105, 110, 113

INDEX

experience (*Cont'd*)
  of reading Derrida 5–6, 31,
    43, 164
  of someone else 73, 77, 82–4,
    86–7

Felman, Shoshana (critic and
    theorist) 167
femininity 153
  and reason 128, 129
  and writing 105
Flaubert, Gustave (writer) 14,
    28, 33, 39, 45
force 5, 8, 17–18, 27–46, 67, 143,
    164–5
  and Artaud 102, 116, 121,
    122, 124
  psychic 109, 113
  see also violence
'Force and Signification' 1, 8, 9,
    24, 19, 27–46, 67, 116–17,
    121, 155, 159
Foucault, Michel (thinker) 1, 2,
    5, 10, 19, 20, 46–59, 100,
    136, 141, 142–4, 169
  The Archaeology of
    Knowledge 144
  Madness and Civilization 1,
    46–59
  The Order of Things 141,
    142–3, 144
freedom 38–41, 45, 58, 61–2,
    99,122, 132, 134–6, 140
  poetic 38–9, 58, 64–6
  of question 93, 98
Freud, Sigmund (founder of
    psychoanalysis) 2, 4, 6,
    17, 21, 22–3, 25, 105–16,
    119, 125–6, 146–7, 148
  and metaphysics 19, 21, 125
  and trace 117, 118, 120
'Freud and the Scene of Writing'
    2, 13, 17, 19, 21, 25, 48,
    105–16, 117, 119, 120, 122,
    148, 154, 157, 164, 168
'From a Restricted to a General
    Economy' 2, 22–3, 25,
    127–41

genesis 6, 10, 12, 21, 28, 78,
    87–91, 97, 102, 116
'"Genesis and Structure" and
    Phenomenology' 1, 6, 21,
    87–91, 101
Genet, Jean (writer) 14, 137
Gide, André (writer) 3, 10
God 19, 24, 40, 62, 64–5, 66–7,
    68, 80, 87, 124, 125, 144,
    155, 156
  death of 126
Granel, Gerard (critic) 165
Guéroult, Martial (philosophy
    teacher) 11–12

Hartman, Geoffrey (critic and
    theorist) 167
haunting 37–8, 42, 46, 49, 94,
    138, 151
hearing-oneself-speak 89, 91–2,
    104–5
Hegel, Georg Wilhelm Friedrich
    (philosopher) 2, 5, 6, 11,
    12, 13, 22, 39, 46–7, 59,
    81–2, 84, 88, 127–41
  Aesthetics 81
  Elements of Philosophy of
    Right 126
  Encyclopaedia 47
  Logic 47
  Phenomenology of Spirit 46–7,
    131
  and philosophy 76, 79, 85,
    165–6
Heidegger, Martin
    (philosopher) 5, 10, 11,
    21, 30,75, 76, 86, 147

INDEX

and being 41, 75, 84–5
and Levinas 74–5, 79–80
Herder, Johann Gottfried
 (philosopher) 143
historicity 18, 45, 46, 50, 56, 61,
 79, 90, 92–3
 and structure 36–7, 41–2
history 1, 5–6, 18, 22, 34,
 45–6, 62–5, 73, 81,
 83–4, 91
 of différance 2–3, 90–1
 of ideas 9, 36, 130
 of philosophy 72, 76, 79, 80,
 85, 89, 92–3, 131, 132,
 142–3, 146
 and structuralism 25, 29–30,
 32, 35–7
 and structure 141, 145, 156
 of the work 41–2, 78–9
 and writing 16, 114
 see also 'Cogito and the
 History of Madness'
Hobbes, Thomas
 (philosopher) 134
Husserl, Edmund
 (philosopher) 1, 4, 10–11,
 12, 19, 20, 27, 29, 44, 47,
 50–1, 59, 73, 74–5, 82–4,
 87–94, 97–9, 156, 160,
 166, 168
 Cartesian Meditations 50–1
 Ideas II 47
 Origin of Geometry 11, 75, 89,
 91, 92
hybris 55
Hyppolite, Jean (philosophy
 teacher) 2, 6–7, 18, 11, 60,
 88, 131
 *Genesis and Structure of the
 Phenomenology of
 Spirit* 6

imagination 35, 36, 38–9

Jabès, Edmond (poet) 14, 24,
 38–9, 59–71, 80, 153–63,
 169
 The Book of Questions 1, 24,
 61, 63, 70, 71, 72, 154,
 158, 161–2
 Je bâtis ma demeure 61, 63,
 64, 70
 Le Seuil et le sable 63
 on Derrida 4, 66, 159
 see also 'Edmond Jabès and the
 Question of the Book;'
 'Ellipsis'
Jewishness 1, 8, 9, 19, 61–7, 70,
 80–1, 87, 95, 154, 160
Johnson, Barbara (critic and
 theorist) 167
Joyce, James (writer) 14, 71
 Ulysses 46–7, 81
Judaism *see* Jewishness

Kafka, Franz (writer) 14
Kamuf, Peggy (critic and
 theorist) 167
Kant, Immanuel
 (philosopher) 11, 13, 38
Kierkegaard, Søren
 (philosopher) 10, 14,
 46–7, 49, 51
 Philosophical Fragments 46
Klein, Melanie
 (psychoanalyst) 116
Kojève, Alexandre (philosophy
 teacher) 130–1

'*La parole soufflée*' 2, 19, 21,
 94–105
Lacan, Jacques (psychoanalyst,
 theorist) 2, 21
Lacoue-Labarthe, Philippe
 (philosopher) 168
language 6, 7, 9, 17, 21, 22, 23–4,
 29, 30, 34, 36–8, 48, 51, 53,

INDEX

language (*Cont'd*)
54, 57–8, 61–3, 68–71, 75, 78–80, 87, 99, 108, 110–11, 124–5, 136–7, 143, 150
   Derrida's relation to 10, 12, 28, 36
   everyday 134, 142–3, 149
   philosophy of 11, 23, 118
   see also logos; signs; metaphor; words
Laplanche, Jean (psychoanalyst, theorist) 2, 96, 99, 101, 112
laughter 129–38
law 12, 14, 18, 21, 44, 60, 63, 79, 101, 126, 131, 140, 145
   divine 44, 64, 65–7
Leibniz, Gottfried (philosopher) 12
letters (literality) 12, 13, 30–3, 36, 38, 39, 44, 46, 54, 61–3, 68–71, 110–11, 116, 157
   Jabès on 159, 160–1
Levinas, Emmanuel (philosopher) 1, 5, 12, 14, 19, 20, 22–3, 25, 72–87, 168–9
Lévi-Strauss, Claude (anthropologist) 2, 9, 23, 141, 147–8, 149–53
life 27, 41, 69–71, 83–4, 89–90, 92, 100–1, 109–10, 115, 118–19, 122, 126, 131–5, 151, 155, 157, 159–60
   and différance 109–10, 120–1
   psychic 106–9, 148
   transcendental 94–9
light 24–5, 34, 44, 72, 77, 79, 81, 128, 149
linguistics *see* Saussurean linguistics
literary criticism 4, 27, 28, 30, 32–3, 36, 37–8, 41, 43, 45
literature 1, 14, 28, 30–3, 43, 45, 71, 100, 162, 166
   see also poetry

logos (concept) 52, 55, 71, 77–9, 81, 86, 89, 91–3, 124, 139

machines 2–3, 106, 107, 113, 115–16
madness 4, 21, 46–59, 94–6, 99–100, 102, 144
Major, René (psychoanalyst) 168
Mallarmé, Stéphane (poet) 14, 16, 19, 39, 116, 166, 168
Marivaux, Pierre (playwright) 28
masculinity 103, 105, 130, 160–1
master-slave dialectic *see* dialectic, Hegelian
mastery 23, 47, 49, 57, 117, 127, 131–4, 138, 140
Mehlman, Jeffrey (critic and theorist) 167
Melville, Herman (writer) 14
memory 3, 47, 63, 78
   and psyche 17, 105, 106, 107, 109, 112–15
metaphor 42, 69–70, 79, 81, 137, 143, 161
   in psychoanalysis 108, 109
metaphysics 12, 19, 21–2, 43, 49–50, 55, 75–9, 84–5, 86, 102, 105, 131, 144, 145, 146–7, 165
   see also 'Violence and Metaphysics'
Miller, J. Hillis (critic and theorist) 167

Nachträglichkeit (concept) 111–13
Nancy, Jean-Luc (philosopher) 15, 168
nature 37, 60, 68, 152
   versus culture 147–8
necessity 18, 40, 89, 100, 105, 117–21, 123–4, 126–7
   and supplement 149, 152

INDEX

Nietzsche, Friedrich (philosopher) 10, 11, 34, 67, 120–1, 146, 160
  The Birth of Tragedy 24, 34, 45, 120, 125
  Thus Spake Zarathustra 28, 67
  Twilight of the Idols 28, 33, 116–17, 121
  nothing 3, 9, 25–6, 39–40, 51, 93, 117, 158
  and Artaud 94, 121
  and Bataille 134–5, 136, 140
  and Foucault 136
  and Husserl 98, 99

oeuvre (work of art) 27, 39, 42, 160, 161
other 1, 3, 17, 21, 30, 58, 114, 119–20, 147
  according to Bataille 133, 134
  according to Cixous 103, 129
  according to Foucault 108, 111
  according to Heidegger 85
  according to Jabès 65, 68, 70, 71, 158–9, 160
  according to Levinas 22–3, 72–4, 77, 80, 81, 82–4, 86, 87
  and reading 48–9, 58, 92

paleonymy (concept) 123
Parmenides (philosopher) 75, 79–80
Pascal, Blaise (philosopher) 54
pathos 7, 50, 55–6, 58–9, 120–1
phenomenology 1–2, 4, 10, 12, 19, 21, 24–5, 27, 29, 31, 44, 72–94, 97–9, 168
  Hegelian 131, 135, 139
  see also Husserl

philosophy 44, 50–1, 57, 72, 73–4, 76–7, 79–80, 129, 134, 136, 140
  see also metaphysics; phenomenology; and under the name of individual philosophers
Plato (philosopher) 6, 11, 76, 77, 79–80, 115, 166
play 6–7, 22, 30, 64, 132, 134, 138, 139, 141–53, 155, 156
  and history 90, 140
  of letters 36, 38, 62, 63, 160, 161
  major 137
  of the world 16, 67, 107, 121
Poe, Edgar Allan (writer) 14
poetry 4, 34, 59–71, 124, 136, 138, 153–63
  see also poetic freedom
politics 13, 15, 39–41, 65, 131, 167, 168, 174n.34
Ponge, Francis (poet) 14
powerlessness 94–5
  see also unpower
presence 55, 86, 95, 116, 120, 138, 142, 144, 156
  complexity of 29, 73, 100, 102, 114–15, 145, 148, 151, 152–3
  and difference 70, 137
  and haunting 37, 42
  and language 24, 110
  self-presence 17, 21, 50, 89, 92, 97, 105, 146, 160
  and writing 35, 60, 112
proper 5, 17, 21, 103–4, 119
proper name 10, 14, 65, 100, 150
property 103, 104
psyche 17, 69, 95, 98, 102, 106, 108–9, 111, 113–14
psychoanalysis 13, 21, 105–16, 168
  and Artaud 125–6
psychologism 41, 95–6, 97

INDEX

question 4–5, 6–8, 20, 25, 32, 66, 72, 73, 74, 76–7, 84, 85, 93, 98, 117
  see also 'Edmond Jabès and the Question of the Book;' Jabès, Edmond, *The Book of Questions*
  reading 4–6, 11–12, 27–8, 30, 43, 48, 51, 52–4, 56–8, 66, 78–9, 92–3, 101–2, 123, 133, 139–41, 156–7
  reason 89–91, 92, 127, 128–33, 150–1
  and madness 46–8, 49–52, 54–6, 96
  repetition 17–18, 21–2, 36, 97, 101, 109–10, 118, 123, 125, 142, 156, 157, 159–60, 161–3
    see also Nachträglichkeit
  representation 3, 109, 111, 119, 120, 125, 156
    literary 70
    theatrical, 21, 121–3, 124
    see also 'The Theatre of Cruelty and the Closure of Representation'
  repression 112, 115, 119, 159
    of writing 109–10, 116, 122
  responsibility 18, 40, 104, 106, 116, 154
Revue métaphysique et morale (journal) 1, 74
Rousseau, Jean-Jacques (philosopher) 10, 60, 117, 120–1, 166
  Essay on the Origin of Languages 23
Rousset, Jean (critic and theorist) 1, 5, 9, 28–9, 30, 31, 32, 37, 38, 41–2, 43, 45

Royle, Nicholas (critic and theorist) 167
Saussurean linguistics 4, 21, 23–4, 29, 30, 141, 151–2
science 16, 17, 18, 19, 113, 139, 141, 142–3, 146, 149
secret 12, 16, 26, 75, 80, 83, 138, 168
self-presence *see* presence
sexual difference 14, 103, 115–16, 128–9, 129–30, 161, 167, 168
Shakespeare, William 14
shaking 12, 19, 30, 33, 35, 37–8, 42, 75, 81, 86, 119, 121, 135, 147
  see also solicitation; trembling
signature 10, 14, 158
signs 9, 23–4, 53, 54, 57, 68, 98, 110–11, 116, 125
  and reading 67, 92–3
  and sense 53–4, 136–7, 140
  and writing, 89–90, 91
  see also 'Force and Signification,' 'Structure, Sign and Play'
silence 24, 25, 47, 54, 55, 57, 59, 63, 64, 68, 75, 90–2, 137–8, 140
  archaeology of 19, 20
sleep 27, 34, 40, 41, 44, 48, 128–9
sliding 22, 27, 42, 137–40
solicitation 33, 35, 86, 121, 159
  see also shaking; trembling
Sollers, Philippe (writer) 14
sovereignty 12, 131–41, 157, 165
spacing 12, 13, 16, 39, 42–4, 65, 66, 68, 73–4, 79, 93, 105, 113–14, 120, 122, 123, 157, 159

speech 19, 34, 37, 39, 40, 49, 66, 70, 80–1, 84, 92, 94–105, 111, 124–6, 138, 160
  free 34, 40
  poetic 136
  speech acts 118
  see also voice
Spivak, Gayatri Chakravorty (critic and theorist) 168
structuralism 8–9, 18, 23–4, 25, 28–32, 35–8, 42, 44, 88, 93, 145, 152, 165
structure 12, 24, 35–6, 42, 27, 28–9, 32, 34, 35–6, 37, 41, 42, 43, 45, 53, 56, 87–94, 111, 141–53, 156
  historical 53–109
  of the mark 35, 49, 123
  psychic 108, 114
  signifying 53, 57, 137
'Structure, Sign and Play in the Discourse of the Human Sciences' 2, 7, 11, 19, 20, 22, 66, 67, 118, 120–1, 134, 141–53, 154, 156
supplement 13, 19, 60, 105, 112–13, 114, 116, 148–52, 153, 154, 163
surprise, 5, 18, 36, 43–4, 53, 77, 87, 165

Tel Quel (journal) 1, 14
theatre 21, 94, 97, 101, 102, 104, 108, 110, 111–12, 116–27, 159, 164–5
  see also drama
'The Theatre of Cruelty and the Closure of Representation' 2, 21, 116–27
theft 95, 102–3, 119, 137–8
totalization 4, 57, 149–52
trace 16–17, 19, 23, 25, 65, 91, 97, 102, 103, 105, 107, 109–10, 112, 115, 117, 120, 138
tradition 11, 12, 56 147
  Jewish 62, 65, 70
translation 6, 76, 80, 111, 125
trembling 5, 6, 37, 44, 81–2, 85–7, 121, 131, 158–9, 172n.4
  see also shaking; solicitation

unpower 96, 103–5
  see also powerlessness

Valéry, Paul (poet) 14
violence 4, 17–18, 25, 37, 72–87, 101, 109, 123, 124
  see also force
'Violence and Metaphysics: an Essay on the Thought of Emmanuel Levinas' 19, 20, 23, 25, 69, 72–87, 158
voice 91, 94, 99–100, 104, 158
  see also speech

Wahl, François (critic and theorist) 165–7
Wahl, Jean (philosophy teacher) 1
Waldrop, Rosmarie (translator) 61, 62, 169
Weber, Samuel (critic and theorist) 24, 164–5, 167
words 7–8, 13, 30–3, 39, 42, 62–7, 68, 75, 92, 95, 99, 100, 101, 114, 117, 123, 124–5, 129, 137–8
  Derrida's relation to 28, 36
  sound of 6, 110, 111, 125
  for structuralism 23, 35–6
  see also language; letters
Wordsworth, Ann (critic and theorist) 167

INDEX

World War II 8, 22–3, 29, 47–8, 84, 154
writing 16–17, 20, 45, 46, 48, 49, 60, 63, 89–91, 105, 106, 114–15, 125, 138–9, 154–6

'Yale School' 167–8
Young, Robert (critic and theorist) 167

Žižek, Slavoj (philosopher) 166